THE TAPROOT OF SOVIET SOCIETY

NICHOLAS VAKAR

THE TAPROOT OF SOVIET SOCIETY

HARPER & BROTHERS, PUBLISHERS • NEW YORK

THE TAPROOT OF SOVIET SOCIETY

CONTENTS

INTRODUCTION

THE LATE JOHN FOSTER DULLES PROMINENTLY DISPLAYED ON HIS Secretary of State's desk a volume of Stalin's *Problems of Leninism*. Mr. Dulles, a man of scholarly and legalistic bent, had read this work, digested its contents thoroughly, and felt that thus equipped with plain insight into Stalin's plans, intentions, and aspirations he was well prepared to cope with any diplomatic problem which the Soviet Union might raise.

The example of the late Secretary of State is perhaps an extreme case of relying upon unadorned Soviet word and Marxist theory as a guide to Moscow's actions and Russian motivations. However, it is by no means an isolated instance. A whole theory of scholarship has grown up around Marxist texts which, in its way, somewhat resembles the kind of scholasticism which is indulged in by the Marx-Lenin (formerly the Marx-Engels-Lenin-Stalin) Institute in Moscow.

The ideologues of the Moscow Institute pour forth a steady stream of texts, studies, collations, interpretations, and revisions which comprise the living body of the Marxist dialectic. If questioned, the Moscow brethren would assuredly declare that this body of rhetoric contains the true, the living body of Marxism triumphant —the faith which guides today's action and directs that of tomorrow.

This confidence that the essence of Soviet policy is to be found, somehow, in a paper structure of logical (or illogical) word formulations is matched on the western shores of this divided and torn world by a similar conviction held by a rather impressive school of Sovietology. Within the school are to be found many men highly trained in the dialectic—men who began their life on either the Communist or Social Democratic side of the barrier; men with a passionate interest in the verbose and ofttimes obscure conflicts which have ravaged the left wing of social thought ever since the emergence of Marx in the middle of the nineteenth century. There are others of what might be described as a teutonic turn of mind, men accustomed to the processes of philosophical thought and eschatological debate, who quite naturally seek to impose upon the house that Marx and so many others have built some logical form or design.

And there is another very human tendency—a tendency to reason by analogy. The dictatorship that is best known and was most feared in the West was Hitler's. Since Russia is also a dictatorship, a simple mental equation operates to convince many of us that we need merely substitute Communist for Nazi, Moscow for Berlin, and Khrushchev (or Stalin or Khrushchev's sucessor) for Hitler. To carry this species of reasoning one step further it is recalled that Hitler wrote a book called *Mein Kampf* in which he outlined his plans and his intentions. If, says this species of analyst, we had only read that book we would have known what he was up to and we could have stopped him in time.

The moral is obvious. Let us not get caught napping twice. Let us read the Russian Mein Kampf whatever it may be—*Das Kapital,* or Stalin's *Problems of Leninism,* or Mr. Khrushchev's latest collection of speeches. There we will find the essence of the danger. Out of the sacred texts of Marxism we will be able to fashion a clear construction of the shape and design of the danger ahead and act accordingly. These are plausible and beguiling ideas. There is even a little logic in them. But only a little.

Heaven knows how many good millions of taxpayers' dollars have been spent in elaborate "research" projects by various military intelligence outfits attempting to winnow out of the Marxist texts "the Kremlin's grand strategy." As anyone with even the faintest familiarity with the endless prolixity of the "texts" is aware, there is something in them for everyone. Out of this amazing dustbin of stale and cloudy language can be fashioned supporting citations for any kind of policy or program which might enter the most aberrant brain of the most far-out inhabitant of the Kremlin.

Not that there are not concealed in the endless procession of words, programs, statements, speeches, glosses, and dialectic certain grains of rare metal. But to refine them out one must, of course, first know what one is looking for.

One would sometimes think in poring through the dreary tomes of western Sovietology that there are no such people as Russians and no such country as Russia. Instead there is an endless paper desert stretching back as far as the mind can reach and stretching ahead in a dazzlingly white vacuity.

This is nonsense, and it is the great gift of Nicholas Vakar that like the little boy who dared to mention that the emperor was, in fact, not wearing any clothes he deigns gently to draw our attention to the inescapable circumstance that Russia is a nation populated by Russians; that most of these Russians were or still are peasant Russians; that regardless of anything which Marx, Engels, Lenin, Stalin, Khrushchev, Suslov, or anyone else has written or said they continue to be affected or even dominated by the indisputable facts of their peasant heritage, their peasant environment, their peasant tradition.

It is Mr. Vakar's genius to draw our attention to the fact that important as it may be for us to know what the Russians think they are and think they are doing it is far more important to know what the Russians *really* are and what they are really doing—and why.

Forty years ago it would not have been difficult to find thoughtful students of Russia who understood the Russian people, Russian history, Russian customs; who had lived in Russian villages, visited Russian estates, talked with the peasants, immersed themselves deep in the unending stream of Russian life and Russianness.

Today this opportunity is far more rare. It is not easy for a foreigner to live among or close to Russian people. The barrages of Party propaganda have so coated the minds of foreigners (and of many Russians) that whole areas of thinking have been wallpapered over and we have even come to believe that all Russian history, all Russian heritage was blotted out somehow in 1917 and that in its place has arisen not only a new Soviet state but a new Soviet man.

But if we attempt to construct a policy or an attitude upon the basis of the cardboard man and the pulp-paper society that he is supposed to inhabit we quickly find ourselves in a Wonderland more strange than anything Alice ever dreamed of.

Russia, as Mr. Vakar so acutely observes, is no longer a village society. It is a village society in transition. But more than 52 per cent of the population is still rural and of the urban hordes the majority is of peasant origin—often first generation. The new generation of Soviet leadership is almost exclusively peasant in origin. Are these men motivated by the psyche of European, intellectualized concepts familiar to a mid-nineteenth century German philosopher like Marx or a turn-of-the-century highly westernized Russian *intelligent* like Lenin? Or are they, inevitably, motivated by the deep primal impress of the village and its ways, of the narrow, paternalistic, master-and-man, patriarchical society in which their mores are inevitably rooted? Is Khrushchev more likely to display the habit patterns of Friedrich Engels or of the *starosta* of a Ukrainian village?

Mr. Vakar would be the last person to contend that his study contains the "hidden key" to Communist policy or Russian action. But it is fair to suggest that for any realistic understanding of how Russians think and Russians act; of what motivates them; of how they view their own inner world and what may impress them in the vast outer world where they still are, for the most part, strangers, this work lays a foundation far more firm than the most elaborate word bricks formed of the clay and straw of the dialectic.

Harrison E. Salisbury

PREFACE

ONE DAY IN THE SUMMER OF 1957 I WAS TALKING TO MY FRIEND, Gordon Harrison, about the Russian village and the impact of its culture on Soviet Communism—a theme generally neglected in efforts to understand Soviet history and Soviet behavior. He proposed an article on the subject; I rejoined that if there was to be such an article he would have to write it. We separated on my promise to send him some notes, and in time I did. But the notes grew uncontrollably into matter for a book. Through many months we collaborated closely (though usually at a distance physically) to shape the work. Thus it is as much Gordon Harrison's as mine, though I, of course, assume the full responsibility for it.

An outgrowth of my course in Russian civilization at Wheaton, it is not intended itself as a text on Soviet history or on contemporary Soviet affairs. Rather, it is the exposition and defense of a point of view which has seemed to yield insights not only into Soviet experience but into some of the problems of these times in which so many new nations have chosen to be born.

The Soviet Union was envisaged by Lenin as a "workers' and peasants' state" to be ruled for at least some time to come by professional revolutionaries like himself who were middle-class intellectuals. It did not work out that way. Instead, under Stalin a new revolution was accomplished in the course of the 1930's by which former peasants engrossed political power, purged the leaders of the November revolution almost to a man, and completed the destruction of what had been known up to 1917 as Russian civilization. This second Communist revolution, marked near its beginning by collectivization and near its end by the great purges of 1936-38, has of course been noted in history books. Because it was unusually spread out in time, however, and because it continued the political language and most of the forms of its predecessor, its distinctness has never been sufficiently emphasized. Crane Brinton, for instance, in his *Anatomy of Revolution* (34) has tried to fit Stalinism into his scheme of uniformities as part of the Thermidorian reaction which, according to him, began with Lenin's New Economic Policy in 1922. But since by this reckoning the reaction has been going on for nearly forty years, Professor Brinton wondered, "Could it not be that the Russian revolution is permanent?"

We see no need to renounce in this way a useful conceptual scheme. The New Economic Policy (NEP) can properly be described as "thermidorian" for it was frankly a reaction to war communism ("extremism," in Brinton's language) aimed, if provisionally, at achieving stability by mixing "the new and the old," the new socialist order with the old middle-class capitalism of small businessmen and independent farmers. But before NEP had run its course the Old Bolsheviks, enfeebled by dissension and personal feuds, deserted by a significant number of intellectuals, saw their government captured by ex-peasants. Though this new revolution was not marked by the storming of a Bastille or a Winter Palace and, in fact, did not reach its climactic violence for more than a decade, it was revolutionary in character. The critical act was the seizure of power by a new ruling class, different in culture, economic status, and political ideal from the Old Bolsheviks they replaced. Their revolution, moreover, had its own "moderates" and "extremists" and, to apply Prof. Brinton's scheme, has recently entered its "thermidorian reaction" under Khrushchev, which aims at stability by mixing again the legacy of the past with the needs of the present.

The new Soviet man who, beginning in the Nineteen Twenties, rose to command a great nation was new only in his occupation of palaces; he was ancient in breed and custom. And he was universal. Having made over Soviet politics in his own primitive image he prepared, far better than Marx or Lenin, the spread of Communism to other nations of peasants who see that the political, economic and ethical model of the U.S.S.R. is readily reproducible in native materials. There lies the essential meaning of Soviet Communism today and its central threat, as distinct from the meaning and peril of the ideas of Karl Marx.

In expounding this point of view we have been aware throughout of semantic difficulties, beginning with the word 'peasant' itself. It is impossible to avoid the various and unpredictable emotional connotations of such a word. It may reduce misunderstandings if we proclaim at the outset two basic intentions: First, that we do not write about all the peasants in Russia but about those who succeeded in making over the new society in their image; and, second, that by 'peasant' we mean a cultural pattern, not a human type. While we regard peasant culture as inferior, the person occupying that cultural level may be noble or base, and as difficult to categorize in his mixture of human qualities as any other person from any other culture.

A list of useful references is appended and, wherever necessary, the name of the author and number of the entry are given in Bibliographical Notes, or in footnotes.

I want to acknowledge my gratitude to the Danforth Foundation and the Wheaton Faculty Research Fund for help in defraying some of the expenses of preparing the manuscript.

Wheaton College   NICHOLAS VAKAR
Norton, Massachusetts
June 1961

THE TAPROOT OF SOVIET SOCIETY

THE VILLAGE MARX

ASKED WHETHER RUSSIAN AUDIENCES WOULD APPRECIATE PERFORM-
ances of *My Fair Lady in English,* the Soviet Deputy Minister of
Culture retorted: "Do you think we are peasants?"[1] His question
was intended to be rhetorical, and there is no record of any
reply. But an honest rejoinder would by no means have been
superfluous. It might have gone something like this:

"No. In fact, we did not think you peasants. Even the word
did not occur to us. It almost never does. We don't use it in
America, except now and then in fun to tease a rather lovable
but uncouth character. We assumed, of course, that the audiences
of Moscow would be like the audiences of New York, or London,
or Paris, or any other great world capital. That is to say, only a tiny
minority would be able to understand plays in a foreign language.
The rest would be content with a translation, indeed, would insist
on one. They would never dream that their linguistic ignorance
might reflect on their culture, which they universally take to be
self-evident from the fact that they live in a great city and attend
its theaters. What does 'peasant' mean to the Deputy Minister of
Culture? Why does he fear that his Muscovite, play-going élite
could be so easily tarred with that brush?"

But possibly this is to ask too much of a minister of culture and
raise questions that had better be asked of Soviet history. For the
inquiry itself already implies history. Clearly there was a difference
of cultural level suggested between peasants and 1959 Moscow
audiences. Clearly, too, there was a connection between them, close
enough to be passionately rejected.

Not to pretend any longer to a mystery, the connection simply is

[1] *The New York Times,* 6 May 1959.

this: most of the Soviet theater crowds are, in fact, former peasants or sons and daughters of peasants who, within forty years or less, have made the colossal cultural leap from the isolation and ignorance of the Russian village to the leadership of a society of some 200 million people. They are now in process of ceasing to be peasant in outlook as they have ceased to be in status. Now, in the transition, one can see everywhere old peasant and new sophisticate jostling one another in the same salons and even in the same persons. The process is so new and as yet so unfinished that those whom it transforms still wish above all to deny it.

These observations are commonplace. No traveler in the U.S.S.R. has failed to note the crudities of Soviet culture as compared with other western nations. Recent visitors have sensed the excitement of a society in ferment as the rural *nouveaux,* the self-made, struggle for the civilization which is literally the culture of cities. Historians have duly recounted the fact that the Russia overwhelmed by the Bolshevik revolution was a nation of peasants, and have recognized that the peasantry and its problems gave distinctive shape to the Marxist experiment. But these admissions formerly have been incidental[2] to a main view of the Soviet Union as a Communist state.

However Soviet idiosyncrasies might thereafter be defined, the empire of Lenin-Stalin-Khrushchev has appeared steadfastly in our history books—and in the eyes of those who make public policy— as a nation of the genus Marxist whose people have been commanded and whose destinies are guided by the imperatives of the "proletarian revolution" described by Marx and modified by Lenin. The fact that Soviet Communists were mostly peasants has, in short, seemed less impressive than that the peasants were mostly Communists.

It is precisely that proposition that this book would turn around. The reason for doing so is not just to be different, nor to indulge

---

[2] Leon Trotsky (285), Vol. I, p. 33, estimated that "in all the enterprises under factory inspection there were . . . about two million [workers] in 1917," that is, only 1.5 per cent of the total population of the Russian empire. In 1928, the numbers engaged in nonagricultural occupations represented 6.6 per cent of the total Soviet populations; cf. Redding (231).

According to official statistics, 42 per cent of the total Soviet population still were occupied in agriculture in 1958 [as compared with less than 10 per cent in the United States]; cf. *Khoziaistvo* (129).

in academic exercise. A point of view is no small matter either for history or for policy. It must largely determine what one sees and, therefore, the data on which one may intelligently act. Insisting on the *peasantry* of the Soviet revolution as its primary color and essential nature does not, of course, deny its communism. What is asserted—and will hereafter be argued at length—is that Soviet communism is also peasant-shaped and can only be understood as a rationalization adopted and adapted by peasant minds. From this point of view the observer will be less fascinated with the Marxist-Leninist vocabulary than with the peasant concepts wrapped in ritualistic words.

The view from the village is cultural rather than ideological, historical rather than literary and static. In the cultural-historical perspective, the minds of men and, therefore, their actions are seen to be ruled by their total experience, not by ideas alone. While radical faiths like the *Communist Manifesto* or the "Sermon on the Mount" may change men in the mass, the mass also changes the faith. The ideology that works is never precisely what its founders had in mind. Communism as dogma is static; but what a society may think of as communistic—and that is their guide to action— must change as the people, and more especially the leaders, grow in experience and alter in outlook. Since the free world's problem is not to coexist with Karl Marx, but to deal with the Soviet Union, Red China, and the so-called underdeveloped nations, which, on the record, are just those most susceptible to communism, we need above all to see the links—economic, ideologic, and especially ethical—between the dogma and the primitive societies to which it appeals.

To insist that the view from the village is cultural is to deny that peasantry is essentially an economic condition. The West has generally underrated that distinction, in part because the West has largely forgotten what peasants are. America, of course, never had any. England has scarcely known one in recent years. Peasants still seen on the Continent have remained, for the most part, outside the consciousness of the intellectuals who have tried to understand communism. The term "peasant" has made us think only of poor, small-scale farmers, handicapped by backward agricultural methods and living dully with few of the advantages of modern life. We have, thus, readily enough accepted the Marxist delusion

3

that bracketed the peasant with the factory worker as a "rural proletarian," one branch of the underprivileged who would—or might not—inherit the earth, depending on how the Revolution went.

The anomaly of communism striking not only first, but exclusively, in backward agricultural nations, instead of in the overripe industrial ones, as predicted by Marx, has therefore not generally seemed interesting. If it happened to be poor farmers rather than poor factory hands who rose against the rich, the conflict nevertheless was "class war," and its consequence, the establishment of that upside-down, unfree social and political system called communism. The essential ingredients of the Marxian revolution— the anti-Communist insists as steadfastly as the Communist—are the existence of a depressed mass and an inflammatory ideology capable of rousing them violently against the old order. It appears to be accepted on both sides that revolutions occur when the have-nots, dosed with propaganda (variously conceived as political education or subversion), rise against the haves.

While not entirely false, this schematic diagram of revolution does not fit the historical facts. It embodies one of Marx's critical delusions: that if the conflicts between men may ultimately be referred to economic differences, then history need reckon with no others. There was in Russian villages in the epoch of revolution a large and growing mass of rural proletarians, the *batraki,* who existed entirely by hiring themselves out to wealthier peasants and landlords. These men and their economic grievances were volatile material for the spreading revolution. But it is false to suppose that they acted as an economic class for class interests or that even with them poverty was the only significant motivation.

These peasants—and, indeed, most Russian peasants—were poor. But they were also as people and as forces in history something much more: not just men struggling for a meager living, not just inefficient agricultural instruments, not just exploited members of the lowest estate in the Tsar's empire, but creators and creatures of a distinctive culture which had been fashioned in rural isolation and preserved against the otherwise pervasive changes of the modern world. The man in the village was a human whole, greater than his economic parts.

It was this whole man whose passions were released by revolution and whose ambitions suddenly found a scope undreamed of during the centuries in which the village hid from history. The Russian peasant who first acquiesced in the Bolshevik revolution, and then took it over was not essentially a proletarian; essentially, he was a cultural survival, in part from the Middle Ages, in part from a primitivism not much changed since the dawn of settled human society.

What exactly the peasant was besides will be a main subject of this book. Here it is enough to observe that the two ways of regarding the peasant—as an economic class or as a cultural estate—produce profoundly different perspectives on the Soviet experience.

From the economic view, the peasantry is seen chiefly as an agent of revolution, expressing peculiar grievances, insisting more or less effectively on redress, employing its mass to help destroy the old order and support the new. It is a force hurrying events along or holding them back. The historian, from that view, will ask chiefly what the peasant wanted of the revolution and what he got.

Regarded culturally, the peasant is the material rather than the agent of revolution. As such it will be not his grievances alone that shape the course of events, but his whole outlook. One will wish to know how he understood the things that were happening and so, literally, what he made of them. The historian will ask not only what communism did to the peasant but what the peasant did to communism.

The two perspectives, of course, are not mutually exclusive. Our object is not to find a point of view from which the whole truth about the Soviet Union might become clear. The object is only illumination. Without derogating the usefulness of any lantern to see by, one would like to stand where the light seems to reach deepest to the heart of the mystery—what Soviet communism is and why it succeeded.

The Bolshevik revolution of 1917 was not, of course, peasant in origin. In fact, the peasant has not anywhere been the cause of Communist uprising and could not possibly be. Although he constituted overwhelmingly the bulk of the depressed Russian population, it was not even his specifically agrarian grievances that provided grist for the Bolsheviks. His predominance was an embarrassment for Marxist theorizers; his characteristic aspiration for land of his own was "petty-bourgeois backwardness" in the revolutionary cant. Lenin borrowed the slogan "All land for the peasant" from the native populist tradition and recognized it as a temporary and essentially un-Marxist expedient. "We know," he said, "that only through an understanding with the peasantry can the Socialist Revolution in Russia be saved until revolution has broken out in other countries." While Grigori Zinoviev described this concession of expediency as an "act of genius," it was to prove fatal for both the old revolutionaries and their ideas. The peasant would save the revolution only *by taking it over*. Twenty years later, of its original leaders only the peasant-born Stalin would still be alive to enjoy the triumph.[3]

As for the peasants, their acceptance of the Bolsheviks was neither general nor spontaneous. Trotsky recalls that "at the May congress of peasant soviets, in the elections to the executive committee, Chernov received 810 votes, Kerensky 804, whereas Lenin got only 20 votes in all."[4] Three to five weeks after the first Soviet government was established, elections to the Constituent Assembly brought out about half the electorate, which was at this time overwhelmingly peasant. The Bolsheviks, who had permitted the elections, confident that they would be confirmed in the power they had seized, received only 9,844,637 of the 51,531,513 votes cast.[5]

After the provisional democratic government was set up in March, rural communities were left to themselves and took advantage of the neglect of the central administration to expropriate land both from the gentry and from about 2 million relatively prosperous individual farmers. But while the engrossment thus of 250 million acres during the Kerensky regime was no doubt agreeable enough to the mass of poorer peasants who profited, it was neither spontaneous nor revolutionary in the sense of action designed to

[3] Leon Trotsky, a political exile since 1928, survived the others, to be assassinated in Mexico in 1943. Isaac Deutscher, in the last chapter of (60), wrote the Revolution's epitaph in the Marxist idiom: "The Russian working class had proved itself incapable of exercising its own dictatorship."

[4] Trotsky (285), Vol. III, p. 18.

[5] Of a total of 707 delegates to the All-Russian Constituent Assembly, only 175 were Bolsheviks. The Assembly was ordered to disband 17 hours after it first was allowed by the Soviet government to meet, on January 18, 1918—for details, see Radkey (230).

transfer political power or prepare a new social order. It was, rather, the traditional reaction of the peasantry to a slackening of the reins of government. As a provincial commissar remarked in the summer of 1917: "The local peasantry have got a fixed opinion that all civil laws have lost their force, and that all legal relations ought now to be regulated by peasant organizations."[6] The peasant asserted not new demands for rights or privileges but his age-old longing to be left alone. When presently the "Reds" and the "Whites" brought civil war to the countryside, the peasants, for the most part, tried to stay out of it.

It is not true that the outcome of the civil war in 1918-1921 was determined by a greater peasant sympathy for the Bolshevik side. Not sympathy but habits of obedience played the decisive role. With greater ruthlessness, unity, and vigor in action, the Reds drafted peasants to fight. The Whites counted on volunteers. Peasants, by nature and training, seldom volunteered, because to do so meant to accept personal responsibility for their actions. On the other hand, they were inured to obedience and therefore, when drafted, felt they had no choice. They would fight for the Reds until captured, then as cheerfully fight for the Whites, perhaps rather more cheerfully in that they were more accustomed to taking orders from the officers of the White command wearing the Old Army uniforms. "Our Samurski regiment was formed of captured Red soldiers," recalls a former White Army officer, "yet that regiment under the command of Colonel Ilyin fought on the White side with unflinching courage and persistence. . . . Thousands of former Reds were the most loyal fighters in our White Army units." There were peasants who would thus change sides several times with, apparently, no sense that in effect they fought against themselves.[7]

Political passivity was the product directly of the peasant's experience. He was necessarily not an initiator. His exclusive attachment to the smallest of human worlds, his own timeless, introverted village, meant that he could neither know nor conceivably care about the larger politics with which revolution was concerned. His uprisings in the past had been formless, anarchical, directed at seizing land and destroying wantonly the people and things resi-

[6] As quoted by Trotsky (285), Vol. III, p. 29.

[7] Cf. Erast Chevdar in *Novoe Russkoe Slovo* (New York), 17 August 1959. See also Denikin (58).

dent in the hostile other world above and beyond his own. He was never interested in new kinds of government, much less in theories about them. His initial role in the affairs of 1917 was similarly chaotic.

Boris Pilniak, a Soviet writer, who may have been shot in 1937 for expressing sentiments of the kind following, specifically contrasted the peasant outlook with the revolutionary spirit. "Peasant life is known," he wrote, "It is to eat in order to work, to work in order to eat and, besides that, to be born, to bear and to die. Our Revolution is a rebellion in the name of the conscious, rational, purposeful and dynamic principle of life, against the elemental, senseless, biologic automatism of life: That is, against the peasant roots of our old Russian history, against its aimlessness, its non-teleological character, against the noddy and idiotic philosophy of Tolstoy's Karataev in *War and Peace*. It will take decades to burn out Karataev's philosophy, but that process has begun."[8]

The fact, however, that peasant roots were "elemental, senseless," did not mean that they would necessarily be burned out by "dynamic" reason. The fact that peasants were politically passive did not mean that they were politically insignificant—a mass to be acted upon rather than acting. What neither Pilniak nor any other Soviet writer observed was the possibility that the peasant point of view, instead of yielding to Marxist enlightenment, might supplant it or at least force an amalgam owing more to the traditions of the village than to the writings of Marx.

While the Bolsheviks, of course, recognized as a special problem the economic and social backwardness of the peasantry, they considerably underestimated its cultural inertia. Or, what comes to much the same thing, they exaggerated the capacity of the Revolution to educate. Trotsky wrote that "the seventeenth, eighteenth and nineteenth centuries of Russian history climbed up on the shoulders of the twentieth and bent it to the ground." But he added that with the Revolution "the twentieth century not only got free of these past centuries hanging upon it, but climbed up on their shoulders to a new historic level."[9]

Ignoring the cultural gap, Marxists and Social Revolutionaries could earnestly debate whether attachment of the peasant to a

[8] Quoted in Maynard (181), p. 301.
[9] Trotsky (285), Vol. III, p. 35.

communal village organization revealed a naïve socialist mind preparing for the direct leap from feudal relations to communism or whether the peasants' petty-bourgeois minds would necessarily doom village socialism.[10] Each missed the essential fact that the village was organized as a primitive institution in a primitive culture equally remote from ideas of socialism or the bourgeoisie. Whether or not the peasant was a species of petty bourgeois had little meaning compared with the fact that at his release in 1917 he was just entering the modern world and bringing to it the traditions and outlook of another age. To ask if he was for Communism was less pertinent than to ask what he could understand by it.

Behind the scenes of Russian civilization as viewed by the world, peasants had lived a life of their own, outside history and even, in some sense, outside time. Laboriously they fed the empire, hardly conscious of what the empire was. Politically ignorant, they did not prepare or expect—or perhaps even want—a revolution. The village had its dreams of better things and from time to time would explode in what Pushkin called "revolts as senseless as ruthless."[11] But it had never heard of "socialism," "democracy," "proletariat," "communism," or of the apostles of change, Kerensky, Lenin, Marx. The words were foreign, the names belonged to strangers. Agitators from the city—and invariably they came from the city—were regarded with indifference or dismay, and often reported to district authorities as outsiders who could not be up to any good. The folk heroes were peasant leaders like Stenka Razin (1667-1671) or Emelian Pugachev (1773-1775),[12] who rose to protect the plain people and their Father the Tsar against the vicious masterfolk—the gentry, the state officials, and the educated—all who belonged to that civilized world from which the revolutionaries also came.

The history of the revolution of March 1917 has been written from Petrograd (as St. Petersburg, renamed in 1914, was called at that time). Seen from the countryside, it presented a much less coherent picture. The origin and meaning of the changes associated

[10] Cf. Wolfe (311), pp. 110-115.
[11] *Russki bunt bessmyslenny i besposhchadny.* Pushkin (226)
[12] See Chapter 3.

9

with the new leaders—Prince Lvov, Miliukov, Kerensky—were scarcely recognized outside a few urban centers. Indeed, the leaders themselves were generally unknown. The fact that Prince Lvov, head of the "revolutionary" government, was appointed by the Tsar himself before the abdication, was confusing, to say the least. The overturn must have seemed to result not from human resolve but from supernatural command, and the consequent efforts of human beings to control events (clumsy enough in fact), were incomprehensible. The Bolshevik riots in July and General Kornilov's rebellion in August-September appear to have irritated the country instead of stirring it. Although apprehension grew with increasing violence and unrest, it seemed that fate rather than human will carried Russia toward the day when, by the convening of the Constituent Assembly, the nation would sit down and solve all her problems once and forever.

Then fate itself faltered. If the people of Petrograd could accept the Bolshevik coup of November as the natural outgrowth of events up to that point, the country in general was stunned. It was impossible to believe that the mighty government of a mighty empire had been upset by a street mob. I can recall the day when the first news reached the war front in the Carpathian Mountains. Our soldiers had never heard the name of Lenin before, and most of the officers knew only that he was some revolutionary recently returned from exile. No one in the higher army command could explain what the "soviets" were or whence came their authority. The more we learned in the days following the more difficult it became to understand how a handful of obscure individuals with the help of a city mob and a moth-balled cruiser from Kronstadt could overwhelm a legitimate government in a few shooting hours. Were there not sensible, responsible people in Petrograd to throw the imposters out, jail them, or shoot them? (Lenin would presently confess that the Bolsheviks themselves were puzzled by their good luck.)

So, as the village saw it, the November revolution, far from arriving like an historic dawn, struck as a thunderbolt—a stunning mystery without rational preparation or justification. Without the data or rationality of historians, people began to seek explanations. What occurred most obviously to the millions as an answer was the new science of Marxism of which they had begun to hear.

10

Karl Marx, they understood, was a prophet, and his knowledge was given to the few who took from it their evidently special and impressive potency.

The fact that revolutionary slogans were sonorous, with words of foreign origin signifying little, contributed to the feeling of awe. All knowledge to the primitive mind is power, the more powerful when it seems to be a gibberish evidently only comprehensible to higher beings. The nation in 1917, it must be remembered, was largely illiterate, and of those who could read and write only perhaps 3 per cent had been educated beyond primary school. In such an intellectual environment, if a new phenomenon could not be rejected altogether it had to be assimilated within the narrow range of things which in the traditional wisdom had meaning.

In this primitive house of the mind, the largest and virtually the only expansible room was reserved for religion and sorcery— the two not subtly differentiated. It was here the Marxist idea could lodge. Marxists had proved by success that they had powerful magic. They had indeed passed a miracle at least as stupendous as any in the Bible. Also like the prophets of tradition, they proclaimed their intention of transforming the world in accordance with truth and justice. (They even called their paper *Pravda*, meaning both "truth" and "justice," especially in peasant usage.) As Jesus Christ had summoned the poor to follow him, so the Bolsheviks addressed themselves to the workers, the peasants, and the common soldiers. *Mystery, miracle,* and *authority*—the three attributes which Dostoevsky had said must attach to a leader whom the multitudes would follow[13]—belonged to Lenin. And by those three marks of leadership the millions who knew nothing more were disposed to accept him.

Acceptance, however, remained largely passive and reserved. "The Soviets . . . took hold rather slowly in the villages," Trotsky confessed.[14] Provincial commissars reported that "all the law-breaking and lawlessness is connected with the appearance within the boundaries of the province of deserters, soldiers on furlough, or delegates from the regimental committees."[15] Peasants joined

[13] "The Legend of the Grand Inquisitor" in *The Brothers Karamazov.*
[14] "Trotsky (285), Vol. I, p. 392.
[15] *Ibid.,* Vol. III, p. 21.

11

the revolutionary movement only as individuals, not in their native villages but in the cities to which they were displaced temporarily as workers, servants, or soldiers.

The peasantry did not constitute a self-conscious social class aware of common interests and disposed to act in solidarity. Every village stood apart from every other, a world to itself. It took years for Bolshevik administration to spread through the country. The process, in fact, was not consummated until the collectivization of agriculture during the 1930's. And by that time the Communists were already a different crew from those who stood by Lenin in the conquest of Petrograd.

In November 1917, power was seized by a handful of middle-class intellectuals—there was not a single proletarian among Lenin's close associates—supported by a somewhat larger handful of factory workers and disgruntled peasants in uniform, and assisted by urban mobs.

The Bolshevik party was small and narrowly based.[16] In contrast to other revolutions, the November coup was the first act of a group of idealists and adventurers aspiring to power, rather than the final act of a social class already dominant in the nation. Once in possession of the government, Lenin's men had not only to defend themselves, as all revolutionaries must; they had to begin the conquest of the country. That was by no means accomplished in the civil war, which achieved only the defeat of overt armed enemies. The larger, still more critical task remaining was to assert effective authority over the millions who, even when not disposed to resist, were nevertheless bound to be uncooperative, since they had nothing in common with the revolutionists or their aims.

In spreading out to occupy the land, the Bolsheviks were like a bottle of red ink trying to stain the sea: they could extend only by dilution. They had increasingly to recruit peasants for the party and to depend on peasant officials to control the peasant masses,

[16] Soviet historians naturally inflate the party membership at that time. More reliable sources estimate its total strength at "something like 5 to 10 thousands" before World War I. By the summer of 1917, the numbers had grown to "about 23,000," and by December—two months *after* the coup— to 45,585—cf. Ivanovich (117) and Dallin (56).

and they had to do so before there was any possibility of educating the recruits to the new philosophy.[17] To put the matter differently, the overriding requirement to complete the conquest of the country outran the necessarily much slower processes of conversion. The result was foregone. The more deeply the new regime pushed itself into the governing hierarchy of provinces, regions, districts, villages —and even in the early days, the regional bureaucracy grew vast and spongy—the thinner the Marxist essence was spread and the more exclusively in practice the party became peasant.

The fact that it was never the village as an economic or social unit that transferred allegiance to the Communists but only individual peasants, had profound consequences. It meant that the Party was selecting out individual types. For the most part these were not the "wise and prudent" but the hotheaded, the self-deluding, the grasping. The evidence is abundant in Soviet literature that many were recruited from the rural scum. Said Lenin: "A vile man may prove useful just because he is vile." Besides them, some shrewd kulaks[18] jumped on the bandwagon early enough to continue their predatory domination of their native villages under Red auspices.

The Soviet revolution had called to the poor to rise up and throw off their chains. But as it turned out not many of the poor either wished or were able to respond. By and large it was not the downtrodden who were drawn to the Party by its ideals or its dialectics of class struggle; it was the opportunistic who caught the promise of personal power and success. The Party, in short, by the nature of its grab for power took in not social classes of mixed individuals but a consistent breed of persons—the *climbers*.

In the Bely region near Smolensk, from which we happen to have detailed records, a 1935 list of 355 party members showed that by social origin 273 were peasants, 63 were workers (a classification which even when not deliberately falsified, was hardly distinguishable in rural areas from peasant), and 19 were employees. But by occupation at that time only 144 listed themselves as still on the

[17] The well of documentation for that period is Soviet literature: the novels, short stories, poetry, and plays of the 1920's and early 1930's.

[18] *Kulak*—Russian for "fist"—a nickname for the well-to-do farmer who profited from the labor of the poorer peasants in his village, generally through usury and economic bondage—see Chapters 3 and 4.

land; 202 were employees; just 9 were workers.[19] The Party was for social climbing and, by the mid-thirties, rustic go-getters were well on their way up.

Indeed, they had the main prize already in hand: They had the Party itself. It was Trotsky who early observed that under Stalin people no longer joined the Party to support an ideal but to secure for themselves positions of authority in the system, and he described this as "bureaucratization" of the revolution. The western term he used would be misleading unless we realize its Soviet rustic connotations. Stalin's mistrust of intellectuals, as well as of the more sophisticated class-conscious workers, was notorious. He was concerned neither with ideas nor with class but with hard work and obedience. Himself of peasant stock he felt more at ease with peasant members, and it was from among them that he set out to choose his household.

Lenin, who had found the tough Caucasian mountaineer useful without ever trusting him, became dismayed shortly before his death at the Stalinist shadow of things to come. He then recommended that the Central Committee remove Stalin from the office of Secretary General. But already, in 1923, most new members felt more at home with that "extremely coarse" but extremely familiar manipulator than they would with the "more tolerant, more loyal, more civilized and human, less arbitrary" leader whom Lenin vainly urged on his heirs.[20]

In the next dozen years Stalin consolidated his personal power, while the Party filled up with peasants. It took time and several purges to complete what amounted, in fact, to the "third" great Russian revolution.[21] From the hands of the middle-class intelligentsia—first the democrats, then the Marxists—the Revolution now passed into the hands of those peasants who adopted the name "Marxists" for themselves. First the dreamers, the adventurers and hotheads, as well as the more impudent ruffians were cleaned out. Then the ideologues of "right" and "left." Theoretical discus-

---

[19] Fainsod (73), p. 130.

[20] Lenin's Testament, 4 January 1923.

[21] Whether the Bolshevik coup in November 1917 was a "second Russian revolution" or the inevitable replacement of the moderates by the extremists, as Professor Brinton (35) suggests, is the subject of considerable debate in the literature; it is generally conceded, however, that the Stalin period must be seen as something else or more than just a Russian Thermidor.

sion virtually ended with the liquidation of the Trotskyites—the term applied to everyone who opposed or doubted the "general line" traced by Stalin. Their places in the party ranks were filled with more disciplined.

The collectivization of agriculture, undertaken against the objections of the Party's last intellectuals, solved the major problem of controlling the peasant mass—by returning it to serfdom. The theory of "socialism in one country" cut the Soviet Union loose to pursue its own development.[22] Stalin was supreme and, in the great purges of 1936-1938, he systematically wiped out the last survivors of the Bolshevik Old Guard along with the less reliable of his newer henchmen. "The victims included 70 per cent of the members (and candidates) of the party Central Committee elected in 1934, the great majority of the highest officers of the army, over 90 per cent of the central trade-union committees, and many managers, intellectuals, and Party and Comintern functionaries. In addition, a multitude of ordinary citizens were accused. . . It has been estimated that eight million people were arrested, and the actual total may well be higher still."[23]

As of November 1938, the changes in the Party leadership can be summed up as follows:[24]

Statutory numbers		Purged
13	Politbureau members	6
140	Central Committee members	125
11	First Secretaries of the Union Republics	9
6	Regional Secretaries (*kraikom*)	6
30	Provincial Secretaries (*obkom*)	26
16	Secretaries of the Autonomous Republics	16
87	Secretaries in larger cities	81
18	Members of the U.S.S.R. Council of People's Commissars	14

[22] The theory of "socialism in one country" is known as Stalin's personal contribution to Marxism-Leninism. The revolution thus became national and domestic, which certainly was not the idea of Lenin and the original Bolsheviks. As a matter of historical record, "up to 1917 the party never admitted even the idea that the proletarian revolution might be achieved in Russia before it was achieved in the West. . . . They rejected as a caricature the idea imputed to them by the Mensheviks of creating a 'peasant socialism' in a backward country. . . . The dictatorship of the proletariat in Russia was for the Bolsheviks a bridge to a revolution in the West. . . . Only in 1924 did a change occur upon this fundamental question"—Trotsky (285), Vol. III, pp. 380 ff.

[23] Treadgold (284), p. 280.

[24] Table drawn by A. Avtorkhanov, in *Posev*, No. 51 (West Germany, 1950).

The character of the change was most strikingly visible in the village. In the Smolensk province, for example, the great purge eliminated almost all the top men in the *oblast* (province) court. Their replacements included semiliterate persons of peasant background and only elementary education. Smolensk University had undergone almost continuous purges, not to wipe out heresy, which most of the accused professors were eager to recant, but to get rid of all who had been born into a superior social class. As rapidly as possible the descendants of noblemen, priests, and civil servants (who in 1930 still had more than a third of the university jobs) were ousted to make way for the sons and daughters of peasants.[25] Indeed, the decimated intelligentsia could be replaced only by recruits from peasant homes. "The dark waters of muzhik Russia have swept and swallowed the Petrine empire," Boris Pilniak observed as early as 1922 in his novel *Goly god*.[26]

The new men and women—some already in possession of secondary schooling, thanks to the Revolution, but many appallingly unfit—who thus entered the Soviet ruling circles are not to be viewed as scrapings from the bottom of the old barrel. They were the chosen advance agents of a brave new world.

The chapters following cannot begin to describe that world in full, much less recount its history. The aim is rather to examine the basic amalgam of peasant and communist, to suggest how it formed, to see where and how Karl Marx as philosopher and the Bolsheviks as rulers found themselves at home in a rustic society, and how that society fitted doctrine to the ethics and traditions of rural primitives.

[25] Fainsod (73).
[26] Pilniak (217).

2

TWO CULTURES—TWO HISTORIES

ABOUT THE MIDDLE OF THE SEVENTEENTH CENTURY RUSSIAN SOCIETY split in two. The city and the village, which until then had largely shared a single national culture, began to lead separate lives.

Lines of cleavage were first marked out by the religious reform of Patriarch Nikon (1605-1681) against which in time large numbers of the population rebelled. They were deepened by the westernizing efforts of Peter the Great (1672-1725) and his successors. Thereafter, Russia had two histories, of which only one, tracing the development of the small sophisticated urban upper classes, has been adequately told. The immense rural mass, along with the closely related townsfolk *(meshchane)*, dropped into a historical backwater. When it emerged again at the Revolution its features had become unfamiliar to most of the world, even to most city-bred Russians.

With the formation of the Soviet state, Russian history became one again, but it did not continue (except chronologically) the history of the Tsarist empire. Rural Russia, having gone underground, as it were, at about the end of the Russian Middle Ages, had not shared in the modernizing and westernizing which produced the distinctive culture of St. Petersburg, capital of the empire. Rural Russia remained instead largely in the medieval mold of the Muscovite state. When the Revolution cracked that old mold a slumbering society awakened to the changes that had passed it by and began acting and developing itself in a new world about where it had left off three centuries before. Thus, in a real sense, the immediate historical background of Soviet society is the history of the Muscovite state—usually dated from the fourteenth century through the formation of the empire in 1721. The parallels and continuities are striking, indeed.

Muscovite society considered itself a religious rather than a national community and was organized politically, as Ivan IV saw it, for the benefit of the orthodox Christians. To be Orthodox was to be Russian; to be Russian was to be Orthodox. The very words, *pravoslavny* (Orthodox) and *russki* (Russian) were interchangeable and continued to be far into modern times.[1]

Christened by the Greeks at the turn of the tenth century, the Russians seem to have received the new faith more readily than most other European peoples. Christianity in the Slavic idiom acted from the beginning as a unifying force, absorbing the loosely organized local primitive cults and creating for the first time a sense of nation through a common religious allegiance, one faith for prince and for slave. Piety and superstition, indeed, took such hold on the land that one historian believes the tradition of "monastic humility" enabled the Mongols to conquer Russia "so easily" in the thirteenth century.[2] It is at least a fact that more than 100 monasteries were founded before the Mongol invasion, nearly all of them in the Kiev and Novgorod regions. And the monkish enthusiasm continued thereafter. In the 100 years after 1340, 150 new monasteries are known to have been established in Muscovy alone, at that time hardly larger than the state of Massachusetts. By the middle of the sixteenth century, nearly one-third of all land was held by the Church. The old word for "peasant," *smerd,* gave way to *krestianin,* a colloquial form of "Christian." In folk tales and songs, the country was referred to as Holy Russia.

Orthodoxy as enforced by the temporal power was, of course, formal and ritualistic. In the normal negative way, authority tried to muzzle other expressions of culture. In Muscovy, science and the arts were valued only as they might aid in salvation. Secular skills and learning were regarded at best as frivolous entertainment. While authorities might tolerate them, "stern church sermons condemned them as harmful fancies and a pastime which can easily become the devil's game."[3] "Abhorred by God is he who loves ge-

[1] Cf. *sovetski* and *russki* in Communist Party usage since the Revolution.

[2] Prince M. M. Scherbatov, historian and writer (1733-1790), as quoted by Miliukov (188), pp. 39-40 and 43.

[3] Quotations are from Kliuchevsky (133), Vols. II and III (Russian text), unless otherwise indicated.

ometry," said a seventeenth-century bishop, "it is a spiritual sin." And officially at least Russians remained innocent until Peter the Great hired a Scot to teach the elements of Euclid in his first "navigation school." The Copernican system, unknown until the end of Peter's reign, was still, a generation later, suspect in the eyes of the official censors.

A medieval state in the midst of a stirring world, Muscovy had to isolate itself. Muscovites were forbidden to employ teachers of foreign languages or to keep in their homes "Latin, Polish, German or other heretical books." Foreigners in Moscow had to live in a restricted section, *Nemetskaia Sloboda* (Foreign Town), and natives were forbidden to communicate with them except on business.

Orthodoxy and isolation together molded a cultural unity. The Muscovite state known as Holy Russia was "a land of innumerable churches and incessant chimes, of long services, pious prostrations and severe fasts."[4] It was a land "as uniform in . . . religious ideas as only an uncultured nation can be."[5] A society of God's children, it was ruled by a prince, who might be stupid or cruel, but ultimately provided "the commn good of all our orthodox Christendom."[6] The prince governed with the advice of the church council (*osviashchenny sobor*), as well as a council of selected nobles (*duma*). In the seventeenth century, the more important government decrees appeared under the signatures of both the Tsar and the Patriarch, representing the temporal and the spiritual powers. Tsar Alexei (1645-1676) formally shared his lay title of *gosudar* (sovereign) with Patriarch Nikon.

The Tsars ordered the provincial governors (*voevody*) to see to it that the people went to church, observed the fasts, and satisfactorily performed the rituals of worship both in public and in private. Even Peter the Great, who regarded the Church as a part of his household, commanded the people to confess and take communion once a year and attend mass on Sundays and holidays. Delinquents were fined. Police enforced the orders of the clergy and persecuted heretics.

After the death of Patriarch Adrian in 1700, Peter the Great joined

[4] Kornilov (139), Vol. I, p. 40.
[5] Stepniak (265).
[6] Metropolitan Iona of Moscow, as quoted by Kliuchevsky (133), Vol. III.

secular and ecclesiastical powers in his own person. The orthodox community accepted the new arrangement without demur. The two powers, separate in operation, nevertheless had always given effect to the same will, like "the two arms of God."

In the fifteenth century, after Constantinople fell to the Turks (1453) and the Russians threw off the Mongol yoke (1480), Muscovy found itself the only politically independent center of Eastern Christianity. In 1472, Ivan III of Moscow married Sophia (or Zoë) Paleologue, niece of the last Byzantine emperor, and thus acquired a claim to direct succession from Constantinople and Rome. He began to use the title "tsar" (from Caesar)[7] and adopted the Byzantine double eagle as the symbol of Russian monarchy. Moscow then stood forth as the champion and guardian of the whole orthodox East, "the last and the only refuge in the world for the true faith and right worship." In a letter to Vassily III of Moscow (1505-1533), the monk Philotheus of Pskov put it this way: "The church of old Rome fell because of the Apollinarian heresy; the gates of the church of the Second Rome, Constantinople, have been hewn down by the axes of the infidel Turks; but the present church of the Third, the New Rome, of Thy sovereign empire . . . shines in the universe more resplendent than the sun. . . . All the empires of the Orthodox Christian faith have come together in Thy single empire. Thou art the sole Emperor of all the Christians in the whole universe. . . . For two Romes have fallen, but the third stands, and a fourth shall never be."[8]

The Russian began to view his local church as coextensive with universal Christian consciousness which it alone embodied in all its original purity and completeness for all the Christians in the world. It alone possessed the whole truth and had, therefore, "nothing more to learn, nothing to adopt in the matter of faith, but needed only carefully to preserve the treasure entrusted to it."

Historians may debate whether the Third Rome was primarily a religious or a political idea; to the Muscovite, there could be no

[7] Adopted officially in 1547.

[8] The original Old Slavic text of two versions of the letter is found in V. Malinin, *Starets Eleazarova monastyria Filofey i ego poslania* [The Monk Philotheus of the Eleazar Monastery and His Epistles], Kiev, 1901. In translations, a combination of the two texts is commonly used—cf. Wolff (313).

difference. History, regarded as the working out of Divine Providence, now appeared to be working through him. The Tsar was the anointed guardian of both the faith and the faithful. Ivan IV made clear in his correspondence with Prince Kurbsky that he did not distinguish his politics from his service to God.[9] Although the notion of Moscow the Third Rome does not seem ever to have been translated into a political theory of the Russian monarchy or even consistently applied in practice, nevertheless from the fifteenth century Russia acted as a political-religious center toward which the Orthodox populations of Lithuania and Poland, and later of the Balkans, gravitated.[10]

Like other medieval kingdoms, the Muscovite state developed from the personal fief of a minor prince. As it grew in wealth and power, it continued to be governed more as a private estate than a public domain. The prince of Moscow was not a "sovereign" in the true sense of the term. He was, rather, a proprietor and manager. In fact, his official title, *gosudar,* meant master, like the Latin *dominus.* The term was used indifferently for "owner," "lord," "father," head of a household, as well as for "prince," "tsar" and "king."[11] It is only in modern times that the words *gosudar* and *gosudarstvo* assumed the public meaning of "sovereign" and "state."[12] To the Muscovite tsar the state was his family domain. "State institutions . . . were nothing but sources of revenue and their sole purpose was to increase his annual income."[13]

Under Ivan III the bulk of the people were reduced to virtual bondage. A portion of the Muscovite lands, as in medieval Europe, was held by the church, and a portion was granted to the gentry in return for services. In contrast, however, with feudal custom elsewhere, universal service was introduced which, instead of being

[9] Cf. Fennell (77).

[10] Nikolai Berdiaev connects the idea of the Third Rome with the Third International, observing many analogies and concluding that "the fact that the Third International is not an international but a Russian national idea is very poorly understood in the West"—Berdiaev (18), p. 144.

[11] Kliuchevsky (133), Vol. III, p. 76; cf. Dahl (54), Vol. I, p. 387, and Sreznevsky (263), Vol. I, pp. 571-572.

[12] In Ukrainian and Belorussian the corresponding terms are still used as of old.

[13] Kliuchevsky (133), Vol. III.

21

tied to rights in land, was imposed directly on persons. Dividing the people into hereditary estates (soslovia), the Muscovite tsars established virtually a caste system, at the bottom of which the peasant, comprising nine-tenths of the population, retained a nominal personal freedom but little scope in which to exercise it. Peasants were to work six days a week on land they did not own, and they were grouped in communities which had collective re-responsibility for catching criminals and for paying royal taxes.

A Croatian patriot, Yuri Krizhanich (1617-1686), who dreamed of uniting all Slavs under the Tsar of Moscow, admitted that "nowhere in the world is there a government as harsh as they have it in Muscovy." At the same time he rejoiced that by the Tsar's orders all difficulties could be resolved and "anything useful introduced, as cannot possibly be done in any other country."[14] The Tsar's people, indeed, do seem to have been prepared to accept anything at all at the hands of the Father appointed to rule them in the name of God. We hear of no popular dissent or significant unrest in the whole Muscovite period until after the death of Tsar Fedor (1592) with whom the Rurik dynasty, begun in the twelfth century, came at last to its end.[15]

That change in dynasty marked the first break in the Muscovite patriarchal system. People then were called upon to elect a new Tsar, and the years following are generally known as the Time of Troubles, a period of many rulers and near-anarchy, which ended in a popular uprising against Polish Catholic invaders and the election of Mikhail Romanov (1613).

An *elected* father made little sense in the Muscovite state, and the new dynasty from the beginning suffered from the weakness of its origin. While the Tsar's authority remained supreme, one could no longer be sure that his will naturally represented the will of God. Popular unrest and riots in the city of Moscow marked the reign of the first Romanovs. People were apprehensive of innovations and suspicious of the influx of foreigners in various

[14] Kliuchevsky (133), Vol. III, p. 270.
[15] Moscow was founded in 1147. The princes were members of the House of Rurik, established in the ninth century in Novgorod and Kiev. The Moscow dynasty derived from a minor branch of the House, and Ivan I Kalita (1325-1341) laid the foundations of the future state by transforming his domain into the Grand Duchy of Moscow (1338).

branches of the new administration. By the middle of the century, the stage was set for a major explosion.

It began quietly enough. Patriarch Nikon decided to purge Russian church books of errors that had crept in over the years through the ignorance of carelessness of copyists. He therefore engaged competent scholars to collate Russian texts with the Greek originals. But scholars running down textual errors were also re- formers proposing to correct Russian religious practice by making it conform to the practice of Constantinople. And there the religious mind might cavil and demand where religious correctness lay. It was Constantinople, not Moscow, that had fallen to the Turks; Moscow, not Constantinople, that had preserved the kingdom of orthodoxy. If Russians had been worshipping in error, then the orthodox community had failed in its duty to God. But had it? How, then, could the Third Rome have survived and flourished?

The points specifically at issue between Patriarch Nikon and the fundamentalists were on the surface trivial: Whether the sign of the cross should be made with two fingers, symbolizing the dual nature of Christ, or with three, symbolizing the Trinity; whether the "alleluia" should be repeated twice or thrice; whether Jesus should be spelled *Isus* in Cyrillic, according to the old scribal error, or correctly, *Iisus*. Yet over such issues thousands of priests and whole monasteries cut themselves off from the Church and neces- sarily by the same stroke from the State. Leaders of the dissent preferred to be burned at the stake rather than make the minute adjustments in the traditional ritual required of them. The point, of course, was that in such matters the trivial had become of the essence. Would it be insignificant to alter a syllable of the com- mand: "Open Sesame," if thereby its magic were rendered in- effective? In the same way it seemed to the dissenters that rituals in the precise form hallowed by tradition were what made their prayers effective. Whether the forms contained rational errors or indeed might consist wholly of nonsense was beside the point. They embodied the lore under which the tribe survived. They worked, and if changed they might cease to work. Was it not clear that the Greeks had fallen because the forms they used did not work?

The schism or *raskol* thus begun became critical for Russian social history because it was so overwhelmingly a peasant movement. No bishop broke with the established church. The passing of a generation or two wiped out the sprinkling of nobility who were among the early enthusiasts. Led in the beginning by the lower clergy and later by laymen able to recite religious texts (since new priests could no longer be ordained), the *raskolniki* developed a lay cult depending exclusively on the intellectual and moral resources of the countryside. It acquired its martyrs and its myths. Monks of the Solovetsky monastery for eight years stood firm against Nikon's reforms and the Tsar's troops in a state of siege. Less militant but no less brave the Archpriest Avvakum died for his faith, and nameless scores of believers united in collective suicide to consecrate the movement. New impetus came from Peter the Great, whose modernizing decrees further exasperated the fundamentalist soul. Peasants and provincial townsfolk rose in revolts against an order to shave off beards and wear foreign apparel. The imperial attack on hallowed customs made many think Peter the Great was Antichrist, and more thousands—perhaps millions—joined the raskol.

No one ever counted the recruits. The Old Believers themselves never knew their exact numbers. But recent estimates reckon them at more than one-third of the Christian population of Russia in the nineteenth century,[16] and about one-fourth at the time of the Revolution.[17] The impact of the raskol, however, was certainly much broader than even these numerical reckonings suggest.

Beginning in opposition to change, the raskol became revolutionary in the changing world. Indeed, it could not otherwise have survived. Old Believers, while preaching nonviolence, had a hand in nearly all the peasant rebellions from the eighteenth to the twentieth century, notably in the greatest of all, Pugachev's, in the reign of Catherine II. While dedicated to preserving ancient customs, their communities served as a focus for protest.

The paradoxes are not hard to explain. Having broken with state and church on grounds that both had been betrayed and corrupted, the dissenters became necessarily a species of passive anarchist in the empire. They found their warmest welcome among the rebellious as, for instance, among the Cossacks. In their turn the more

[16] Zenkovsky (319, 320).
[17] Miliukov (190).

24

remote Old Believer communities harbored escaped serfs, deserters, the hunted. Within the Russian state, they did not belong to it. They made a world of their own in which they recognized no law but their own customs and beliefs. For the most part they tried to live with the other world as with hostile nature, making use of what they could, opposing what they must, looking always for an escape.

Adjustment was essentially by withdrawal. They established small agricultural colonies in the wilderness of the northeastern forests, in the Ural and Altai Mountains, in Siberia and in the Caucasus, along the Volga, in the depths of the interior provinces. Some were able to hide themselves even in the suburbs of Moscow. In relative seclusion—sometimes in total isolation—they lived and prayed, concealing their communities from state authorities as best they could. In our day villages have been reported in North Siberia where people speaking an outdated dialect knew nothing of the world outside.[18] As late as the first Five-Year Plan, Soviet novelists described the peasantry as "continuing to live in the fashion people lived in the seventeenth century.[19]

But some communities fending for themselves grew strong enough to stand forth in more open defiance, and missionaries went out from those in the guise of peddlers and itinerant laborers to sow "the living seed." One on the Vyg River, not far from the western shore of the White Sea, became more famous than all the rest. Here a monastic community, founded in 1694 to escape "from the heresies and temptations of the world of the Antichrist through common life and prayer," collected within a few years more than 1,500 inhabitants. Under the paternalistic rule of first Andrey (1702-1730), then Semyon (1730-1741) Denisov, scions of an impoverished gentry family, the community prospered. It developed

[18] The notes scribbled by Grigori Rasputin were in style and vocabulary strikingly reminiscent of the old vernacular used by the founders of the raskol —cf. Archpriest Avvakum (11). Cf. also the attempts of Alexei Remisov (1877-1957) to blend in his writings that strain of the Russian speech with the modern Russian standard.

[19] Cf. Pilniak (219): In 1959, a colony of Old Believers secretly practicing its seventh-century Christian faith in Turkey came for the first time to the attention of church authorities when the members petitioned to move to Brazil. The community on the shores of Lake Iznik consisted of 1,000 farmers and fishermen (see *The Guardian*, Manchester, England, 12 November 1959).

industries to make leather goods, clothes, ironware, agricultural implements and, most famous of all, brass castings. So useful were the Vyg manufactures to the empire that Tsar Peter winked at the presence of outlaw artisans and left them in peace and production.

In the course of the eighteenth century, the Vyg community became "the wealthiest joint-stock company in the empire."[20] More importantly, the brothers Denisov laid down the spiritual and moral foundations of the whole raskol movement. Under their pens, the negative attitude of the dissent toward enlightened, or westernized, monarchy was first rationalized in positive terms. Having rejected the Tsar as the spiritual leader of the nation, they substituted the concept of "orthodox Russia"—the association of orthodox Christian congregations—as collectively constituting the supreme authority in both spiritual and temporal matters. The term *sobornost*, in the sense of the collective mind and will, which became later the darling of the Slavophiles, appeared first in the writings of Denisov and, in some sense, in the practice of the Vyg settlement.[21]

The settlement was a federation of monastic and peasant communities, represented by their elders, who elected a cenobiarch. Under his authority the elders formed something like a board of trustees. Decisions were by majority vote and, formally, the cenobiarch's voice was decisive only in a tie. The political reality, however, was not democratic. It represented a mixture of the monastic tradition and the town meeting government, *veche,* inherited from ancient Novgorod, Pskov, and Viatka. The Vyg administration dealt with communities and households, not with individuals. The cenobiarch and the elders were all elected for life and could not be removed except by revolution. General meetings were called only at the discretion of the cenobiarch and exercised only advisory powers, like the family council in a peasant household. The elders' decisions were not subject to appeal to the general meeting, and dissent was not tolerated once a decision had been made. The community thus governed and owning its lands, industries, and even merchant and whaling fleets in common, more nearly resembled a miniature socialism under a "collective leadership" dominated by the unquestioned authority of the top man.

[20] Stepniak (265), p. 467.
[21] For detailed discussion, see Zenkovsky (320).

Defense against the Antichrist was the main concern of the Denisovs. They wanted to save the true faith, so that they might assure the salvation of mankind. Their perspective was not national but universal, even though their actions at first had to be limited to uniting the faithful in one country. They set great store by education, which consisted chiefly in indoctrination in the old religious texts. It was training in dogma, but its more important by-products were a much higher rate of literacy among the Old Believers than among the rest of the peasantry, livelier imagination as expressed in folklore and artisanship, greater prosperity, greater readiness for leadership.

The Old Believers came to dream of finding the Kingdom of God on earth somewhere beyond the political realm of St. Petersburg—in the mythical White Waters (*Belovodie*) governed by the White Tsar.[22] This kingdom of God was, of course, a kingdom of peasants, for peasants working God's land were the beloved of God. One day, they believed, the White Tsar would extend his domain to the whole of Russia—a kind of peasant Messianism which perhaps helped prepare the countryside to receive the Revolution.[23]

In the meantime, the Old Believers and the law-abiding Orthodox lived side by side, sometimes in different sections of the same village, sometimes even more closely intermixed physically. Yet the sectarians held themselves apart. They had little respect for the indifferent mass of the peasantry. Intermarriages were rare. Mutual distrust and hostility plagued rural life. Only in the customs inherited from pre-Christian time and in their almost instinctive hostility to outside authority were the villages at one. Among the peasants at large the age-old habit of obedience prevailed, and they continued to regard the Tsar, however tyrannical, as Father and undoubted master of life and property. For oppressions they suffered they blamed not the Tsar but his "drones and parasites."

[22] In Russian folklore, "white" (*bely*) has always been a symbol of purity, innocence, and freedom.

[23] Leon Trotsky, explaining the success of the Bolshevik revolution, says: ". . . And to this we must add the work of the sectarian ideas which had taken hold of millions of peasants. 'I know many peasants,' writes a well-informed author, 'who accepted . . . the October [November] revolution as the direct realization of their religious hopes' "—(285), Vol. III, p. 30. Ample evidence is found in poetry and prose by peasant authors in the early Soviet period; cf. Zavalishin (318).

Indeed, the worse the imperial officials and the clergy behaved the stronger grew the peasants' conviction that the Tsar, if only he knew, would turn the rascals out. But whether the Tsar blundered or sinned, his rule enforced in all peasant minds much the same conclusion: that the world had been run too long by city people who humiliated peasants, exploited them, deprived them of hope, and ignored their most elementary needs as human beings.

And it was all true. The upper classes in the course of time had developed almost wholly out of contact with the rural world. While both Old Believer and Orthodox in the village retained remarkably the medieval vision of a single religious-temporal community paternalistically governed, the gentry and city folk were becoming secularized, westernized, creating a new and distinctive culture, brilliant in its artistic and philosophic accomplishments, but desperately thin and remote from the mass of the people.

Secularization, begun under Peter the Great, was confined to the principal cities and the homes of the larger landowners. In 1790, there were still only 269 schools, 629 teachers, and 16,525 students in the whole of the empire of 29 million. Readers of *War and Peace* seldom realize that the well-educated Russians about whom Tolstoy wrote numbered at that time only a few hundred, not many thousands. Several decades later, when the total population had grown to 75 million, the circulation of all Russian periodicals together did not exceed 12,000 copies.

Under increasing western influence, a new cultural élite was being formed. First a product and tool of the modernizing government, it soon cast loose and developed that curious, unique, brilliant, and tragic misfit the Russian intelligentsia. Existing between the unenlightened government, on the one hand, and the dark masses, on the other, it made a kind of world of its own and, in two centuries, not only caught up with the level of civilization in the rest of Europe but began in turn to influence European literature, arts, and certain branches of science. The new capital of Russia, St. Petersburg, rivaled London, Paris, and Vienna in its beauty and air of sophistication. Modernized Moscow and Kiev were at least the equals of western European cities of comparable size.

But Russia westernized was Russia still. Despite the reformed and modernized institutions; the new trends in literature, arts, and science; and the changing economy and ways of life among the educated, which marked Russian culture at the beginning of this century, the new élite displayed certain distinctive, apparently un-European, mental traits which it has been tempting to think of as uniquely Russian. In fact, they were more likely anachronistic reminiscences of an earlier cultural age. Nikolai Berdiaev has remarked "the characteristically Russian search for an integral outlook which would give an answer to all questions of life, unite theoretical and practical reason and give a philosophical basis to the social idea."[24] Generally viewed as a manifestation of "Russian messianism," could that search not be more plausibly explained as a subconscious memory of the historical time when Russian society was in fact embraced in a system having "an answer to all the questions of life"?

While a Henry Adams in quest of ideal unity had to look back 500 years and to a foreign land and alien tradition, a Kireyevsky or a Danilevsky[25] could tap a native tradition at a distance of hardly more than 200 years and with the aid all around him of cultural survivals of the medieval idea.

To those recent—and in significant ways still current—Middle Ages might be referred that extreme dogmatism to which "Russians are fundamentally disposed," and which was "characteristic of the Russian intelligentsia, dominated as it was by social motives and by a revolutionary frame of mind." The frame of mind, it should be noted, was also passionately religious. Indeed, to study the Russian revolutionary tradition is to see political parties uniformly behaving rather like sects than clubs. "Russians are always inclined to take things in a totalitarian sense," Berdiaev writes. "Among the Russian radical intelligentsia there existed an idolatrous attitude to[ward] science [natural and social alike]. . . . What was a scientific theory in the West, a hypothesis, or in any case a relative truth, partial, making no claim to be universal, became among the Russian intelligentsia a dogma, a sort of religious revelation."[26]

But if the intelligentsia may thus be said to have had a medieval

[24] Berdiaev (18), p. 38.
[25] Ivan V. Kireyevsky (1806-1856) and Nikolai Y. Danilevsky (1822-1885), leaders of the Russian Slavophiles.
[26] Berdiaev (18), pp. 20-21.

cast to its thinking, it did not in that regard discover any sympathy with the medievalism of the countryside. Quite the contrary. It was living and thinking in the modern world. The "reminiscences" of a lost unity became revolutionary when compared—and this for the nineteenth-century intelligentsia was the whole point—with the decadence of the modernizing, industrializing society being constructed on the western model. Between two worlds, the Russian intellectual was alienated from both. His passion for a kind of medieval restoration of unity had nothing in common either with the medieval social and political forms of the village or with the peasant's chronic irritations over his chronically depressed and stagnant role in the world. They wanted the ancient unity reconstructed on a new rational or, as they would put it, "scientific" basis.

For almost three centuries the urban cultivated stratum of Russian society and the rural masses had lived almost wholly separate lives, hardly even conscious of belonging to a single national body. Only on the abolition of serfdom in 1861 did they meet again, as it were, as a common citizenry. Then, writes Stepniak, the passionate nineteenth-century chronicler of the peasants' woes, "It was as though two cultures, two different universes, we may almost say two different types of human nature, as strongly individualized as they were incompatible, had suddenly been brought face to face."[27]

Thereafter the cultured world extended itself a little, undermining rural tradition here and there. But the force working to bridge the historical gap was too small, and the gap was too wide. At the moment of revolution the provincial world and the urban élite were still, as Berdiaev said, "on different planets." In the revolution the planets collided in open war.

[27] Stepniak (265), p. 154.

BATIUSHKA[1]*:* LITTLE FATHER

THERE WERE RICH PEASANTS AND POOR PEASANTS. KULAKI, WHO MIGHT
have large acreage under long lease and by usurious loans hold
whole villages in virtual bondage, were a true if singularly unat-
tractive rural plutocracy. *Batraki,* at the other end of the social
scale, the landless ones who cultivated for landlords and kulaks,
were a true and miserable rural proletariat. In between were the
large bulk of the peasantry, the *seredniaki,* or gray *muzhiki.* These
middling men might live in the most abject poverty; they might
be in debt and have to hire out their labor in order to live at all,
but they had land of their own under cultivation and possessed
cattle and farm implements.

Nearly all peasant families lived in the traditional peasant cottage
(*izba*), comprising two or three rooms, only one of which was
heated. The richer peasants might have two huts connected, but
larger dwellings were rare. The main room was dominated by a
massive clay stove (*pech*) for cooking and heating. In big families—
and a family that flourished was inevitably numerous—the grand-
parents and sometimes the little children slept on top of the stove.
Typically, the only other furnishings were an unpolished table in
one corner, with the indispensable sacred ikons hung above it,
and around the walls wooden benches for sitting and sleeping. For
extra bunks, shelves might be built in tiers as in a forecastle, but
more commonly the preferred bed was a pile of straw on the floor.
Overcoats served for blankets. The unheated rooms were the *seni,*

---

[1] Grammatically defined as the diminutive of *batia* (father, dad; cf. Hindu-
stani *batu*), the word is endearing, not diminutive in any logical sense; somewhat parallel to our "daddy," though less intimate and informal, it expresses
wholehearted filial devotion, respect, and awe at the same time, e.g. *Tsar-
batiushka.*

properly the entrance hall but used in summer for sleeping, and the *klet*, which, when it existed, often served as the bedroom for the married son. The izba gave on a courtyard (*dvor*) commonly enclosed by the cattle and implement sheds. But many peasants lived in what were called open courtyards, whose outbuildings had been burned for firewood.

Open or closed, the courtyard rather than the hut was home. "Out of doors" in Russian is *na dvore* (in the courtyard). A village is reckoned as comprising so many *dvory*. The unit was not a residence but a domain—tiny, cramped, crude, but nevertheless a whole and, ideally, a self-sufficient colony of people and beasts. In the wedding folk songs the bride and bridegroom are serenaded as king and queen—the custom being observed throughout the period of serfdom! Behind the poetry lay some literal truth: the married couple could start their own economy (*khoziaistvo*) and, however poor they might be, they would be sovereign within their dvor.

The striking fact of peasant life was its primary communism. The basic social unit was not the person but the household. The basic political unit was the village. To each of these an individual inextricably belonged, and could not act or be thought of in his daily existence apart from them.

In the enforced intimacy of the tiny izba there could be no room for privacy or even the notion of privacy.[2] Instead of "leave me alone" the Russian says, "leave me in peace," (*ostav menia v pokoe*) and he may expect to be left in peace even when physically in the midst of a group. In the izba where there was no corner to which a member of the family could withdraw to mark his separateness, to be left in peace could not be claimed as a right but only as an indulgence from a benevolent father who would not ordinarily care what an individual did with his spare time provided that he was trusted.

Peasant life, however, did not encourage individualism. Farming techniques were so archaic and inefficient that it just barely paid men to go to the trouble of cultivating the land. The average yield of grain available to the cultivator for food at each harvest was a little less than threefold the seed planted, and rarely exceeded six-

[2] In fact, there is no adequate term for "privacy" in Russian, and the descriptive phrases used in literature are not found in folklore.

fold. No other long-settled country, including India, did so poorly.[3] To subsist at all on such meager bounty, the peasant needed continuous productive labor as well as more than a reasonable share of good luck.[4] One man could not make it. Even man and wife together could hope at best only to keep alive. But with three or four workers, men and women, able to exploit a larger holding of land, care for animals, and manage the household, there was a chance for small surpluses that might be sold; and the money received, put out at usury. The marginal conditions of life which kept the bulk of the peasantry desperately poor also provided opportunity for wealth for the few. The majority who had to borrow to get through the winter alive could be and were persuaded to mortgage property and labor at rates which usually guaranteed default. Thus, to become a creditor in the village, even if one began on a very small scale, was the path to wealth and power and virtually the only one. Since surplus labor alone made that possible, it followed that numbers in the patriarchal family were literally riches.

In everyday Russian usage a child is called *rebenok* (cf. the standard Russian *ditia*). Historically, it is a diminutive of *rab*—Old Russian "worker"; modern standard, "slave"—and grammatically, it belongs with a class of words denoting the young of animals, like *telenok* (calf), *zherebenok* (colt), *tsyplenok* (chicken). Language here accurately reflects the interest of the farmer in children as little workers—a universal bias in agricultural societies—and his disposition, otherwise, to reckon them with the livestock. Indeed, the young of other animals could commonly expect greater solicitude. As a Siberian peasant once remarked to explain the relative value of horses and people: "A man—any of us can make a man. But a mare—just try to make a mare!"[5]

It was primarily to produce workpower that peasants married. A woman's beauty and personal charms were little valued. Customarily, if she proved unable to bear children the marriage was

[3] Maynard (181), p. 30.

[4] The word for luck or chance, *avos*, has almost idolatrous connotations; cf. *avoska*, the "shopping bag" in Soviet Russian parlance.

[5] Maynard (181), p. 175. See also the peasant poet Sergei Essenin who in one of his most moving poems sees the ultimate horrors of the civil war in animal rather than human slaughter—when hungry peasants kill their working animals and, like cannibals, partake of their flesh.

annulled—simply by sending her back to her family. Marriage was essentially a contract to establish a mutually profitable association to multiply—crops and workers.

Evidently the productive unit thus formed had to function as a unit dedicated wholly to its objective and disciplined effectively to the task. The family was unified under the absolute authority of the head. A *totalitarian* society in miniature, it demanded ideally not only the obedience of all members to the head of the group but the devotion of each to the purposes of the whole.[6]

Legislative, judicial, executive, and moral authority all merged in the head of the household. He disposed the tasks, judged the performance, flogged the recalcitrant. Nothing could take place in the realm he controlled without his knowledge, let alone without his permission. He guarded the family's traditions and its morals. It was his unquestioned right to know what every member did and thought, and the unquestioned duty of each to keep him informed. Since the individual had no independent standing, secrecy could only be regarded as disloyalty to the group.

Although in the presence of difficult problems the father might call a family council and permit argument, criticism, and even recrimination, the power of decision was his alone and subject to no appeal. A decision might be made contrary to some opinions expressed; but, once made, it was understood to have unanimous support. The notions of consensus and majority rule were foreign to the peasant world. Like the modern dictator, a father was held to act as trustee and embodiment of the will of all. Right answers—the *volonté générale*—were to be found not by polling the members but by perceiving directly their higher good. To turn the comparison around in its proper historical order, the totalitarian leader, like the peasant father, does not just take care of his subjects; he knows and exercises their true will by doing for them what they want done even when they do not themselves know their own

[6] Totalitarian society can be defined as "a society all of whose activities, from the rearing of children to the production and distribution of economic goods, are controlled and directed from a single center"; cf. Moore (194), p. 31; Friedrich (85), p. 47; Friedrich and Brzezinski (86), pp. 9-10. The contention that "no known society of course has ever coincided exactly with this conception" is erroneous unless, as a matter of definition, family is considered not a society.

minds. The fact of unanimous consent may then be celebrated in appropriate rites, such as elections in the totalitarian state or exercises of personal subjection in the household.

The head of the peasant household was not necessarily the natural father. "It is quite common among the peasantry that when a father or mother pass the farm to the son, then the son and his wife become masters and the old folk have to earn their bread as best they can."[7] If the father died, his eldest son, as a general rule, took his place. "He's a man, the stupidest of the stupid," says a peasant in a story by Ivan Turgenev. "His brothers are lively lads, I'm told . . . nevertheless, he is their head.

"Why is that?

"Because he's the eldest! That means . . . younger lads, obey."[8] So it is in the Soviet Communist party: "When there are elder brothers and younger brothers in a family," said Soviet Marshal Bagramian, referring to the Party affairs, "the elder ones agree and the younger ones do not quarrel any more."[9]

In the farm household there was no time to waste in persuasion. The duty of all members was to obey. Whoever balked must be forced into submission, and no one doubted that this could be done. "A rabbit can learn to strike a match if you beat him hard enough," said Anton Chekhov of this educational method, and the phrase has assumed the currency of a proverb. A rustic character in Ivan Bunin's novel, *The Village,* praises another for the way he "has educated those brats. . . . He's a soldier. He beats them unmercifully, but he has them well trained in all sorts of ways."[10] This—it should be noted—is not the old-fashioned school of child upbringing. It is the much more ancient, not to say atavistic, harking back to a trust in physical pain as the normal path to learning. Anton Chekhov describes in a story a good-natured peasant attendant at a mental hospital who regularly beat the patients on principle: "When he beats somebody he beats him about the face, the chest, the back—wherever his blows may fall—and he is convinced that without this there would be no order in this place."[11] It was customary

[7] Tolstoy (281).
[8] Turgenev (287).
[9] At a reception at the Turkish Embassy in Moscow (Associated Press, 29 October 1958).
[10] Bunin (37), p. 207.
[11] Chekhov (43).

in the village for the bride's father to give her husband a new knout which was often hung over the bridal bed. Symbolism, to be sure, but symbolism that was never far removed from the literal reality.[12]

Beatings, of course, were not merely educational; they also provided an emotional outlet for men who typically were both frustrated by the conditions of their life and inarticulate. The village was accustomed to physical expressions of a man's will and temper. Kulak meant "fist," and kulak was the symbol of both physical and economic dominance. A blow of the fist was the natural assertion of authority—Nikita Khrushchev has been seen pounding his desk at the United Nations with his fist, not with the palm of his hand. Stories of Russian rural life without brawls or beatings are nearly as rare as Westerns without gun fights.

Women, of course, took more than their share of these beatings, and their submissiveness is proverbial in Russian literature. Yet women on the whole did not occupy an inferior position in the peasant household. They might be whipped in fury because they were weaker, or disciplined because they were subordinate to the head of the house. But as women they did not have special disabilities. They were regarded as equal both in their essential obligations and in the rewards they might expect therefrom. Girls, in fact, enjoyed more freedom in the peasant household than boys and were even allowed to have some personal property which was recognized and protected by customary law. While as marriageable and therefore temporary workers they did not share equally in the inheritance, brothers of an unmarried girl were obliged after the father's death to outfit her suitably for marriage.

Wives shared in the authority and dignity of their husbands. However submissive to the master in the management of the economy, they reared the children and directed the work of women as though supreme in a separate domain. Custom distinguished the tasks proper to men and to women. Thus, a man might clean pigsties without shrinking, yet feel it degrading to sweep the floor of his own cottage. Correspondingly, a woman would feel not only put upon but debased if she had to plow and sow when there was a man about the house. On the other hand, in the absence of men, women were prepared to do all the work at home and in the fields

[12] Cf. for instance, Chekhov (42) or Gladkov (89).

—as they did during World War II. A capable widow, with help from her sons, could run the farm herself and would then exercise the full authority of a head of household.

When the Marxists came to preach sexual equality they found themselves more at home among Russian peasants than in some more sophisticated circles. It was not in emancipating women that the revolution upset traditional arrangements but in forcing women to work outside the home. Here the change has been great. Women now make up 48 per cent of the work force in Soviet industry. They constitute 75 per cent of the medical doctors; 70 per cent of the teachers; 40 per cent of the judges. Against the few who have found rewarding careers must be set the many whom the new dispensation has put to pushing wheelbarrows on road construction jobs, driving trolleys, laying bricks, painting, working lathes and power tools, and shucking grain and stacking hay on collective farms. In Soviet cities women, not men, collect the garbage, shovel the snow, and sweep the streets. To a shocked American tourist, a Soviet official explained from the characteristically homely point of view: "Isn't it the woman's job to keep the house clean?"

In other ways, too, peasants in Russia—as everywhere else in the world—practiced Communist principles long before Karl Marx made ideals out of them. "From each according to his ability, to each according to his need," for instance, has been pragmatic household doctrine for as long as the family existed. It was the father's privilege and responsibility to use the abilities of each member of the household and meet their needs as he judged fit. Of a peasant father, Gleb Uspensky writes, "He took all the money earned by his sons. One brother earned more, another less, for equal skill was not required for their respective work. They were all put on equal footing by the absolute rule of their father."[13] Fedor Gladkov testifies that—fifty years later—all money earned in his own family was turned over to the grandfather, the head of the household.[14]

[13] Uspensky (293).

[14] Gladkov (89). The Chinese father before the Revolution also had the right to appropriate the earnings of his sons for a common purse for the expenses of all; cf. Su (269), pp. 47-50. So could the father in ancient Rome's agrarian days. In some sense members of the family might be regarded as chattels; cf. Queen (228).

37

In practice, both peasant and modern communist have valued and therefore tended to reward the effective rather than the merely needy. Those whose abilities the farm household could not use—the very young, the very old, and the sick—were provided little more than bare subsistence. Custom held that a man need not feed his wife and children if they refused to work.[15] An idle child might be disinherited in favor of an outsider working without wages. So the operative principle became, "To each according to his work." That is also how it has read in Marxist orthodoxy since the Soviet Constitution of 1936, which capped Stalin's rise. "God likes labor," says the peasant-born Russian proverb. "Work in the U.S.S.R.," proclaims Article 12 of the Constitution, "is a duty and a matter of honor for every ablebodied citizen." And the state, like the father of course sees to it that the duty is performed.

In rural society father's authority was natural, not legal, and it had natural, not legal, limitations. As an individual outside his household he was tightly bound by laws, regulations, and customs. But within it he answered only to God, and even there rather for his devotion to proper ends than for the humane exercise of his powers. If he failed the family it was too bad for the family. They had no effective redress. The village would not interfere, unless the father needed help in flogging his sons. Peasant courts seldom acted on complaints against husbands or parents. The common view was that father was necessarily right, that his authority was sacred, and that resistance to his will was worse than a crime: it was a sin.

In 1911, a Belorussian peasant drowned his disobedient son. Tried by a rural court, he was found guilty and sentenced to three months in jail not for murder, but for "failing to bring the boy up in the sacred virtue of filial obedience." Although the case was re-tried three times, the peasant verdict remained the same. To get a conviction for murder it was necessary at last to hale the accused before an imperial court in the city.[16] Twenty years later, another man shot his wife for refusing to give up an outside job and return

[15] The principle, of course, is very old indeed and unarguable in a primitive agricultural society. St. Paul, writing, "If any would not work, neither should he eat" (II Thess., 3, 10), stated a maxim much older than Christianity. In American Puritan households, "a master was required to give a certain basic minimum to all, but beyond that he gave different kinds of compensation to different kinds of servants"; Morgan (195), p. 69.

[16] Vakar (295), p. 23.

to her household duties. Peasant jurors, both men and women, held it to be justifiable homicide. Sovereign within his household, man had the right to deal as he pleased with a refractory wife.[17]

The cases have an outlandish sound that tempts us to exclaim, "How Russian!" But in fact they are remote in time, not space. In colonial America, wrote a contemporary observer, "Without exception [the husband] is master over the house; as touching his family [he has] more authoritie than a king in his kingdome."[18] The Puritan child was taught that it was his scriptural duty to obey, and his will to resist, according to one historian, "was broken by persistent and adequate punishment. He was taught it was a sin to find fault with his meals, his apparel, his tasks, or his lot in life."[19] And in this the Old Testament, written for another agricultural society, offered stout support: "If a man has a stubborn and rebellious son, which will not obey the voice of his father, or the voice of his mother, and that, when they have chastened him, will not hearken unto them: Then shall his father and his mother lay hold on him, and bring him out unto the elders of his city . . . and all the men of his city shall stone him with stones, that he die . . ."[20] The echo of this prescription in a seventeenth-century Connecticut "blue law"[21] owes perhaps more to religious fanaticism than to parallel economic conditions. Yet the economic basis in the hard, primitive life can at least be negatively demonstrated: the autocratic Puritan family proved it could not survive the receding frontier. The autocratic Russian family has fared no better with urbanization and rising standards of living; but in the isolation of the Russian countryside it has survived to our day.[22]

[17] Maynard (181), pp. 177-178.
[18] Lumpkin (173), p. xiii.
[19] Earle (67), p. 214.
[20] Deut., 21:18-21.
[21] "If a man have a stubborn and rebellious son of sufficient years and understanding, viz. sixteen years of age, which will not obey . . . then may his father and mother lay hold on him and bring him to the magistrates . . . such a son shall be put to death"; J. Hammond Trumbull, ed., *The Blue Laws of Connecticut and the False Blue Laws Invented by the Rev. Samuel Pebers* (Hartford, 1876), quoted in Queen (228), p. 256.
". . . But rather than apply this extreme penalty, the courts directed another law against parents whose affections blinded them to their children's faults"; Morgan (195), p. 38.
[22] Cf. some survivals in the United States: "Obedience to [parental] authority necessary for the well-being of the Highland family and community

39

The patriarchal family developed to save the individual by suppressing him. In some measure it succeeded. Foreign observers for centuries have been impressed with how much more docile to command are the Russian masses than any other European folk. Russia's long tolerance of despotism, under Tsar and Communist, is indeed remarkable. But historians who have written that the tyranny of the Tsars conditioned the nation to accept the tyranny of the Communists have missed the fact that Russian habits of obedience have been the cause, not the result, of political autocracy. The autocrat was the image of authority which each child learned to accept in the family, where his first and most durable political concepts were formed. "The physical superiority of the father . . . is the child's first experience of authority. In the patriarchal family . . . the father is the breadwinner. . . . The father is bigger, stronger, wiser and wealthier than the children. Conflicts with him have consequences. As a result of a long and painful process the individual learns in the family not merely to take account of authority but also to respect it. He adapts himself to circumstances by rationalizing his dependency and finding his satisfaction therein."[23]

The "long and painful process" shapes personalities at least as permanently as a tight boot habitually worn from infancy shapes a foot. As a rationalized rule of behavior the habit of ready obedience tends to subdue the self. One learns not only to accept command but to require it. The typical child of contemporary Western parents, even when "well brought up," feels free to do whatever is not explicitly forbidden. A person reared in the dependency of a patriarchal household is schooled to act only in ways explicitly permitted. He tends to abdicate his will power and even his desires, and to function as an agent of necessities for which he can feel no personal responsibility. Once accustomed to moral dependence he can hardly escape it.

Typically, the peasant declined even such free choice as might be open to him and demanded that all his action be covered by higher authority. Even in rebellion he sought out the familiar pattern of

---

becomes a pleasure, an obligation, a part of life. . . . The Ozark social organization is one which has existed undisturbed for a long period in a situation where the aims of the individual and of the family were fused"; Zimmerman (322), pp. 283-285.

[23] Horkheimer (107), pp. 905-907.

command and submission. An old revolutionary recalls that before the Revolution a worker came to him, wishing to help in underground conspiracy against the Tsarist regime. The worker said: "When I was a boy I obeyed my father, and since I have begun to work I have obeyed my master, and now I am going to obey you. You know what to do and I don't. Just tell me."[24]

This craving for command, it should be noted, was a craving only for command by a father or father figure. Lacking any abstract notion of institutionalized power, the peasant was loyal to God rather than to the church, to the Tsar rather than to the imperial government, to Stalin rather than to the Party. Father was always right; not so his agents. Old Believers had felt it their sacred duty to resist both Tsar and Patriarch because these, as they saw it, were appointed by God and had betrayed Him. An Orthodox peasant who would not dream of resisting the Tsar knew that often enough the Tsar's agents, his police, his clerks, his minor officials, were corrupt and inept. He reasoned that if the Father of all the Russians were not so far away and also knew the truth he would repudiate those who acted harshly or unworthily in his name. Thus the habit of absolute obedience to the supreme authority, so long as it was reckoned natural and true, by no means prepared the kind of disciplined society which is sometimes associated with German culture.

Russian history is crowded with pretenders. Nearly every rebel leader felt he had either to claim royal blood or attach himself to a claimant. The mass of the peasantry would burn and pillage with enthusiasm if convinced they had the Tsar's permission or, better still, his command. So Ivan Bolotnikov (1606-1607), an ex-serf who preached class war in the Time of Troubles, nevertheless associated himself with a false *Tsarevich* (son of the Tsar). When in an extremity, under siege in the city of Tula, he sent word to the Poles to create another, more powerful one. (The Poles obliged, but too late to save Bolotnikov.) The Cossack brigand, Stenka Razin, who between 1667 and 1671 led uprisings of peasants in the lower Volga, claimed to have the Tsar's son on his side as well as the Patriarch of the Church. Emelian Pugachev (1773-1775), in the greatest revolt of the three, himself impersonated Tsar Peter III and created a bogus court. All led specifically rural uprisings pre-

[24] *Novy Zhurnal*, 46, (1956), p. 133.

cipitated by peasant grievances. Pugachev's took on the proportions of a peasant war. Yet none in fact challenged the existing system of power: neither the despotic rule of the Tsar nor the communal bonds of the village.

Peasants hated men, not institutions. In individuals the hate could run very deep, as deep as the total frustrations endured by those whose whole life experience was a lesson in inferiority. Fedor Gladkov, the late Soviet novelist, who was born a peasant in the Volga region, has told of his boyhood in the house ruled by his grandfather. One day the grandfather sent Fedor's father to town on an errand. On the way back the horses died of exhaustion. Fedor's father, having reached home on foot, fell on his knees before the old man and in the presence of the whole family reported his loss and begged mercy. But, Fedor recalls, instead, "Grandfather brandished the knout and my father tried to seize it with trembling hands to avoid the blow. Seeing that, my grandmother ran up to my father and shouted at him angrily, 'Damn you! Trying to stand up to your own father? Have you lost your mind?'" The old man by then had spent his energy and, after cursing his son, turned away. "After that night grandfather never noticed my father who now was like a stranger in our home. When he ate with us he sat at the end of the table, never lifting his head." And thereafter, Fedor concludes, "He nourished in himself a constant resentment against grandfather. . . . He bore himself with contempt toward grandfather in his absence, but to his face he expressed devotion and unconditional subordination."[25]

Some forty years later a refugee from the Soviet Union, describing life on a collective farm, reported the same mixture of outward submission and inward fury. "If the chairman of the village soviet comes around and abuses a peasant verbally for something the peasant is not guilty of, he will be silent and will wear a face of guilt. But inside . . . he will be furious and hurt. . . . When he comes home he will drink, if he can get it, or he will fight with his wife."[26]

When these locked-up furies escaped they ran wild in orgies of plunder and destruction. That is what happened in the Bolshevik Revolution. But when the struggle for power was settled the peas-

[25] Gladkov (89), pp. 313 ff.
[26] Dinerstein (62), p. 127.

42

ants, as practical men, made their peace, on the whole, with the winners, whom they accepted as new masters in the old way, without prejudice to either past or future allegiance. It is notable that although the German invasion in 1941 released an immense amount of dissatisfaction against Communist rule, the peasants in occupied Belorussia and the Ukraine did not always seek vengeance on the few Party members who stayed on in the village. Often, indeed, the local Communists were sheltered from the Germans and given their share of land and cattle from the redistribution of the collective farms. In the autocratic pattern of administration impressed on the peasant mind, all responsibility rested with those at the top, who exercised all power. The instruments—all who obeyed— might be abhorred personally if they were arrogant, but they suffered no guilt by association.

When Nikita Khrushchev denounced the sins of Stalin to the Twentieth Party Congress in 1956 it would not seriously have occurred to him or to most of his listeners that having served Stalin as obediently and efficiently as he did he shared in the master's guilt. On the contrary, from his point of view exposure of the crime after the fact—that is, as soon as Khrushchev became a free agent—wiped the slate clean. It dissociated present rule from past error and promised that as responsibility shifted so would policy toward a better day.[27]

To the civilized mind, trained to consider all men morally responsible for their own actions, this was hypocrisy. If Khrushchev acquiesced in Stalin's sins from complacency, he proved his own moral delinquency. If he acquiesced from fear, he testified to the desperate helplessness of men and nations in the grip of the new absolutism. By either view he confessed that neither the system nor its men could ever be trusted to behave justly. He proved, in short, what we always knew, that men being capable of evil cannot be trusted with unrestricted power.

But to a mind shaped to consider autocracy the natural order of families and states, a contradictory first principle seemed no less axiomatic: that no man may resist the command of him whose position requires him to rule. This is the practical justification of unfreedom in primitive conditions of life where the need for survival is paramount and the margin for error almost nil. What

[27] For further discussion of de-Stalinization, see Chapter 6.

Khrushchev did as a member of Stalin's household he did to uphold the established order which, subsequently, as boss himself he proposed to improve. For the promised improvement one could only be grateful. Did the system not demonstrate double virtue in purging its own error while retaining its omnipotence? There was after all something god-like in the free disposition of reform, and the face of the past as publicly washed by Khrushchev could indeed seem less like a man corrupted than like a god cleansed. At least, the faithful might feel that without rebellion the father grew in wisdom and the family prospered.

However bitter the memory of the late Master, it has remained sacred. He personified family—the Party—and when he sinned the family sinned with him. Whatever the collective burden of sin, it was to be lifted after his death, and the family redemption would be his redemption, too. Khrushchev performed the rite. Everybody felt purified, and the family was restored to grace. In the cult of ancestors thus adjusted, the monuments to Stalin can stand not as a reminder of his errors, but as symbols of eternal family "unity and greatness."[28]

Everywhere, not in Russia alone, people at a certain level of cultural development "act together under the benevolent domination of a parent-autocrat who, by his success in commanding the respect and loyalty of the members, has made his will and the wishes and welfare of the group identical. When issues arise, therefore, [the members] look to him to settle them; when choices are to be made, they turn to his authoritative word; and when the law is spoken, they regard it as their duty not only to obey it but to agree with it as right."[29] What is difficult for the civilized mind to encompass is the appearance of the Little Father system as the governance of a major nation in the twentieth century.

[28] See, for instance, the issue of *Pravda* dedicated to Stalin's memory, 7 March 1957.
[29] Lumpkin (173), p. 28.

4

MIR: LITTLE WORLD[1]

TO PASS FROM THE PEASANT HOUSEHOLD TO THE PEASANT VILLAGE IS
to seem to leap from autocracy into a perfect democracy. Those
who, like the populists (*narodniki*) of the late nineteenth century,
idealized the Russian peasant as the uncorrupted child of nature
found in the communal organization of the village (*mir*) an expression of natural equality, togetherness, unselfishness, coopera-
tiveness, and that specifically Russian mystical notion of sobornost
(see Chapter 2), the dogma that truth exists indivisible in the
whole council or congregation. In the village council each man
counted for one, no matter who he was. No chairman directed the
proceedings. Since all decisions had to be unanimous, no majority
tyrannized over dissenters. The mir's executive agents, the elders,
were only servants employed to carry out orders so minutely defined
as to leave no discretionary authority. In the extensive economic
affairs which the mir managed, even the idea of private property in
land was banished. The common interest unanimously agreed upon
was commonly administered on behalf of all.

That was the ideal, the model mir. The real mir was not only
something less than that; it was something radically different.

The idealistic intelligentsia looked at the Russian village the way
Western romantics regarded the noble savage, from an immense
cultural distance and with unreasoned and unreasonable faith in
human goodness. From a sophisticated urban civilization they
transported their generous spirits to the village in order there to
listen to echoes of their own noble sentiments. They forgot that
before they came no such spirit spoke to the primitive world. They
failed to note that it was this spirit of theirs, developed in civiliza-

[1] *Mir* is Russian for "peace," "world," and "village community of farmers."

tion, which was basic to democracy, not the traditions of the village. They found, therefore, much more in the mir than was really there and saw much less.

Mir in Russian means "world" and also "peace" in the sense of orderliness and harmony.[2] The peasant's village mir was a little "orderly world." A federation of sovereign peasant households, it exercised collective authority over every matter of joint concern to villagers living in intimate relationship with each other and in isolation from the rest of the world. It acted as a town meeting of the heads of households, who decided everything unanimously by custom and common sense.

Essentially, the mir existed to distribute land in the open-field system of husbandry (*obshchina*). Land was unfenced and cultivated in strips under rotation. Since a third of it always lay fallow and since the arable was necessarily of unequal quality, a central authority was needed to apportion the land fairly. As households fluctuated in the number of working members and as new land was brought under cultivation, the mir was periodically called upon to redistribute holdings. Before emancipation all land belonged to the crown, the church, or the gentry. But it never seemed so to the peasant. The practical attributes of land ownership were after all the right to assign it to use, which the peasants exercised through the mir, and the right to take produce from it, which each family acquired by its work. For the peasant, the land was his who worked it. "We are yours," said the serfs to their masters, "but the land is ours."

The Emancipation Act (1861) gave each village the option of breaking up the land into privately owned parcels or of keeping it as common property. Communal tenure was accepted by 73 per cent of the peasantry, but none anywhere questioned the right of each family to the products of its labor. The peasant regarded land not as property but as sustenance to which each man must have access so long as he was ready to devote his labor to making it fruitful. Thus the peasant who said, "The land is ours," could as well say, "The land is God's." And in fact he did say that.

Collectivist theory would conceive the village commune as having abolished private rights in land. The mir, or association of households, would appear as a resolution of the natural conflict between

[2] It does not have connotations of rest and quiet (in Russian expressed rather by *pokoy*).

selfish and community interests. But it was not so historically or psychologically. The peasant's primary interest was in having as much land as he could work and in restraining others from engrossing any more. His idea of his natural rights exactly coincided with that interest. It was to assure those rights that the machinery of the mir existed. There was, therefore, no concept in the village of subordinating self to the greater good of all, and no grounds in history to assert that such subordination had taken place. Only after the wage-money economy began markedly to differentiate between men of unequal abilities did ideas of private property come into conflict with the communal arrangements of the mir. Then the appeal to primitive communism, or "peasant socialism," was seen to be frankly regressive. As expressed finally in Soviet collectivization, it rationalized the disorderly relations between the poor and rich, the lazy and the ambitious, by returning all to serfdom.

In the mir, as in the household, all decisions had to be unanimous. But the demand for unanimity no more signified the spirit of democracy in one institution than in the other. The guiding principle in both was that authority once established must not be questioned. While village meetings were often the scene of heated discussion and even brawls, opposition would collapse if it could not prevail. No vote was taken. The business of the mir was not to find a consensus: it was to locate the collective will and activate the collective authority. When objections were no longer heard, a decision became unanimous and binding on all villagers whether present or not.

A decision was binding in a way that majority votes never could be: it was both practically beyond appeal and morally conclusive, not subject to review by court or conscience. In fact, the mir absolved villagers of all individual responsibility. "No man is responsible for the mir," according to a proverb. And no man could criticize what the mir decided, any more than a subordinate member of a household could criticize the father.

Unanimity was valued not as an expression of universal consent but as a formal abjuration of the right to dissent. This is also the significance of Soviet elections and of the Soviet use of certain quasi-parliamentary machinery to endorse decisions of the executive.[3] The purpose—authoritarian, not democratic—echoes the aspirations of a primitive political body. In French Guinea recently the Secretary of the Democratic African Union proclaimed that "unanimity in government is necessary in an underdeveloped country" precisely because a decision once made must not be discussed. "Our objective is unity of concept and unity of action from top to bottom," said Premier Sékou Touré. "We have been violent and we shall be violent again if necessary."[4]

In making decisions, the mir did not feel itself bound either by law or by its own precedents. Even custom, which of course in large part regulated life in the village, put no rigid restraints on the mir's deliberations. Each case was judged afresh by common sense, which is to say by a sense of the moral order of village society in which the peasant had his place and felt secure. The law, resistant to such manipulation, inflexible and external, was commonly conceived as the enemy of justice and morality.[5] At best, the mir without guidance of a code exercised rough and ready good sense; at worst, it was merely arbitrary. In either event, it was absolute.

The powers of the mir in fact had no recognized limits. It was analogous in many ways to a tribal organization, or a family of families, charged not only with managing the common economic interests but with preserving itself as a community. Because it controlled the distribution of land none could settle in a village without the mir's permission. Because it was collectively responsible for taxes and debts no peasant could leave without the mir's permission. Every peasant knew what was going on in all other households in the village, and any problems that concerned others could be brought before the mir.

In the fall of 1917, by means of the mir the peasants divided the

---

[3] Cf. Carson (41); also Berman (26). "After the expulsion of Trotsky . . . there was no instance in the Party Congress of even a minority vote against an official proposal"; Maynard (181), p. 205.

[4] *The New York Times,* 16 March 1958.

[5] The concept of a formal set of rules to be obeyed in all circumstances was alien even to sophisticated Russian thought. To the Russian liberals, the inability of the imperial government to grasp the idea of law was the prime cause of the Russian Monarchy's downfall; cf. Maklakov (176). The attitude is common in folklore. Cf. the American Highlands where the families and communities prefer to settle their problems without the aid of the "furriner's" law; Zimmerman (322), p. 283.

"appropriated goods" from the plundered country estates; and through the mir they conducted negotiations "with the landlord and overseers, with the county commissars and with punitive expeditions of all kinds." Trotsky saw in this "a temporary retirement of the representative organs in favor of primitive peasant democracy in the form of the assembly and the communal decree."[6] In fact, this "primitive democracy" continued until suppressed by Soviet collectivization of farming.

So long as it lasted the mir's power was an ever-present reality for every villager; but its collective exercise was a myth—a myth strongly believed in and always to be reckoned with by the real rulers, but a myth nevertheless. Within a few decades after emancipation, three or four kulaks in each village had come to dominate most of the mirs. The submission of the individual to the community, which had appeared ideally democratic so long as all men were more or less equal, now facilitated the kulaks' capture of power and strengthened their despotism.

Kulaks can be thought of as prototypes of the self-made man—the first to rise above the multitude in a society just liberated from the equality of serfdom. They began by saving a little money through superior industry, thrift, or good luck. That beginning might be hard, but advancement thereafter was swift. A little money loaned to those less thrifty, less able, or less lucky multiplied rapidly. The poorer and more desperate the bulk of the peasantry the greater the opportunity of the money lender to exploit a meager capital by exacting usurious interest rates. It was not unusual for peasants needing food to carry them through the winter and spring to pledge repayment, usually in crops or labor, of three or four times the original loan.

When kulaks had squeezed capital in this way out of the misfortune of their neighbors they might accumulate enough to make loans on similar terms to whole villages which, through the mir, would grant long-term leases of land as collateral. Since the interest rates were generally ruinous and the borrowers optimistic, large tracts of common land thus came into the practical possession of kulaks and were worked by poorer peasants paying off their own

[6] Trotsky (285), Vol. III, p. 32.

debts. Kulaks might also buy acreage from landlords who found the management of estates profitless or tiresome. In these ways by the time of the Revolution many kulaks had succeeded in their natural ambition to replace the landlord, and were fastening on the peasantry a new and crueler system of tenancy managed by men who knew exactly how to extract the last kopek of profit and were on the spot to do it.

Of those predatory men a Russian observer writes: "The distinctive characteristic of this class is very unpleasant. It is the hard, unflinching cruelty of a thoroughly uneducated man who has made his way from poverty to wealth, and has come to consider money-making by whatever means as the only pursuit to which a rational being should devote himself."[7] Other Russian writers wondered why the "increased material well-being among the peasants should invariably bring moral deterioration in their brains."[8] But so it was. The ablest and shrewdest man in the village nearly always ended up a kulak. "I have known that type very well," recalls a former Russian landlord. "As soon as a peasant acquired wealth his attitude toward his fellow-laborers entirely changed, as well as his standard of requirements. The peasants obeyed him and feared him and hated him perhaps more than they did the landlord; yet they knew very well that any one of them would comport himself exactly in the same manner should he have the same good luck."[9]

Peasants also found the power of the kulaks all but irresistible. A man in trouble preferred to ask help of someone he knew in his own village rather than tangle with distant authority. He did so out of primitive fear of the foreign, especially when it threatened him with incomprehensible documents. He did so, even though he knew that the distant landlord or state official could easily be cheated of his due, while from the ruthless creditor next door there was no escape.

At the village meetings, a kulak had only the same formal rights as any other peasant. Since most of the poor were apt to be his clients, however, he could in fact bend the will of the mir exactly to fit his own. The ordinary peasant knew that, if he resisted, the kulak could find hundreds of occasions for revenge. Even if he

[7] Stepniak (265), pp. 54-55.
[8] Uspensky (293).
[9] *Novoe Russkoe Slovo*, 5 May 1958.

himself were not at that moment in the kulak's debt who could tell how fortune might turn?

People called the kulaks "mir-eaters," because economically and politically they engorged the villages. In that they had some help from the old government, first through a law that gave independent power to the elder *(starosta)*. Originally the elder was the executive of the mir's collective will, a mere agent who carried out what was decided. The position conferred no distinction and entailed considerable unpleasantness, since it brought the peasant into frequent contact with landlords and officials. In many villages it was filled in rotation on the theory that everyone should have his share of misfortune.[10] But after emancipation the imperial government, unable even to conceive of power emanating from below, assumed as a matter of course that the elder ought to be an executive in the sense of presiding officer and local boss. He was therefore given police powers, and was authorized to impose fines, imprisonment, or compulsory labor on any member of the commune for any infraction of the imposed rulings. This power the elders exercised at their own discretion without appeal. They might, and did punish slights to their own dignity. "A meeting assembled without their authorization is declared illegal, its resolutions void, and its conveners liable to severe penalties. By withdrawing from a meeting the elder can break it up whenever he considers that the debate is taking an unlawful turn." Although still elected by the mir, he became under the new order the "master of the body which elected him."[11]

The elder developed into a local despot, but he answered to others bigger than he. By law he was subordinate to the district superintendent *(ispravnik)* of the imperial police. The ispravnik, who was basically responsible for rural administration, was permitted at will to indict, fine, and imprison the elders. And so the bigger fish swallowed the littler, and the mir—its despotic control over the individual still intact—passed gradually under command of the police. Their abuse of power and their brutality toward the helpless peasantry have been perennial themes of literature and

[10] Cf. the practice revived under the German occupation (1941-1944) in Belorussia and the Ukraine where the institution of the mir was spontaneously restored in spontaneously decollectivized villages; Dallin (55), Vakar (295).

[11] Stepniak (265), pp. 160-161.

folklore. They could enter anyone's house any time, examine anything, interrogate whomever they pleased on the merest suspicion or pretense of suspicion. They could arrest and jail any in their district.

Since the rural constables *(uriadniki)* were underpaid, they lived on tribute from those in their power. It was, therefore, not hard for a kulak to buy the police, including sometimes the ispravnik himself. It was even easier for him to manage the election of one of his henchmen as elder. So, with police and elder in his pocket, the kulak emerged in the new dispensation as the local overlord, manipulating the mir and ruling and exploiting his little world as he pleased.

A kulak's power in fact was limited only by the rival power of other kulaks in the village or in the region. These rivalries sometimes broke out into open hostilities, sometimes were patched over with agreements to divide the spoils, arrived at in "summit conferences" of local bosses over a bottle of vodka. In his own world, the kulak developed a shrewd and cynical capacity to size up the balance of power. But since there was no trust anywhere, a bitterness underlay the rural scene—"harsh, cruel, cynically egotistical" —a source of instability, and invitation to turbulence.[12]

The narodnik novelist Gleb Uspensky wrote a quarter-century before the Revolution: "Every time I happen to meet or speak to peasant Havrila Volkov I invariably think how dreadful it will be to witness the time when this Volkov shall let loose the fierce hatred and rage which lie hidden in the depths of his heart, and are at present only discovered in the cruel expression of his eyes and mouth and in the harsh tones of his voice. For when the outward pressure which holds him down shall be removed his hidden passions will immediately assume the form of a powerful, revengeful and pitiless giant, raising an enormous cudgel against everything and everybody."[13]

Volkov's release came in 1917.

A decade earlier the mir had taken what should have been its deathblow at the hands of Nicholas II's liberal Minister of the

---

[12] Stepniak (265), p. 119; also Bunin (37).
[13] Uspensky (293).

Interior, later Minister-President, Peter Stolypin. In the aftermath of the abortive revolution of 1905, he undertook a program of land reform aimed frankly at strengthening the landed gentry and creating peasant allies for them. By a series of decrees he confirmed peasants in the permanent possession of the land they farmed at that moment, released new state lands for sale, required the villages to split up the old common lands when two-thirds of the villagers wished it, and allowed peasants to claim their individual shares in one holding instead of in strips.

The reform aimed at nothing less than the total revolution of agrarian society. The mir was to lose its primary reason for existence in the abolition of common lands and so either atrophy as a political organ or merge, like a town assembly, with the system of local self-government (zemstvo). Distribution and sale of lands to individual heads of household without regard for the number of workers attacked the foundations of the patriarchal family. Consolidation of holdings inevitably favored some peasants, handicapped others; it also permitted more efficient farming decisively to benefit the more efficient farmers. Opening lands for sale profited the kulak who had money to buy. So the rich got richer, and the poor got poorer, just as Stolypin intended. His aim to develop and attach to the established order the "strong and the sober" carried the necessary implication that those neither strong nor sober would sink into the ranks of the rural proletariat or move to industrial centers rapidly growing in the country.

As the Stolypin reforms began to work out, they split the peasantry, often with incidents of violence. Peasants in need of money might be bribed to make up the majority necessary to approve the division of the common lands and then induced to sell their new property. Land began to accumulate in a few hands. New social and economic distributions began to crack the village community. Money alone could now assure peace, security, and the respect of one's fellows. Labor lost much of its former dignity, scope, and attractiveness. Rural society became polarized as never before between the haves and the have-nots.

In time, through hardships and some great injustices, the reform would have permitted Russian agriculture to take modern form and so to serve the needs of the nation and ultimately of the peasantry as the ancient system never could. With these developments, however, World War I and the Revolution decisively interfered. During the period of economic chaos and confused experimentation, the old ways and old institutions in the countryside revealed their continuing vitality, as well as their usefulness to the new revolutionary despotism.

If kulaks, by and large, were recruited by natural selection from those fittest to survive in the acquisitive jungle, one should not be surprised to see them emerge victors from the still crueler jungle of civil war. While individual casualties were enormous, in twenty years of ups and downs the human type proved its hardihood.

At the beginning kulaks shared in the 1917 revolts against the landlords from which, as Trotsky has admitted, they mostly "got the best of it."[14] Then came their first trial. Under the Bolshevik decree of 7 November 1917, which gave all land to those who worked it, some two million of the biggest peasant landowners were expropriated. Those who survived, however, had a fresh opportunity five years later, when Lenin inaugurated the New Economic Policy (NEP). In an effort to revive agricultural surpluses on which the whole Communist program of industrialization depended, the village was granted virtual autonomy; and the kulaks stepped back into their old positions in local institutions, dominating and exploiting the poor for their own profit. The poor, though made equal in the eyes of Karl Marx, were as reluctant as before to assert their equality against the men of whom they might have to borrow farming tools or beg for work. As for the local soviets, which retained nominal supervision, when they threatened the kulaks' interest, it was usually possible to set up the old mir against them. The mir, as before, represented the ordinary peasants' dream of equality and the rich peasants' reality of power.

The New Economic Policy, making at first a reluctant retreat from socialism, forbade the hiring of farm labor and the leasing of land. But by 1925, under the continuing pressure to increase production, both restrictions were relaxed. The growing reliance on the more prosperous peasantry was attested by statistics which, in 1927, revealed that no more than 3 per cent of cultivated land was collectively held and worked, and that almost as many farm

[14] Trotsky (285), Vol. III, p. 17.

54

laborers were employed as before the war. NEP continued the prewar disintegration of the middling class of gray muzhiks. Kulaks dominated the rural soviets, just as they dominated the mirs. No one took seriously the "committees of the poor" *(komitety bednoty),* by which the government tried to counterbalance the rich with the rich man's clients.

In 1927-1928, peasants to get better prices held grain off the market, threatening both the food supply of the cities and exports on which the Communists depended for industrial capital. More serious still was the threat that the few who had prospered by NEP might soon be in a position to dictate terms to the Revolution. That was a question not of socialist theory but of survival. The government, in January 1928, reacted with a decree excluding "kulaks" from the village soviets. It was the forerunner of expropriation under the first Five-Year Plan (1928-1932) and of the ruthless "liquidation of the kulaks as a class."

Theoretical debate of that policy was conspicuously strained in Party circles, but there was no ambiguity in action. It is possible that a dictatorial authority had no choice in the circumstances but to accept the gage to all-out war or risk losing political control of the land. The collective farm, by which the problem was finally solved, was not essentially a mechanism to set up communistic society. It was a device to extend the state power effectively to farm production, on which the state absolutely depended. Significantly, when the Germans occupied the Ukraine and Belorussia (1941-1944), they tried to preserve the collectives, although they had obviously no interest in them as Marxist communities.[15]

In January 1930, the liquidation of the "kulaks as a social class" was announced. By official count, that meant dispossessing 5 million independent farmers. In fact far larger numbers were eventually involved. Some observers have calculated that more than 2 million persons were driven out of Belorussia alone, where the whole population hardly exceeded 10 million at that time. In the Don and Kuban regions and in the Ukraine, whole districts were depopulated and resettled by exiles from other parts of the coun-

[15] Compare the Red Chinese use of the commune. Whether expressive of a "purer" or merely more primitive communism, the Chinese organization imposed a military discipline on the peasantry—and that was its appeal to the state.

try. Millions were taken off the land to work in factories or in labor camps. Since the objective of the state was absolute subjugation of the peasant population, "kulak" became a term denoting all who resisted collectivization. As such it was constantly redefined according to the needs of the moment until the nonresisters had been segregated and safely herded into the new enclosures. In the end, the rural population of the Soviet Union was cut in half, and the half remaining on the land was reduced to a serfdom in some ways more onerous than that which they had escaped some seventy years before.

Although imposed on the people with extraordinary ruthlessness, collectivization undoubtedly appealed to many poorer peasants. Certainly, the process of dispossession was helped along by the envious in each village who saw another opportunity to get rid of rich oppressors and divide up their lands. In Communist usage "kulak" became a simple smear word, as "Communist" has sometimes been in American usage, to condemn anyone who for any reason resisted official policies in rural areas. The government, declaring war against its own enemies, encouraged the villagers to join up and, in order to take fullest advantage of all the local hates, left it to the discretion of local agents to select the victims.

Collectivization had also an important assist from the fact that it was not a revolutionary idea but a very old one. It hustled the peasants back into their age-old communes, where they rediscovered the equality of poverty and unfreedom and resumed their positions as the lowest social estate.[16] Where the system of obshchina had never existed or had disappeared long before, resistance was stronger. Elsewhere the forms were new, but the substance familiar. Familiar, too, were the new bosses. A good many kulaks in fact became active collectivizers, shrewdly adapting them-

[16] Some twenty years after the abolition of serfdom, Count Dmitry Tolstoy, Minister of Education under Alexander II, predicted that if monarchy should fall in Russia it would be replaced by Communism—"le communisme de M. Karl Marx de Londres, qui vient de mourir. . . ." (*Memoirs of Prince von Buehlow* (Boston, 1931-32), Vol. I, p. 575). Similar views were expressed by other Russian statesmen, who knew the village life very well. Significant was the report submitted to Nicholas II by Peter N. Durnovo, his Minister of the Interior (1906); cf. "Zapiska Durnovo," *Krasnaia Nov*, 10 (1922), pp. 178-179, English translation in *Documents of Russian History*, ed. by F. A. Golder (New York 1927); comments by Mark Aldanov, *The Russian Review*, Spring 1942, pp. 31-45.

selves to the new paths to power. Thousands of the clever ones were discovered in positions of authority during the great Party purges of 1936-1938. And the cleverest of all, of course, were not found out at all, but survived in the Party hierarchy into our day.

Nominally governed by the assembly of members, the collective farm (*kolkhoz*) is actually ruled by the chairman of its management committee, elected by the assembly to serve two years. In the selection of the chairman, however, peasants have at most had an advisory voice. From the beginning he has been so far as possible a Party man, chosen by the Party, often brought in from the outside and, in the early days particularly, often totally ignorant of his job. In position and function he resembled an overseer or manager hired by the absentee landowner in the Tsarist past— a familiar type in the village and a familiar authority.

Until 1950 the kolkhoz tended to be coextensive with the village. Some large villages might contain two or three kolkhozes, but few collectives included scattered villages. Amalgamation, begun in that year, has steadily increased the size of the kolkhozes as administrative units. But like other Soviet enterprises, they continue to be run essentially like overgrown households in which members have the obligation to work and the right to be rewarded according to their work. The chairman, like a father, sees to that. He must also represent the state, however, much as the old starosta did and in much the same atmosphere of mutual distrust and insecurity. "We are afraid of each other," confess the villagers in a recently published Soviet story:[17] the chairman because his position is never really secure; the villagers because, as before, they can count on no legality, no rules of correct and safe behavior, but must simply do what they are told and stand ready to answer for offenses that may not even have been proscribed in advance.

In this atmosphere no one wants to call attention to himself. Yet there remain grievances which cannot be accepted without protest. At a typical kolkhoz meeting, as described by one who has attended them, the peasants do not address the chair. They begin to talk to each other, and presently there arises a rumble of

[17] Yashin (316).

57

sound in the midst of which some remarks can be distinguished. But the chairman will not be able to tell who is talking. Then a political leader, usually from outside the kolkhoz, may say: "Well, I hear that the *kolkhozniki*[18] are complaining about the distribution of rye. Will the comrade chairman please explain?" Thus encouraged someone—perhaps an old woman with little to lose—will put the complaint directly and specifically to the chairman and someone else may shout for a new "election." In this way the complaint is made general, and no one can be singled out as the trouble-maker.[19]

Even that much popular participation in government, however, has been exceptional. In most collectives it has been hard to get a two-thirds quorum for even the annual meetings in which the accounts are reviewed.[20] Peasant members charged with various review responsibilities in the complicated Soviet system that sets watchmen to watch the watchmen typically shirk the job. They are disposed rather to accept the pattern of paternalistic rule to which they have been accustomed.

The father figure in the collective or in the factory is not merely a cultural survival; it is also idealized as a Soviet type. In the Soviet novel, the kolkhoz chairman is portrayed as a successful peasant patriarch, shrewd and resourceful, maintaining his own position and protecting his domain by his personal skill in fending off rapacious authority from above and intimidating the dissidents below. The ideal has been thus described in *Pravda*: "He is not a large man, but he is a well-built man. He is lively as mercury; he is cheerful and understands everything quickly . . . There are united in him Bolshevik passion and muzhik calculatedness, bold directness and slyness, the capacity to look directly into the heart of an individual."[21] Under the retouching for propaganda, one may recognize instantly the features both of the old village boss and of Nikita Khrushchev, the chairman of them all.

[18] The term *kolkhoznik* (collective farm member) was introduced to replace the historical *krestianin* (peasant), but the familiar term reappeared after World War II and has been increasingly used in Soviet literature and in the Party's public statements.

[19] Dinerstein (62), p. 68.

[20] *Ibid.*, p. 67.

[21] Galina Nikolaeva, writing about "Features of the Future," as quoted in Dinerstein (62), pp. 52-53.

The Communist war against the "kulak" had generally the ironic consequence of raising the most successful of the breed to positions of command in the nation. Through constant redefinition of peasant classes, in order to segregate those on whom the Party could rely, the Soviet state has selected both for subjugation and for preferment not economic classes but appropriate *human types*. The type which advanced under the brutalizing and immoral terms of the struggle could not help being just that kulak whose shrewd, hard, cruel, grasping nature earned him the fear and hate and envy of the villages he ruled. Counting only his own interests, paying lip-service here to God, and there to Marx, never handicapped by any sort of idealism, he was perfectly suited to the dog-eat-dog times of purge and liquidation. With a sure sign of which way the battle went and a dark corner in which to change his uniform, he could be counted on as a vigorous supporter of the winning side.

In the Soviet dispensation, the kulak type found he could do rather more easily and effectively what he had always done—make his fortune at the expense of his fellows. Under the developing capitalism effected by Stolypin reforms, it had been necessary to get money first in order to acquire power over people, then to squeeze out of them significant wealth. Under Communism, the road was political and more direct. One joined the Party and acquired at once the necessary power over people to build and feather one's own nest. This to the wise man was the sense of the Bolshevik revolution. He would thank his luck that he had been too young or too poor to have made the fatal mistake of becoming a kulak too soon, and so was saved to become a commissar in good season.

5

PEASANT BORN AND BRED

THE COMMON INSTITUTIONS OF PEASANT LIFE COULD BE EXPECTED TO produce a common mark on the man. The culture of the village must be at least as ubiquitous as the village itself. The human qualities needed to survive in conditions varying very little throughout rural Russia must be the qualities universally most in evidence among the living—and especially among the prospering. In generalizing about the peasant character or the peasant mind, one does not forget that individuals remain unique and unpredictable. In generalizing specifically about those peasants who, as the new élite, have set their mark on Soviet society one does not forget that there are other peasants whose dominant human qualities are different. Finally, what is said *about* the peasant is not said *against* him or without full consciousness that in another context for other purposes of description and analysis a different emphasis might with equal truth be given. What is affirmed is the existence of cultural forms more or less rigid, more or less controlling on persons living together. The peasant village, small, isolated, shaped by tradition, all but closed to strangers, devoted to the all-consuming, jealous tasks of subsistence farming, may well have formed a society as homogeneous and inescapable as any in the modern world.

Primitive rural life is not simple and idyllic as the romantics have made it out. Just the reverse. Its complications overwhelm primitive man with tension and anxiety. The peasant almost from birth is on the defensive against a hostile environment and typically develops the traits to protect himself against a hard father, a sharp neighbor, a powerful landlord, a meddling official, and all the manifold catastrophes of nature. He learns to practice patience, caution, suspicion, shrewdness, ruthlessness, even treachery, to endure or subvert the forces that are inherently stronger than he, yet must somehow be overcome. The physical power of nature and men threatens the fruit of his labor at every turn. To the power of nature he must in part yield, submitting himself to the tyranny of the seasons, doing the back-breaking work of tilling and harvesting with primitive tools day and night if need be when nature commands, literally exhausting himself in the service. "The land is the peasant's master," writes one observer, "and it imposes itself upon him like a fate."[1]

The quality of his endurance is proverbial. Sir Bernard Pares recalls that "the Russian soldiers of the Great War would go four days without food, though they would say that they could not go for more than four days without sleep."[2]

The peasant's fortitude, however, had no flavor of equanimity. He submitted to the exactions of a kulak or the lash of the police as he submitted to the seasons, only because he figured that by accommodating himself, like grass to the wind, he might survive. He played the role of a lowly one, but would rather play the master. At the first opportunity he was ready to seize the whip of power and lay on.

As suggested earlier, despotism in Russia was prepared at bottom by the habit of obedience. Because the habit of obedience was engrained in the mass, the whole society was despotically organized. The Tsar, in absolute command of the nation, was only the diadem of tyranny. Under him lay the interrelationship of command that made of every man both slave and master—a linkage of arbitrary power which, historically, extended unbroken from the Tsar's ministers to the peasant flogging his work horse. Each, within limits imposed here by law, there by custom, was supreme and irresponsible. Difference in rank affected not the kind of power wielded but only its extent.

Below the top, however, all despots were timid. The peasant near the bottom was most conscious that his power, though unrestricted in exercise, was nevertheless small. A despot to the weak, he was a coward before the strong or, as he describes himself frankly in a proverb: "A man against lambs, and a lamb against men." In

[1] Maynard (181), p. 31; also (182).
[2] Pares (214), pp. 47-48.

folklore he pictures himself not as brave but as cunning. One of the popular heroes is Ivan the Little Fool—*Ivanushka Durachok*—a simpleton who invariably outsmarts the wise and powerful. Daring is envied but as a virtue belonging to another world. It is common, for instance, to attach an endearing suffix (in which the Russian language abounds) to the word for "highway robbers" producing something that sounds like "little old robbers"—*razboynichki*. But robbers too often are caught and punished. Their adventurousness is not to be emulated by men of good sense, though women may still in the end shed a tear for "the dear unlucky ones"—*neschastnenkie*.

Good sense, variously interpreted as self-serving—not morality—is the limit on action. On a farm, the good and the expedient are the same. The peasant will dare to grab what he feels pretty sure of getting away with, but he is soberly aware that he has small margin for error. If he tries for too much he may lose the little he has. He plainly cannot afford failure. Indeed, by his code of behavior, failure is worse than crime. In making his fortune he will typically move by small steps, digesting his gains before moving on.

Infinite patience, uncomplaining hard work, caution, but within safe bounds entire ruthlessness—these are the natural responses to a hard environment by a people still preoccupied with problems of physical survival.

Caution for the peasant requires knowing all he can know of the perils that might threaten, and of avoiding so far as possible any venture into the unknown. His greatest fear is of being caught unprepared. Because to some degree he cannot help himself, but must face the sudden devastating storm or the onfall of the police as blows of fate, he seeks out and shelters among the familiar when he can with a yearning for something more precious than economic security. He will literally guard his cows and pigs with his own life. He will deal with the devil he knows—or the local kulak—in preference to good people he does not know, regardless of the terrible price he may expect to pay.

In his own home he demands to know everything. Members of the family as a matter of loyalty to the group as well as fear of the father inform on each other. The debt of loyalty is owed not to the heart but to the hierarchy. When the Communist Party came to appeal and serve as a larger family it expected as a matter of course to command similarly exclusive loyalties. School children were trained to inform on their teachers, their mothers and fathers, brothers and sisters. The child who reported his mother for stealing grain was a hero. In a Soviet play a sister denounces her brother at Party meeting, "instead of discussing their differences at the breakfast table at home."[3]

Propaganda to make stool pigeons of Soviet youth is less strident now than in the beginning, when it was perhaps encouraged by early idealistic attacks on the family as one of many archaic human institutions that the Revolution was to wither. Nevertheless, Soviet school textbooks still glorify the memory of one of history's most terrifying brats, Pavlik Morozov, who having got his father arrested and shot for withholding grain was killed by his grandfather in a justifiable rage. Pavlik's statue still stands in Moscow; as late as 1953, a Soviet poet published a poem about the "heroic little boy."[4]

Against the temptation to find communism, as a theory, chiefly responsible, one must observe that in three-generation peasant families, children were expected to report on their parents as on each other because all were inferior members of the group over which the grandfather-patriarch ruled supreme. In European literature there are landlords and priests who turned village children into informers on their own parents. When crusading against gambling in 1947, Mayor Fiorello LaGuardia asked New York children to let him know if their fathers were losing money on the horses.[5] Despite some moralistic and sentimental overpainting, the model remains recognizable. In each case the appeal is from a lesser loyalty to a greater; in each case a paternalistic figure asserts his right to know and his responsibility to provide in a larger society which overrides the normal filial loyalties.

Properly to discharge his responsibilities the peasant patriarch had to know more than what had happened. He had to know so far as possible what to expect. His inquisitorial rights were, in theory at least, as sweeping as his powers. He demanded to know

[3] Simonov (257).
[4] Shchipachev (250).
[5] *Life,* 5 May 1947.

63

and would punish disloyal thought as well as action. He regularly acted on suspicion without bothering with proof. From the standpoint of maintaining absolute authority, a criminal thought was as dangerous as a criminal act. Indeed, it was worse, since God knew how deep secret disloyalty might run or what ultimate catastrophe it might prepare.

Every primitive mind occupying a tiny village in a wilderness of ignorance must reckon so. It must be less concerned with present evils than with nameless ones to come, less impressed with crimes committed than with crimes possibly contemplated, less interested in punishing guilty men than in identifying dangerous ones.

In sixteenth-century England, under the benevolent despotism of the Tudors, any man could be charged by his neighbor with treason, and none could be sure of proving innocence. The Act of 1534 made it a crime "maliciously to wish" the death of the king. "The determining factor in most cases," writes one historian, "was not whether the individual had committed treason, but whether he was too dangerous to the state to be allowed to live."[6] This, of course, has also been the guiding judgment in Soviet purge trials. It is the principle that gained such frightening currency in this country among the followers of the late Senator Joseph McCarthy. That it exists pure and without scruple in the peasant household is hardly more surprising than that poison ivy has roots.

A member of a rural household or of a totalitarian state becomes a menace to the organization whenever he falls under suspicion. It matters little how or why suspicion is aroused. Once aroused it must be explained, which is to say justified, and once justified it must be removed. It does not occur to the simple mind that what he suspects may simply not be true. That he is suspicious is sufficient evidence of his peril. "Where there's smoke, there's fire" is a Russian as well as an English proverb. While in both languages it purports to state an obvious relationship between cause and effect, in practice it argues a naïve confusion of perception with fact. The real meaning is, "Where I see smoke, there is fire," quite a different matter.

Suspicion will always be justified, but still it is not the same as knowledge. A father may act on suspicion alone and often must, since it is proof enough that action is needed. But he acts then

[6] Smith (260).

partly in the dark. It is better to know. Suspicion becomes knowledge through confession. By confessing, the guilty outline their
guilt, making the worst *known*. Only then can the father feel sure
that the evil has been discovered in full and retribution duly
weighed.

As for the suspect, he may be persuaded to confess by the
knowledge that his silence or denials will be regarded as proof
of guilt, not innocence, and by the hope that by seeming to re-
pent he may soften his punishment. More fundamentally, however, he is likely to share the delusions of which he is victim. He
does not himself consider his feeling of innocence a sure support.
He may actually have sinned in spite of himself.

The Russian peasant lived in a world more impressively peopled
with evil spirits than presided over by God. Man all too obviously
was not in control of his environment or his destiny. Was there any
good reason to suppose that he was in control of himself? If he
had the appearance of guilt might it not be that while he slept or
thought of other things he had become possessed? At least there
was no way to prove that he had not. The presumption of guilt
rested on suspicions which the victim, too, was accustomed to accept
at full subjective weight. In rebuttal, he had only the inner consciousness of conscious innocence. But that might mean only that
he had not intended to sin. This is not such incomprehensible
reckoning. Modern psychology has made us familiar with all degrees of division of the self, from the rebellious subconscious of
most of us to the schizophrenia of the madman. If the devils that
now possess us are differently defined, they probably make much
the same kind of hell.

When not voluntary, confession has regularly been extracted by
physical and psychological pressures. The means never mattered.
A confession wrung by torture served as well as one freely offered,
since the object was not to determine guilt but to purge it. So in
confession the accused invariably admitted not only his crime but
his prior corruption, and affirmed that being now purified he
welcomed his punishment as just retribution and a warning to
others.[7] From the viewpoint of authority, confession repaired the
torn fabric of despotism—familial or communal, royal or communist—by making it appear again to be a unity in which re-

[7] Cf. for interesting parallels, Smith (260) and Leites (160).

bellion could not happen because there is only one word and one way. Despots have understood very well the threat of treason, which is so much greater than the immediate challenge of power. They have wisely feared above all the deadly seed of independent, individual judgment, which cannot grow in the partriarchal household or the totalitarian state—without destroying them.

Actually, the village felt little need for independent judgment. The peasant, fearing it in others, also distrusted it in himself. He relied rather on the strategy and weapons inherited from the collective wisdom of his forefathers who, for centuries, had been coping with just his problems and had found ways of dealing with them. Maybe they were not absolutely the best ways, but they worked well enough, and the weight of experience was heavily in their favor. If new ideas were to be tried at all the peasant preferred they be tried on someone else.

In familiar surroundings, with familiar answers to familiar problems, he could normally feel sure of himself and ignore the limitations of his competence. But he has been correspondingly afraid of people and experiences he did not know. Though hospitable to strangers that came to his village, he insisted that they remain strangers.[8] If they tried in any way to meddle or make friends he became suspicious. Peasants have consistently maltreated teachers, doctors, relief workers, technical counselors sent out from the city by benevolent organizations or by the spirit of benevolence itself. Why should anyone wish to give away something for nothing? It is a stupid fish not long for this life who believes that worms swim down to him, desiring only to be eaten.

The peasant felt safe only in his own village, among those he knew personally and intimately. And he knew his neighbors very intimately indeed. Few secrets could be kept in the village about the things that counted—the economic things. Each man knew precisely what the others had and, says Stepniak, "could give an inventory of each household in turn, by heart."[9] Each was curious not like an intelligence agent or a tax collector, but like a cat that is uneasy until every bit of home has been sniffed, catalogued, and memorized in its proper place.

[8] Cf. Sprott (262), p. 81: "In Norfolk (England) within living memory no young man would venture into a neighboring village unaccompanied. In Sussex every stranger was a foreigner—' 'eave 'arf a brick at 'im!' "

[9] Stepniak (265), p. 301.

Characteristically, a peasant thrown out of his familiar environment sought to transfer the old forms to the new world. He would often in effect adopt a new father, a relative or friend chosen of his own will, or perhaps a factory foreman, a gang leader, a party boss, a military commander, imposed on him by authority but reinterpreted to fit his own psychological needs.[10] Conscious of his ignorance and accustomed to mistrusting his own unaided judgment, he wanted to find someone who knew and had already developed the techniques needed to get along. To that knowing one, he would yield almost filial obedience, but only in those areas where he felt his own ignorance and only for as long as he felt it. As soon as he thought he knew as much or more than his new master, he would go his way without any question of gratitude for past help or any sense that loyalty was owed out of affection: "Friendship is friendship, and business is business."

In the business of rural life paternalistic attachments did not bind the heart. They were only the cement of society. The family principle was the principle of subordination. Village solidarity was the solidarity of herd rather than of tribe, and reflected no corporate spirit. Outside of his native village, the peasant preferred to do business with other peasants, not because he trusted them more than other people, but because the human type was familiar to him.

A former prisoner in a Soviet labor camp tells of seeing a sick peasant, who could hardly move after a day's work in the woods, bend down by the roadside: "He took a pinch of dirt and put it in his mouth; he chewed it slowly, and his solemn face brightened as though he were taking communion."[11]

Land was the mother, the provider, the savior. The peasant might kneel and kiss it, or he might curse it, but he could never leave it. Like Antaeus, he drew from the earth all his strength. But not from any particular portion of earth.[12]

From the beginning to the present, the Russian folk have been one of the great migrating peoples. Expansion of the state histori-

[10] Handlin (99).
[11] Shiriaev (252).
[12] Russian has the same word, *zemlia,* for "earth," "land," "soil," "ground" and, in ancient literature and in folklore, for "country."

cally has followed restless peasants in search of better lands. Peasants in fact wandered so far, so often, and in such numbers that they disturbed the state in the sixteenth century, when the state was ready more or less to settle down. It was mostly to pin the peasant in place and establish a reliable supply of manpower that serfdom was by degrees fastened on the country. But the serf would not be bound. Dissatisfied, he fled into the southern steppes or into the northern wilderness by himself or in bands to begin again his primitive economy in the seemingly endless virgin lands. Pioneers had just begun to open up Siberia at the beginning of serfdom; less than a century later settlers had reached the Pacific. After emancipation, pioneering by individuals became the exception. But whole villages moved frequently in quest of their collective fortune in greener fields.

The combination of extreme cultural isolation in the village with extreme geographical mobility over the vast spaces of Russia seems like a paradox until one observes that travel in this form is no more broadening than the movement of armies over endless battlefields. The peasant's normal way of life was so primitive that he suffered little change in transferring to the wilderness and had little difficulty in re-establishing his institutions in new soil. The migrations thus normally brought him into no new, significant contacts with either men or nature. In so far as his departures were forced by a threat of extinction it could be said that his own mobility and the space of his motherland conspired to preserve his primitiveness, extending and perpetuating the traditional rural pattern. In any case, the important psychological fact was that however tightly the peasant was bound to his village by fear and ignorance, he was emotionally attached only to the land. When transplanted, he craved contact with the earth—even some educated Russians carry a box of Russian soil with them to be put at last in their graves—but unlike the Chinese he did not usually yearn to revisit his ancestral home.

Rodina, ordinarily translated motherland, reflects in its roots and connotations something of this special sense of the earth as home and womb. The root is *rod* (essentially the idea of birth) from which are also derived words for nature, people, nation, family, breed, harvest, and so on.[13] Unlike *otechestvo,* from *otets*

[13]Cf. Latin in *nativity, nature, nation,* etc.

(father)—historically, a translation of French *patrie*, German *Vaterland*—the word *rodina* had no precise political meaning until Soviet times. To the peasant it was his native village, or the province in which he lived, or even an ill-defined region for which he felt some attachment, like the Volga River, the Ural Mountains, Siberia, or the Ukraine. Almost never did it include the whole of Russia. Peasant-born poets like Alexei Koltsov, Sergei Essenin, and Nikolai Kliuev used the word to indicate an almost physical passion or attachment, without bothering to define precisely the object.

This supercharged emotional content the Communists tried to capture and harness to their purposes, especially in World War II, by making rodina synonymous with the Soviet state. What success they have had is not easy to judge. It is at least a fact that communism is still challenged by Soviet defectors in the name of love for rodina.[14] But in time the symbol may change, perhaps most profoundly, as contact with the land weakens among the transplanted peasants in factories and offices, and the political use of the term wears out its emotional content.

Nature is cruel. Or, rather, nature is quite literally inhuman. The more tightly obedient a man is to the compulsions and rhythms of nature the less can he be expected to exhibit the gentler human qualities called civilized, because civilization alone is friendly to their exercise. A peasant may often be kind or generous to both man and animal. He does not, however, accept the obligation to be kind and generous except in well-defined situations, usually where his self-interest is not essentially involved or where tradition has shaped customs of mutual aid.

Literature is full of poor peasants who give away their last crumbs of bread or take the shirt from their backs to clothe a beggar. These acts are perfectly characteristic, yet it is a mistake to generalize from them a noble moral order. Although large with the promise of man's civilizing soul, they remain small clearings in the jungle in which the peasant spends most of his life and whose amoral laws of survival he on the whole obeys. So little does he feel any general moral suasion that he does not even realize

[14] For attempts of the Germans to exploit this sentiment against the Soviets in World War II, see Fisher (82), Dallin (55), and Vakar (295).

the contradictions of his behavior, which so often amaze the observer.

Pushkin tells of a group of peasants who set fire to the house where they locked up some district officials. The victims moaned and groaned, cried for help, howled from fear and pain, while peasants listened "with malicious smiles." When they saw a cat on the burning roof they laughed. But the blacksmith, who had led them to burn the officials alive, said angrily: "What are you laughing at? Do you not fear God? One of God's creatures is perishing and you laugh!" Setting a ladder against the burning roof he climbed up and at last, badly burned, brought the kitten down in his arms.[15]

Dostoevsky tells another story: "That same evening I [Prince Myshkin] stopped at a small provincial hotel, and it so happened that a dreadful murder had been committed there the night before and everybody was talking about it. Two peasants—elderly men and old friends—had had tea together and were to occupy the same bedroom. They were not drunk, but one of them had noticed for the first time that his friend possessed a silver watch which he was wearing on a chain. He was by no means a thief and was, as peasants go, a rich man; but this watch so fascinated him that he could not restrain himself. He took a knife, and when his friend turned his back, he came up softly behind, raised his eyes to heaven, crossed himself and, saying earnestly, 'God forgive me, for Christ's sake,' he cut his friend's throat like a sheep, and took the watch."[16]

For most peasants, of course, a man would be worth more than a kitten or a silver watch. But not intrinsically. That is the point. During World War II, Soviet commanders marched their men through German minefields as though the mines weren't there, calculating—as Marshal Georgi Zhukov afterward told General Dwight Eisenhower—that they would lose no more of their men than would have fallen before German guns if guns, instead of mines, had defended the ground. General Eisenhower correctly observed that this tactic did not necessarily prove "that the Russians were cruel or were innately indifferent to human life." But he was mistaken in attributing their harshness to their experience in war.

[15]Pushkin (227).
[16] Dostoevsky (64).

The significant facts are that Zhukov is of peasant birth (as most of the Soviet officer corps have been since Stalin's great purges of the late 1930's) and that, among the ranks, the World War II armies were still overwhelmingly peasant. The peasant, rather than the Russian, attitude toward human life was shaped not by four years of war but by a lifetime in the village. The key to it was practicality. A man was to be valued for what he could do. If in the attack what he could do best was explode mines with his naked flesh, so that his comrades might pass, then let him. Thus he made himself useful, serving the greater good of the group.

Superficially we do not disagree. We, too, send men to die for the greater good of the nation. But two things, as a civilized people, we do not do—nor did the Russians in World War I: We do not order any man to sure death; we do not ordinarily and by general assent expend life when by using other means life could be saved. Furthermore, we regard the necessary sacrifice of one life for many as self-sacrifice, insisting both that it is voluntary in some meaningful—though sometimes remote—way and that we care about the individual as an individual even though we may use him like a pawn. The difference, even in war, is not academic. In peace, it is the palpable kernel of civilization. By his unconcern with persons the peasant shows most clearly his closeness to nature, which counts sheep but does not name them. Soviet society, driving faceless men through minefields or through production lines, shows most clearly its peasant origins and its real retrogression from human ideals.

Humanism and liberalism are urban, not rural, products. Indeed, how could they have been born on a peasant farm? In the village there was no view of mankind, only a number of men and women whom one knew well and some of whom only too obviously were not worth a horse or a cow. "Take example from an animal," says old man Eroshka in a story by Leo Tolstoy.[17] "What do you think? You think the beast is a fool? No, he is wiser than a man, though you do call him a pig. He knows everything." And man? What is so precious about a man? Eroshka says, "When you die the grass will grow on your grave, and that's all." . . . That's all. There is nothing in man either to be proud of or to despise. The failure to perceive and generalize any specifically human quality is nicely observed

[17] Tolstoy (280).

71

in *War and Peace* in the first characterization of the peasant Platon Karataev: "Attachments, friendships, love, as Pierre understood them, Karataev had none; but he loved and lived on affectionate terms with every creature with whom he was thrown in life, and especially so with man—not with any particular man, but with men who happened to be before his eyes."[18] If he might freely kill a beast in his need, should he suffer any greater compunction in killing a man?

Birth and death belong to the routine of any farm. A peasant lavished care on his animals to prepare them for slaughter. He would pet his calf and cut its throat. Neither gesture could move him deeply. "Everything lives to die." He included himself hardly less calmly than his animals. Turgenev and Tolstoy were fascinated and puzzled by the simple and calm way the Russian peasants prepared for death. They could contest a high death rate only with a high birth rate. Survival was by numbers: out of many born some would surely live. The odds that any one person would endure were relatively poor compared to the probability that a family would grow up. That, moreover, was the important thing.

Most men are likely to give back to their environment as good as they get—hardly ever anything better. In part the reaction may be deliberate. Victimized by arbitrary power the peasant is perhaps driven to exercise it where he can, if not in revenge, at least in compensation. Having been humiliated he may wish to humiliate; having been subjected to brutality he may wish to torture. Or it may only be that finding himself of so little account in the wider world he must display as vigorously as he can his power over the world of the courtyard. In part, however, he undoubtedly acts simply as he is conditioned to act, without any kind of malice. He is cruel because he is himself inured to cruelty. He inflicts suffering as he takes it without emotion. He does not spare himself in his work, submitting his own flesh to whatever agonies are demanded by the struggle. Why should he spare others, or even think of sparing others? If he stupidly beats his wife and children, pitilessly drives his horses till they drop, he also stands ready to give his life for them.

[18] Tolstoy (279).

For his enemies nothing that imagination can devise is bad enough. Arsonists and horse thiefs—the bad men most hated in the village—commonly suffered prolonged torture before being lynched. Atrocities during the civil war were far too common to be attributed to the madness of individuals. Torture has been a routine instrument of the Soviet police. German cities were given to the victorious Soviet armies for three days to sack, plunder, and rape. A total ruthlessness toward the helpless remains the policy of the Communist state, as the massacres in Hungary showed.

Characteristically Soviet policy in ex-peasants' hands has not reserved force as a last resort. There are no "emotional fixations for or against force as such," writes one critic. "The Soviet machinery of power is geared to use force at any given moment . . . It is not limited to any inhibition regarding the extent to which force is to be used."[19] Nor has it any inhibition as to timing, but will employ force and persuasion in any order and any mixture that seems expedient. This routine, as distinguished from the ultimate, or exasperated, use of force is very difficult for Western civilized man to understand. The civilized habitually hold force back, feeling, with something like the compulsion of instinct, that in any dispute other means of settlement must be tried first.

As the poor have always known that poverty is brutalizing, not challenging, so the downtrodden know that to be forever stepped on is not fitly humbling but just humiliating. In the literary view of the peasant, submissiveness has loomed as his most distinctive quality, for this is the face he has turned outward whence the literary light in general came. But the inside view through his own folklore shows, instead, his vanity. He is contemptuous of all who are not peasants and do not know what he knows, and especially of foreigners "who can't even speak Russian." In a popular tale, rewritten by Nikolai Leskov,[20] illiterate Russian artisans in the town of Tula put British skilled workmanship to shame. "What a foreigner (*nemets*) would die of," a proverb proclaims, "a Russian would eat and feel better for it."[21]

[19] Niemeyer (201), p. 54.
[20] Leskov (164).
[21] *Chto russkomu zdorovo, to nemtsu smert.* In modern Russian, *nemets* is a "German," but historically, every foreigner was *nemets*—a derivative of *nemoy* (mute, dumb)—that is, as good as a mute, for he doesn't know Russian.

Soviet boasts that everything worth inventing or discovering was invented or discovered by the Russians are typical extravagances of the village braggart. They only stretch the primitive fantasies a little. Even if Russian folk did not actually do these things they could have. And was that not brilliantly demonstrated at the launching of *sputnik?* What a triumph for men like Khrushchev, born in a village, poor and semi-literate! The fact of achievement is impressive enough. The sense of it to ex-peasant Soviet citizens must have been immeasurably grand.

Years before, a *Pravda* editorial had claimed: "We, the Soviet people, successors and continuators of everything best, everything progressive that has been the glory of our Motherland in the past, we did not squander our heritage but increased it manifold. Our socialist culture is the most advanced culture in the world, and it is our legitimate pride that our country has become the beacon of world civilization, the standard-bearer of advanced ideas."[22]

Catching up with America evidently has been all along a slogan, appealing not merely to greed for material things but more powerfully to the collective desire of self-made men to prove themselves. That the goal has repeatedly seemed nearer than rationally it should have, even to the more sophisticated, may be partly because they wished to stretch a point for propaganda; but it may also have reflected the disposition as consistently to underestimate the prowess of the foreigner as to overestimate their own.

In the village, justice was practical and utilitarian. To the peasant mind the law was a swindler's weapon. Justice was something apart. It was the common sense judgments of the peasants' courts (*volostnoy sud*) which protected the village and its inhabitants, and it was also the body of traditions by which men protected themselves. In the Caucasus, the code of vengeance endured, and wise men— like Iosif Vissarionovich Stalin—did not leave their enemies at large any longer than they could help. In some cases murder in the village, causing material damage to the household by depriving it of labor, might be settled in the medieval fashion by paying wergild. Universally, the major crimes were those most dangerous

[22] *Pravda*, 6 June 1949.

to men's property. As in the old American West, and for similar reasons, the horse thief was one of society's worst enemies. If caught he had ordinarily no hope for trial. He was promptly tortured and lynched. So were arsonists in a land where thatched cottages burned like brushwood, and a village could be consumed in a few hours.[23]

But if an avowed horse thief came from a distant province to dispose of his stolen property he would be regarded with respect and envy. After all, he did not take from the village but by his daring brought wealth to it. Stolen goods could often be had quite cheap. The peasant, despite his sincerely professed faith in the Christian code, never considered crime in the abstract. He saw only criminals, and the criminals that impressed him as evidently evil were those who injured or threatened him. Stealing wood from the state or the lands of the gentry was against the law but certainly no crime. Stealing even the smallest object from a fellow villager or from the commune, on the other hand, would bring the culprit, at the very least, a severe beating—possibly, mutilation or death. By the same reckoning, a stranger who transgressed could expect no leniency, and one who complained against a villager was unlikely to get satisfaction.

Justice, in short, consisted very largely in keeping straight the ordained relations between persons. The very definition of a crime depended on who the culprit was and who his victim. Crime was not conceived of as individual wrong but as social danger. Exactly so is it conceived in Soviet law, with an ideological bow to Marx and an even deeper ethical obeisance to the primitive custom of the village. By Articles 6 to 19, Section III, of the Criminal Code of the Russian Soviet Federal Socialist Republic (R.S.F.S.R.)[24] the severity of crimes was made to depend on the social status of the accused and the practical consequences of his criminal act for the state. Soviet courts have routinely considered the ancestry as well as the profession of the defendant, making one rule for the son of a "bourgeois survivor" and another for the kin of a Party member in good standing. Courts deem the murder of an important man more heinous than the murder of a nobody. Common thieves,

---

[23] Significantly, the Russian phrase for "warmongers" is *podzhigateli voiny* —literally, "war arsonists."

[24] *Criminal Code* (51).

robbers, and murderers have been more gently treated, as the "socially close element," than even innocent members of the "hostile social classes."

Similarly, the Soviet government values its own property and protects it by laws far harsher than those safeguarding private possessions. Separate decrees of June 4 and June 9, 1947, dealt respectively with crimes against "national and communal property" and "citizens' personal property." If the distinction may be rationalized by Communist theory, it also accords with the peasant disposition to prefer the security of family and community to the rights of individuals.

Stealing from the state, including pilfering grain from the collective farms, may be punished by death. So, of course, may treason, which still includes "flight abroad or refusal to return from abroad."[25] Four times since 1920 the Soviet government has decreed the abolition of capital punishment and four times restored it, most lately by decrees of January 12, 1950, and April 30, 1954. Under the revised code, about thirty crimes are punishable by death, compared to seventy in the first R.S.F.S.R. Criminal Code (1926).

If there is here some quantitative reduction in barbarity the underlying legal concepts remain archaic. Whatever the law says, it is well understood that no means are denied the state to enforce its authority and protect its own. Law is an instrument of the sovereign will and does not bind the sovereign. By the U.S.S.R. code of 1958 criminal penalties were forbidden except by court sentence. That would appear, on the surface, to restrict the activities of the secret police. But in the official Soviet cant what police do to discipline or reform citizens in their custody is not called "punishment" but "repression" or "measures of social defense." The code, moreover, does not undertake to define pretrial procedures, which are not supervised by the court nor restricted by regulations nor subject to appeal. Arrest is still permitted without warrant, and prisoners have no recourse against indefinite confinement. For the first time in 1958 the Soviet Union adopted the principle that a person may be punished only for acts defined as crimes—a principle accepted by all civilized nations, including Russia before the

[25] Cf. Gsovski (95).

Soviets, and rudimentary to the rule of law.[26]

Of course, a uniform rule of law could hardly be expected in any arbitrary system of power. Like every other institution in totalitarian society, law must serve the master. But the characteristic communist degradation of law is not fully understood if it is viewed only as an expedient of power. It is part also of the exaltation of the primitive.

Soviet modern law is more like Russian medieval than Russian imperial law. Analogies abound. The medieval code, *Russkaia Pravda*—drawn without benefit of Marx's theories of class struggle —provided three schedules of punishment for murder, depending on the social status of the corpse.[27] Soviet law is like medieval English law. In the tenth century, "the bishops and reeves" of London ordained that anyone over the age of twelve who stole more than twelve pence should be put to death.[28] One thousand years later in Russia, by decree of the Presidium of the Supreme Soviet on July 7, 1941, an earlier Soviet decree was reaffirmed to read: "Those twelve years old and older, whether their crimes be premeditated or inadvertent, shall be subject to all the provisions of the Criminal Code on an equal footing with adults."[29] This article, involving punishment by death, stood in subsequent revisions until 1958, when the age of majority was raised to fourteen for most crimes, including destruction of government property. What makes these and other analogies significant is the *continuity* traceable from medieval codes through the traditional customs of the rural world to Soviet times.

The modern idea of law as a continuing, dependable, uniform guide to action has yet to be accepted. In forty years Soviet legal shelves have filled with legislation, but the country continues to be governed by decree. No Soviet citizen abiding by the law can feel secure. On the contrary, he sees on every hand the evidence that the smart and successful are those who circumvent the law and those who, by acquiring a little power and substance of their own, can

[26] Only Germany under the Nazis rejected the maxim; Red China still does not accept it and recognizes "crime by analogy"; cf. Gsovski (95) and Tao (273).

[27] *Russkaia Pravda* (239).

[28] Queen (228), p. 189.

[29] *Criminal Code* (51), Art. 12.

divert the law like a stone in the current.

Marxist theory that law in a bourgeois society was an instrument of class struggle fitted providentially with the traditional distrust of the peasant. Legality, sent packing by the Revolution, has not yet returned. Even the Soviet press discusses "socialist legality" mostly in the future tense. It awaits in fact the maturing of Soviet culture.

6

"HE LOVES HIS PEOPLE"

WHEN THE STALINIST REVOLUTION WAS COMPLETE, WITH THE COLLEC-
tivization of the rural multitudes at the bottom and the final
extermination of remnants of the old revolutionary élite at the top, a
kind of seventeenth-century Muscovite society was re-established
in Russia—in rather more thoroughgoing and stable form than had
existed four hundred years before.

The new society was "classless" in the sense that persons of
peasant stock occupied all positions in its hierarchy, but the stratification was actually more rigid than in any bourgeois country. At
the top, the new Party aristocracy, consisting of Stalin, his henchmen, and his top generals, emerged out of the human stuff of the
kulaks of other days. A new middle layer—which in the nature of
middle classes everywhere has steadily grown in numbers and
weight ever since—settled in the bureaucracy. A new intelligentsia
was formed almost wholly of a few technicians and was inadequate
at first to the nation's most elementary needs. A new military caste
grew out of the ranks and, as could be expected, developed a still
more rigorous exclusiveness than the old. The reconstructed master
classes, created in the image of the medieval *soslovia*, rested as of
old on the mass of the citizenry returned to virtual serfdom in both
industry and agriculture. The whole nation was governed as
though it were the household of the Communist Party, and from
top to bottom rulers and ruled were bound together by mutual
obligations.

The principle of universal service written into the Soviet Constitution of 1936 as the creation of socialism was also a resurrection
from the Muscovite state. In both worlds it functioned essentially
as the principle of the patriarchal household. The point that the

Communist Party and its chiefs serve the people and therefore have the right to command the people to serve them has been made incessantly by the Soviet press. But it has been still more convincingly made by the practice of government, which in scores of ways has impressed on the citizen its intimate, detailed, fatherly concern.

Like most languages, Russian has a status symbol in the familiar form of "you." Russian *ty*, like French *tu* or German *du*, before the Revolution was used by educated people chiefly between intimates and particularly within the family circle. Its connotations are loving between friends but patronizing between strangers. Thus in pre-revolutionary society it might be used by the gentry in addressing their domestic servants, by commissioned officers addressing men in the ranks, and by officials and landlords addressing peasants. The March revolution, as a token of the new democracy and a tribute to the dignity of man, decreed that the formal *vy* (French *vous*, German *Sie*) should be used exclusively by superiors talking to subordinates. The peasant revolution reversed that. Stalin in his character of socialist father came to address everybody as *ty*, and to expect in turn that everyone should deferentially reply *vy*. Khrushchev apparently follows the same pattern.[1]

The customary peasant use of the pronoun has spread throughout Soviet society. Marshals say *ty* to generals, generals to colonels, party bosses to lesser party bosses, foremen to workers, and so on down the line until the kolkhoznik at the bottom once again has no one to patronize but his child or his beast.

"Comrade," or *tovarishch*, the old revolutionaries' most attractive gesture toward the ideal of the brotherhood of man, has characteristically been turned into a rhetorical flourish reserved for official pronouncements. In everyday use the style of address has come to follow the servile pattern of rural society. In Soviet novels, party officials speak about their superiors only in the polite form, by first name and patronymic. Thus, in the novel *Not By Bread Alone* by Vladimir Dudintsev (1956), the surnames of the state minister

[1] Exactly the peasant household pattern. In sophisticated urban families, the personal pronoun *ty* was used for the father as well. On the other hand, Russian emperors in the modern time invariably addressed their state ministers and subjects (except the soldiers, servants, and peasants) as *vy*. They themselves were called "Thou" on solemn occasions but "Your Majesty" or "You, Sire" in normal discourse. Eventually, the ritual form "Thou" was revived for Stalin in poetry and in public addresses: "Dear beloved Comrade Stalin, thou art our leader, teacher, and father!"

and his deputy are never mentioned. To refer to a respected man in the village by his surname would be unseemly. It has been said that Soviet citizens in conversation treated the surname "Stalin" as though it were taboo. He was referred to rather as Iosif Vissariono-vich, in the conventional way, or as Vissarionych (a kind of peasant blend of respect and affection), or as *Khoziain* (Master), or oracularly as *Sam* (himself). Officially, of course, he was *tovarishch* Stalin and, in the Soviet press, he was the only one who rated the full title. Others were cut down to one syllable (*tov.*) or all the way down to a bare "*t.*" Khrushchev rates "tovarishch," but the current official style seems to prefer "N. S. Khrushchev," the pre-revolutionary form, though not infrequently he also appears in the Soviet press simply as "Nikita Sergeyevich."

Official meddling in the private lives of citizens has been gener-ally associated with totalitarianism as a political system, and viewed as the effort of the state to ferret out disloyalty in the most intimate corners of daily life where it might otherwise grow formidable in obscurity. But in the Soviet Union meddling goes far beyond any conceivable need of the police state and beyond anything that might be justified by a political theory or idea.

Mikhail Koriakov, a former captain in the Red Army who for a few months was attached to the Soviet Embassy in Paris after World War II, has reported that he and every other member of the staff were under the constant surveillance of the secretary of the Embassy's communist cell. The secretary, Panchenko, a Ukrainian peasant who had been a railroad worker before the Revolution, regularly searched their rooms, opened their letters, and occasion-ally at least had them shadowed.[2]

Among the Russians in Paris there was a widely circulated story of a young man, new to the staff, who was summoned one day to Panchenko's office:

"How old are you?" the secretary asked.

"Twenty-six," said the man.

"I know. Twenty-six and not married. That ain't good. What have you been thinking of? At your age!"

[2] Cf. his article "79, rue de Grenelle: Kak zhivut i rabotaiut v Sovetskom posolstve [How They Live and Work in the Soviet Embassy], *Novoe Russkoe Slovo*, 17, 18 and 19 April 1949; see also Koriakov (138).

The young man, who was only recently transferred from the Army, pleaded that there had been a war and that, besides, he did not happen to have been in love. The secretary observed that the war was over and all decent men of his age were married.

"As to love," said secretary Panchenko, "there is no time to waste. I'll tell you. There are two young girls right here at the Embassy. Both are good and loyal Soviet citizens. You can take my word for it. It's really a shame they aren't married yet. Well, don't argue. I give you two weeks to make your choice."

When the victim protested that he did not even know the girls and they might not want him, Panchenko laughed: "Leave it to me," he said, "I'll see that one of them will. Oh yes, she will!"

The young man, with more reason than most bachelors, chose freedom. He fled the Embassy—and at last married into a foreign family.

Vladimir Petrov, a code clerk at the Soviet Embassy in Sweden, tells that in similar fashion he kept his eye on the whole Soviet colony in that country in 1942. Five years later, he was overseeing the loyalty as well as the moral conduct of Soviet seamen visiting foreign ports, and still later was watchdog in the Soviet embassy in Australia. Although his reports were of course available to the NKVD, he was not a secret police agent himself and actually was not primarily functioning as one. He was the eyes of a paternal government that took for granted its right and need to be informed in every particular about its children. In a Soviet novel, a party secretary who pries into everyone's affairs declares that it is his job on behalf of party and state "to penetrate into the very essence of a person's soul, not his work."[3] No other country holds such complete personal files on its inhabitants. The archives are indeed so stuffed with domestic trivia as to be almost useless to the police, who frequently ignore them altogether.[4]

In the village it was customary to ask the stranger "*Whose* are you?" not "Who are you?" The answer took one of three forms: It was a possessive adjective formed from the father's name, like Ivanov, Petrov, Alexandrov ("John's, Peter's, Alexander's");[5] or a

[3] Koptiaeva (137).
[4] Petrov (216).
[5] Cf. *Ivanov dom* (Ivan's house), *Ivanov lug* (Ivan's meadow), etc. Note that the patronymic Ivanovich, Petrovich, etc., means merely "son of" (cf. Johnson, Peterson) with no connotations of possession or ownership.

possessive adjective from the father's occupation, like Kuznetsov, Melnikov, Pastukhov ("blacksmith's, miller's, shepherd's"); or it was an adjective from the name of the person or institution to which the family or village belonged, like Romanovsky, Smirnovsky, Monastyrsky ("Romanov's, Smirnov's, the monastery's"). The idiom neither began nor ended with serfdom. Even in current usage the peasant may identify himself as attached to a collective farm just as formerly he might have named his overlord. The common phrase *sovietskie liudi* (Soviet people) connotes attachment besides nationality.

Belonging in the village had been enforced by law as well as custom. No peasant could leave home without authorization of the head of the household, and even then a passport was granted only if it appeared to be in the community interest. At any time, on complaint of the father or the mir, a passport could be revoked and the man arrested by the imperial police and returned home at public expense. Similarly, rigid controls over the movements of all citizens were established by the Soviet govenment in the fall of 1933. Citizens of unquestioned loyalty were issued passports good for three years and were permitted to change residence. Students and others who, though outwardly loyal were inherently suspect, could get passports for only one year. Others less reliable had to reapply every three months. Modified in some details, the system endures to this day. As already noted, the Soviet government continues to claim the unlimited right to recall any citizen from anywhere for any reason or none.

Such control has little to do with national security, and may often be exercised at the expense of national interests. *Psychologically*, it seems justified by an irrational desire to hold on to one's own. The frenetic, undignified pursuit in the United States of the defected school teacher, Oksana Kasenkina, some years ago, for instance, can hardly have profited the Soviet government; and Soviet authorities, moreover, gave no sign that they recognized or cared about its political repercussions. The story is worth recalling. Miss Kasenkina, who was teaching children of Soviet employees in New York, refused to return to Moscow and fled instead to a farm in New Jersey. For the Soviets, the prudent course would have been to repudiate her openly and pursue her quietly. Instead, Consul General Lomakin in person went out after her to the farm and demanded delivery as though she were a stray cow. Rebuffed by the American police, he used other means and, finally, lured the fugitive back to New York where he locked her in a room on the fourth floor of the consulate. Form there Oksana Kasenkina made her famous leap to freedom. Only then did Consul Lomakin limp home in disgrace—not for the black eye he had given his country in the world press but for having lost Soviet property.[6]

Unquestionably, behind such incidents as the pursuit of Oksana Kasenkina lies the basic disquiet of a crowd of usurpers still relatively new to power, still conscious that being illegitimate they can rely on only their own talents for survival. They stick together because they obviously cannot get along separately, yet they cannot trust each other. When one of the family breaks loose, tremors of dissolution pass through the body politic.

Like the ancient patriarchal household, the totalitarian state is held together essentially by fear and ignorance in the citizens, which together give effect to absolute power at the top. For over forty years Communist Party members have been conditioned to feel alone in a hostile world, where the penalty for weakness was death. "It's either we or they," Lenin said; and Gorky repeated the aphorism of extremists: "He who is not with us is against us and must be crushed." So it had been literally in the beginning, as in all revolutions. But the state of civil war was abnormally prolonged in the Soviet Union. When the external danger to Bolshevik rule eased off, the internal stress tightened under the Stalinist terror. While tensions have slackened somewhat since Stalin's death, the insecurity remains—in part because it is still cultivated as an instrument of control, in larger part because it is inherent in a system lacking two principles essential to stability: legitimacy and the rule of law.

Revolutionary intellectuals of the first generation, like Lenin and his associates, rationalized their right to rule by historical inevitability. They were the inheritors of the kingdom which, according to Marx, had been building for them since the beginning of human society. It is doubtful, however, that this faith has ever been effective among the rank and file in legitimizing the Soviet

[6] Kasenkina (126).

regime. To believe in history and to act effectively as its servant one must at the very least have read it. The bulk of the Communist Party came to be drawn from semiliterate (though often extremely intelligent) peasants who did not read. They could derive no sense of historical mission or immanent security from Lenin's idea that they belonged to the world proletariat and were the vanguard of destiny.

An Austrian Communist, associated for a number of years with the Soviet government, wrote of Stalin's henchmen in 1935 that they were men "for whom the ideas of the great Revolution meant absolutely nothing . . . The higher they rose in the hierarchy the greater became their privileges. And they could rise only on the backs of others. This system resulted in a sort of natural selection of the most ruthless."[7] Stalin himself cared little about theory. His biographers—the unofficial ones, of course—note that he not only contributed not a single idea to the lively debates of the pre-revolutionary ferment, but was often missing altogether from the forum, busy with incessant intrigue behind the scenes. He was the practical man, a kind of rural boss, with his mind and energies firmly fixed on the main chance of engrossing power. Son of a rural cobbler in the Caucasian Mountains, reared by a drinking father and a devout mother, he was "a totally different type of Bolshevik, both in his psychological makeup and in the character of his party work; a strong but theoretically and politically primitive organizer . . . Without a theoretical viewpoint, without broad political interests, and without a knowledge of foreign languages, [he] was inseparable from the Russian soil."[8] In the summer of 1917, recalls another revolutionary, Stalin "during his modest activity in the Executive Committee produced—and not only on me—the impression of a gray blur, looming up now and then dimly and not leaving any trace."[9] General Charles de Gaulle, visiting in Moscow thirty years later, remarked: "During the meal Stalin acted the part of a primitive and uncultured rustic. . ."[10]

[7] Weissberg (304).
[8] Trotsky (285), Vol. I, p. 288; other pertinent remarks, Vol. III, pp. 164 and 416.
[9] Sukhanov (270), p. 230.
[10] *War Memoirs*, Vol. III. See also the studies and reminiscences by Basseches (14), Deutscher (59), Lyons (174), Ludwig (171), Serge (245), Souvarine (261), and Trotsky (286); official biographies give a different picture of course.

Yet, being successful, Stalin proved to his followers that he possessed theoretical as well as practical wisdom. They were compelled to believe that he was the best of them in every way, the greatest philosopher as well as the greatest statesman, military leader, economist, scientist, literary critic, and protector of the arts. He was supreme because he had been infallible, and he had to be infallible because he was supreme. If he did not become omniscient through his secret police, at least one could hardly depend on his ignorance in any particular. He was all-powerful, surely, when he exterminated his personal enemies in great purges, and the enemies of Russia in a great war, or when he not only made the law but unmade it at will. And was his presence not ubiquitous in every home where his picture hung, in every corner of consciousness where his name penetrated whenever a man read or listened?

Observers of Russia under Stalin have often enough been impressed with the vastness of power so manifested, and with its evils. But more impressive still was the need it answered. For the peasant born and bred, Stalinism in fact was only the magnified "father cult" found in all primitive agricultural societies. It had grown so impressively large in the Soviet Union because never before had the peasant underworld stood forth to make over a nation in its own image.

Lenin was still living, although incapacitated by illness, when *Pravda* described a Moscow district party meeting where a worker delegate concluded his speech by remarking, "Comrade Stalin told us 'The less democracy the better,' and I say this is very true." The audience applauded enthusiastically until Stalin himself stood up and said: "The comrade is mistaken; I said the more democracy the better." The audience laughed, applauded again, and gave Stalin a standing ovation.[11] The press at that time was concerned with rebuking the party rank and file for their uncritical readiness to follow the leader wherever he went. But Stalin understood that readiness as a national need and exploited it to an extent that a civilized man like Lenin would not have believed possible, much less desirable.[12] What Friedrich Engels once called the "primitive sheep instinct of the Russians"[13]—and he meant of course the mass

[11] *Pravda*, 9 December 1923.
[12] Cf. Lenin's testament (see above, Chap. 1, n. 20).
[13] Quoted by Souvarine (261), p. 193.

of Russian peasants—would inevitably yield strength to the strong-est, and especially to a man like Stalin who, unhampered by ideals, combined the cautious rapacity of a kulak with the cunning and ruthlessness of a bandit. (As a matter of historical record, bossing a gang of bank robbers, who looted to fill the party's treasury, was one of Stalin's most notable contributions to the Communist cause before 1917.)[14]

Although it would be difficult to imagine a character less lovable or a career less attractive than Joseph Stalin's, once he be-came Father, the peasant members of his family (the Party) felt as strong a compulsion to worship him as to obey. Indeed, the two absolutes—total obedience and total attachment—went necessarily together. Even an outside observer under the romantic spell of paternalism elevated to Olympian dimension could write of the supreme predator of the Russian nation: "He loves his people."[15]

Significantly, Stalin nourished and enlarged his image by bor-rowing from Russian history and folklore. The heroes of the his-torical past, condemned as feudal and decadent by the founding fathers of Bolshevism, were resurrected by Stalin to create an apostolic succession. A selected group of rulers of medieval Russia appeared beside Marx and Engels in the Soviet pantheon: Prince Alexander Nevsky (1220-1263), who was canonized by the Russian Church as protector of the Russian land and faith against the Swedes, Germans, and Mongols; Grand Duke Ivan III, founder of the sovereign Muscovite State (1440-1505); Ivan IV (the Terrible), the first Russian Tsar (1530-1584); and Peter the Great, founder of the Russian empire (1672-1725). Except for Peter the Great, all these refurbished national heroes were despots who ruled over "Holy Russia" before the seventeenth-century *raskol*. Toward later, more enlightened Tsars, whose achievements were no less large or significant for the growth of the Russian empire, the Soviet attitude remained as negative as before. Why? If Catherine II might be

[14] The most successful was the hold-up in 1907 of a military convoy taking money from the post office to the Tiflis (Tbilisi) branch of the state bank. Stalin's men used bombs and guns: "In that attack some completely innocent persons lost their lives. More than fifty passers-by, including women and chil-dren, were injured"; Basseches (14), p. 38.

[15] Maynard (181).

87

disqualified for having been born a German, what of Alexander I, who defeated Napoleon; or Alexander II and Alexander III, who added the Caucasus and Central Asia to the empire; or Nicholas II, who granted the country its first parliament in 1905?

Clearly they provided no fit model for Stalin. The heir of the Revolution hankered after the Muscovite glory because there he found the last despots who could be shaped like demigods. He was himself near deification. After the last war, *Izvestia* printed a song about him, purportedly improvised by Siberian fishermen: "Do you ask where the Sun comes from? Listen to the song of the birds, listen to the language of our rivers, and you will know who set happiness in our land and how the sun came to shine over it. The Sun is given us by Stalin. Yes, this is the greatest Truth."[16] In a play performed during his lifetime, Stalin appeared in a vision to a girl working on a collective farm, exactly like a holy visitation. As deity he was incomparably remote and powerful, yet could be adored by everybody. Soldiers on the march sang to the "Great Friend and Father of the Soviet peoples, Iosif Vissarionovich Stalin."[17] In 1960, as part of the campaign to rebuild his image, *Pravda* printed the recollections of a Soviet poet, who wrote:

> . . . It was just natural
> That, through the smoke of his pipe,
> He personally supervised the world
> And ordered everything like god.
>
> . . . .
> We called him—why not admit it?—
> Father in our country-large family."[18]

With sure instinct for the peasant taste, Stalin had laid the groundwork for idolatry at Lenin's death. The embalming of Lenin's body and its public exhibition were gestures of barbarism, which symbolized the transformation of revolutionary ideals into talismans for the medicine man. As the "endless procession of superstitious peasants" filed by the glass tomb of Lenin, the saint who was dead prepared the sanctification of his successor. Lenin's likeness was

[16] As quoted by E. Kuskova in *Novoe Russkoe Slovo*, 26 February 1947.

[17] A Soviet movie, *Shchit Dzhurgaya* (1950).

[18] Alexander Tvardovsky, in the poem *Za dal'iu dal* [Distant Visions], published in *Pravda*, 30 April and 1 May 1960.

molded into a thousand relics to succor the ignorant. "Under the varnish already disappearing of imported Marxist theory, there reappeared the familiar face of ancient barbaric Russia."[19]

The myth of Lenin's infallibility was created after his death. Stalin's was made alive. Lenin while he lived was the chief, the first among several leaders who tried by various expedients to bring a nation successfully through revolutionary trials to a previsioned ideal. Stalin, on the other hand, was the Master (Dominus, *khoziain*), owner, and ruler of the Soviet land and people, absolute head of the Party household. His entourage, rearranged now and then by purge and shaken constantly by fear, consisted of trusted superintendents and managers (*khoziaistvenniki*) without independent authority and without influence over policy, except as they might intrigue at the risk of their lives.

While Stalin lived the party seniors vied with each other in extolling the master from whom all power flowed. It was necessary to his position and, therefore, to their own dependent one that he be the ideal authority. But when god died no notorious mortal could take his place. The heirs had therefore to *deflate* the divinity they helped create in order to make any succession at all adequate in the eyes of the Party and the people. This was necessary to make way for a collective regency or equally to prepare for a new Leader.

"Those who sell idols," says a Malayan proverb, "do not believe in gods because they know what these are made of." So Khrushchev in his assault on the Stalin myth evidently underestimated the dangers of image-smashing. Foreign observers, on the other hand, greatly overestimated them. No doubt the Soviet people were shocked at hearing that father on high had now and then sinned; but they did not suffer the shattering disillusion that to the outsider had seemed inevitable. They were conditioned to accepting Khrushchev's performance as an act of piety, not abuse. In revealing Stalin's errors, the new leader began the purification of a saintly image which had regrettably tarnished in contact with facts.[20] Kings after all have been discovered to be murderers and idiots without destroying the notion that royalty was a gift from God.

[19] Souvarine (261), pp. 350-351.
[20] Cf. *Great Soviet Encyclopaedia* (Moscow, 1957), Vol. 40: "The sworn enemies of the people and the party . . . wormed their way into his confidence."

So Stalin, his heirs confessed, had certain qualities of highway rob-
ber mingled with his greatness. It was necessary to distinguish these
in order to remove them from the governing symbol. Nikita Khrushchev was as interested in restoring that symbol to its traditional
purity as he was in toppling Stalin's ghost from the empty throne.
For the father image was—or at least might turn out to be—the
essence of the inheritance.

Significantly, "de-Stalinization" was accomplished in a single
stroke in Khrushchev's speech to the Twentieth Party Congress.
Gradually thereafter the positive image began to be reformed, as
a new cult of personality began to emerge around Khrushchev.[21]
"Stalin made many mistakes in the latter period of his activity" is
the gist of the heir's repeated statements, "but he also did much
that was beneficial to our country, to our party, and the whole
international workers' movement. Our party and the Soviet people
will remember Stalin and give him his proper due." His due is
the purely sentimental attachment owed to a master who is quite
dead.

The relative ease with which the transition between dictatorships was made was thanks largely to the power and discipline of
the Communist Party. Since its early days as a band of crusaders
preparing the way for world revolution the Party has narrowed
and hardened into the governing instrument of the Soviet Union.
It acts something like an army command, something like a *curia
regis,* but most strikingly like its master's household.

A young Texan, Robert Minor, who joined the party in New
York, was asked by a reporter whether he considered the party
his employer. "A benign smile spread across his face. 'The Party,
he said softly, 'is father, mother, brother and sister. It is not an
employer."[22] Hede Massing, who joined the party as a young Austrian student after World War I, has written of the pain of
leaving it at last: "To leave the warmth, the safety and friendship
that have been given you is a tragedy. You have been imbued with
the communist spirit to such an extent that for a long time you

[21] Khrushchev became dictator, but not quite father, of a society significantly
matured since Stalin's accession—see Chapter 9.
[22] *The New York Times,* 30 March 1947.

90

see yourself as a traitor, as do the comrades you have left . . . It is like renouncing your religion, your family, your life's work, the taking leave from all your friends—all at once."[23]

The emotional childishness of these two converts is characteristic. On the part of persons born into sophisticated cultures, it is a sign of a pathetic personal failure to mature. But among the true primitives the emotional craving is counterpart of the physical need. Persons are prevented from outgrowing their emotional dependency because in fact they are unable to fend for themselves. Their own immaturity echoes the immaturity of their culture.

Since *family* was a natural association and the only one with which the primitive was familiar, its pattern was naturally adapted to any group engaged in common enterprise—religious sects, military units, bandit gangs, or political parties. A man might choose to join or not to join these other groups; but once accepted, he was identified with it in the same sense and the same terms as he was with his natural family—working, sharing, investing, benefiting, relating himself to others outside, not as an individual but as a part of the group. As a family substitute, the Communist Party—to paraphrase Prof. C. C. Zimmerman[24]—became the group functioning as a collective agent with unlimited responsibility for the well-being and existence of its members. Created for revolutionaries, it developed under the peasant counterrevolution as a refuge for cultural primitives.

Characteristically, successive revisions of the Soviet Communist Party by-laws moved the group away from the band of free associates of early revolutionary days. Amendments to Article 3 have redefined the duties of a Party member to bind him to the patriarchal society.[25] He is commanded "to guard the unity of the Party in every way, as the prime condition of the Party's strength and might; to be an active fighter for the fulfillment of Party decisions; to set an example on the job and to master knowledge of it, constantly increasing his working skills; in all ways to safeguard and strengthen public socialist property as the sacred and inviolable basis of the Soviet system; to observe Party and State discipline,

[23] Massing (179).
[24] Zimmerman (322).
[25] By-laws of the Communist Party of the Soviet Union (CPSU) as revised in 1952, amended in 1956—English text as in Meisner (186); see also Reshetar (235) and Schapiro (242).

obligatory to all Party members alike . . .; to report to leading Party bodies, right up to the Party Central Committee, short-comings in work irrespective of the persons involved; to be truthful and honest before the Party and never permit concealment or distortion of truth; to keep Party and State secrets and to display political vigilance; at any post entrusted to him by the Party, to carry out without fail the Party directives on correct selection of cadres with regard to political and working qualifications . . ."

While defining the duties of party members, characteristically the regulations set no bounds to the authority of the head of the group, the First Secretary. Although formally answerable to the Central Committee, he can in fact ignore its suggestions, decide everything himself, and proscribe criticism. On paper, the Central Committee may remove him by a two-thirds vote, but he alone may call the Committee into session. Indeed, party regulations are no more binding on him than a family council on the head of a rural household. He is supposed to work in council with elders (*presidium*), but their authority as well as personal security are hardly any greater than those of the boyar council (*duma*) in the Muscovite state. In case of disagreement, he stays, and they go. When, in June 1957, Khrushchev found himself outvoted in the Presidium he had only to call the Central Committee to have Georgi Malenkov, Vyacheslav Molotov, and Lazar Kaganovich expelled by unanimous vote.

The original structure of the party, defined by Stalin in military terms, as befitted a Generalissimo, has not changed since: "Three or four thousand men of the high command—the generals of our Party. Then thirty to forty thousand intermediate commanders—these constitute the officer corps of our Party; and a further 100 to 150 thousand of the leading elements of our Party—these are, so to speak, the subaltern officers of our Party."[26] While total membership has fluctuated (from under 400,000 in 1924 to over 8 million in 1961), the party is still an exclusive officer corps within which the ruling élite, including the senior bureaucracy, police, and army bosses, remains a comparative handful—perhaps 10,000 in a society of 200 million.[27]

The Ten Thousand, led by the First Secretary, can be very

[26] Quoted in Monnerot (193), p. 86.
[27] Bauer (15).

nearly identified as members of the central committees at every echelon of the party organization—union republics, autonomous republics, regions, and provinces. According to Article 11 of the Party by-laws, they cannot be censored or removed except by a "two-thirds majority" of the respective membership. In fact, if not in law, they have been and are removed only by orders of the Secretariat of the Communist Party of the Soviet Union. As the "immediate family" of the First Secretary, they form an extraordinarily homogeneous, powerful, and efficient clique, governing the larger party household and, through it, the nation.

7

THE NEW CULTURE

AT THE END OF 1958, A *New York Times* REPORTER WROTE FROM Prague: "Life in Eastern Europe is shaking down into a recognized pattern . . . The capital cities have acquired a proletarian mark. The population have a distinct working class flavor in dress, manners and taste . . . Physical fatigue is written on faces of people. Weary eyes and lined jaws and necks are the recognizable stigmata. The middle-aged people seem much older in Eastern Europe than in the West."[1]

So do they in any village. If civilization is essentially a process of freeing mankind from the all-consuming toil characteristic of primitive agricultural societies, then Communist reversal of that process might usefully be regarded as "ruralizing"—not only in the literal sense of manning the cities with countryfolk, but in the cultural sense of decivilizing the city to the standards of a village.

The culture of the cities in Russia before 1917 was largely confined to St. Petersburg, Moscow, Kiev, and a few other provincial capitals. Outside them the nation was one great village: "All Russia is nothing but a village; get that firmly fixed in your noodle," wrote Ivan Bunin on the eve of the Revolution.[2] Industrialization, even though making very rapid progress after 1880, had scarcely begun to urbanize the hereditary peasant. Most who worked in factories retained their ties with the village, either returning to the land in the growing season or holding to the dream of return. There was virtually no urban artisan class at the base of the newly growing proletariat. When Lenin spoke of "workers and peasants" he meant,

[1] M. S. Handler, in *The New York Times*, 7 December 1958.
[2] Bunin (37).

94

in fact, peasants removed from the land along with the peasants still on it. A tiny—though for its numbers powerful and influential—bourgeoisie and intelligentsia were the sole bearers of urban culture. These the Soviet Revolution exterminated, exiled, or enslaved.[3]

Being a peasant is not, of course, a human condition that prohibits an individual from acquiring culture. There have been in Russia as elsewhere rustics who became great scholars, statesmen, sponsors of arts and sciences, creative writers. Like the self-made men in other countries, they rose by exceptional talents schooled through established civilized institutions and traditions. What happened after the Revolution, however, was that the Communists, inviting the peasants to move "from huts to palaces," condemned and rejected the world that had built palaces. While a few "proletarians" in the cities experimented, chaotically trying to create a new "proletarian culture" (whatever that might mean), the fury of the unleashed peasantry was turned not only against the old masters but against the master civilization.

Much, perhaps most, of the brutality with which the intelligentsia was treated paralleled the experience of other major revolutions which, beginning with attack on privilege, have universally loosed a more indiscriminate violence against all those whose superior attainments have made the mass man feel inferior. In any leveling movement, by revolutions or bulldozers, the untenable position is to be outstanding.

In addition, however, peasants traditionally believed that the city was the abode of the devil. Nestor Makhno, a leader of the "green" peasantry, which in the Ukraine fought both Reds and Whites, wished to destroy all cities as "the horrible boils swelling on the skin of mankind."[4] The peasant poet, Sergei Essenin, wrote: "Oh city! city! Even the earth under you is not like earth. Satan has murdered her, trampled her down with his iron hoof, leveled her down with his iron back . . ."

[3] While individual members of the old intelligentsia, who survived, were able to preserve in themselves and in their children some of their heritage, they were excluded absolutely from authority—political, economic, moral, or cultural—in the new Soviet society.

[4] A curious and ironic echo of Thomas Jefferson's famous gentleman-farmer remark: "The mobs of great cities add just as much to the support of pure government as sores do to the strength of the human body"; *Writings* (Washington, D.C., 1904), Vol. II, p. 229.

When, in Russia, the country turned on the city, the offensive was vast and the defenders few. The Russian muzhik, Trotsky wrote, "was fulfilling his progressive historical task with the only means at his disposal. With revolutionary barbarism he was wiping out the barbarism of the middle ages."[5] Whatever in fact he was wiping out, he made a clean sweep of it. No revolution before had ever so changed a society.

"Sometimes I feel that the old Russian people is gone and a new people has come to inhabit Russia now," muses a character in Marc Aldanov's novel. "It seems that a new race has been bred, perhaps very good in some respects, but a different and vulgar race leading a coarse life and making it coarser every day."[6] A similar sense of dispossession grips Dr. Zhivago in Pasternak's novel, "All customs and traditions, all our way of life, everything to do with home and order, has crumbled into dust in the general upheaval and reorganization of society. The whole human way of life has been destroyed and ruined. All that is left is the naked human soul stripped to the last shred."[7]

The lament ran much deeper than against the temporary disorder of the civil war itself. What made Zhivago despair was the feeling of rootlessness and emptiness, as though a scythe had swept the nation, cutting the present from the past—the *modern past* into which civilized men were born. "Revolutions are made by fanatical men of action with one-track minds, geniuses in their ability to confine themselves to a limited field. They overturn the old order in a few hours or days, the whole upheaval takes a few weeks or at most years, but the fanatical spirit that inspired the upheavals is worshipped for decades thereafter, for centuries."[8] The spirit is worshiped because the worshipers endure, and it takes time for them to grow into the larger world they have seized.

Civilization at last is the best cure for fanaticism, because it opens broader fields, extends the range of human activity and interest, discourages the delusion that there is only one path to the kingdom.

[5] Trotsky (285), Vol. III, p. 32. Trotsky, of course, would be among those wiped out. Exiled by Stalin in 1928, he was murdered in Mexico in 1940.
[6] Aldanov (2).
[7] Pasternak (215).
[8] *Ibid.*

The process is visibly going on in the Soviet Union and has, indeed, made some remarkable progress in forty years. However small or limited that progress may seem by western standards, it is remarkable because the new society took over little more than cultural ruins, and had not only to rediscover traditions but to adopt or create its own models of civilized behavior. It was as though a school had been left without teachers, and the students had not only to educate themselves but decide what they would learn and why. In a Soviet novel, for instance, it was "a peasant girl Dunia," quick with her curses, blowing her nose in her sleeve and proud of it, who was charged with "cultural" work among the women workers.[9] A small sign of the chasm between the old society and the new were the reissued editions of Russian classics—Pushkin, Turgenev, Chekhov, Tolstoy—printed with footnotes to explain the more difficult words.[10]

Western travelers in the Soviet Union within the last decade have reported in various ways on the crudity of the new world. In the most expensive restaurants the new Soviet aristocracy appear in sweaters without ties. "One evening," writes an American visitor, "in one of Moscow's most luxurious restaurants, the Ararat, I watched a Moscow citizen at the next table finish his chicken by throwing the bones over his shoulder [Shades of Henry VIII!] then grasp a generous steak in his right hand and alternate its dismemberment with full slices of bread uninterruptedly supplied to his mouth by his left."[11] Manners are more conventional at the Kremlin, but the spirit has at times been as exuberant at official receptions where, Joseph Alsop reported, "The crowd tucked in the eatables and drinkables . . . with cheerfully visible enthusiasm," and Comrade Khrushchev behaved with the voluble good humor of a guest at a country wedding.[12] Another seasoned reporter commented that immediately after World War II the manners of Soviet diplomats—thirty years after the Revolution!—"were appalling. At diplomatic dinners they acted as though they had never

[9] Voinova (302); cf. Luke (172).
[10] Conversely, it would have been hard for Turgenev or Tolstoy to read Soviet writings. Maxim Gorky (92, 93) was outspoken in his criticism of the new literature, full of regionalisms, vulgarisms, and cant. The campaign in the Soviet press for "more cultured" speech has continued to this day.
[11] *Life*, 8 February 1954.
[12] *The New York Herald Tribune*, 16 January 1957.

seen such food before. Probably some of them hadn't. Their table manners were rudimentary. And when they had literally polished their plates they sat glowering at the company or drank themselves insensible."[13]

Now that has changed, and the change is dramatic enough, being all on the surface and all visible. The new generation of Soviet diplomats is polite, sober, well-dressed. They are not often seen any more in their pompous uniforms designed by Stalin, with golden epaulets and elaborate embroidery. To consider the change insignificant would be as false as to see in it reliable evidence of inward civilization. It marks in fact some progress out of primitivism. But while pointing hopefully in the direction of social maturity, it shows at the same time how close even the new Soviet man is to his rustic origins.

Because both civilization and the civilized manner had been identified with the *"bourgeoisie"* and condemned, and because the leadership of the old intelligentsia was rejected, the post-revolutionary generation has had to reach for its ideals in part into the literary past, in part into the Western world, and in part into some first principles of good health and good neighborliness. In 1958, in Moscow, the state published a book entitled *For a Healthy Way of Life;* a chapter on good manners reminded those aspiring to "culture" not to blow on soup "or you will soil the tablecloth," never to eat from a knife, "usually" not to drink out of a saucer, and, as a general rule, to refrain from taking food from platters "with your own spoon or fork"[14] There has since appeared in the Soviet press a column on Lessons in Cultured Behavior. Letters to the editor ask "How to furnish an apartment nicely, with taste? . . . May we wear narrow trousers? . . . How about a 'curl' in the hair-do? . . . And thick-soled shoes? . . . Is sentimentality something quite normal, and to what extent? . . . Generally speaking, what is good taste? . . ." To the last the editors answered, "Simplicity, comfort, hygiene—that's what good taste basically is. Books, radio, TV, and an ordinary but comfortable lamp—that's what beautifies your modern apartment in the first place."[15]

[13] Drew Middleton, *The New York Times Magazine,* 7 December 1958.
[14] See *The New York Times Magazine,* 16 November 1958.
[15] *Komsomolskaia Pravda* (Moscow), 1958.

A German writer, not long ago, who was cordially welcomed to a party in the Moscow suburban home of privileged Soviet citizens, remarked caustically about such old-fashioned manners as kissing the ladies' hands which, he said, reminded him "unpleasantly of Tsarist days." His host bridled: "We are progressive, not conservative," he said, "This is culture!"[16]

Culture is the word, if not quite the universal fact, of the day. The word *kultura* is as common in the press as the names of Lenin and Khrushchev. It covers everything that can be construed as self-improvement, decent manners, literacy, style, even sanitation. It is "cultured" to have clean fingernails, to wear a well-cut suit, or to refrain from getting drunk. "The new Soviet man is said to be *kulturny*," that is, "he doesn't spit in the streets, he gives his seat on the bus to old ladies laden with bundles, and he wears a tie on formal occasions."[17] In Soviet novels, characters talk of buying a "cultured suit" or of failing to treat a wife "culturally enough." An American visitor writes, "The false gentility of Russian 'culture' in this limited sense of the word is one of the most depressing aspects of Soviet life."[18]

Yet it should not be a surprising aspect, nor does it warrant this observer's conjecture that the government is manipulating the symbols and allure of culture in order to distract the people from political concerns. Here rather is *a stage* of civilization whose characteristics can be paralleled wherever a society or an individual has begun to emerge from the primitive preoccupation with acquisition. The most conspicuous forms of civilization attract first, and these are tried on by the ascending barbarian like masks in a play before he has any idea of what they signify. Only in playing the part does he begin to feel and understand it.

The Soviet man tries on not only new manners but new moral attitudes. "A point of interest about the upper stratum of Soviet society," writes a British observer, "is its curious similarity, in tastes and moral outlook, to the Victorian bourgeoisie of the nineteenth-century Britain and Western Europe. There is the same dreary puritanism professed (if not actually practiced) in private life, the

[16] Hans Zerer, *Die Welt* (Hamburg) 1958.
[17] Cf. Harry Schwartz, *The New York Times Magazine*, 7 September 1958.
[18] Hans Rogger, *The Reporter*, 17 October 1957.

same moralizing literature and 'nice, catchy tunes.' The difference is that whereas self-made businessmen had no power in nineteenth-century England to dictate what should or should not be written, painted or composed, a monolithic committee of Soviet politicians has precisely such power."[19]

A difference no less significant is that the Victorian bourgeoisie climbed in an already mature civilized society, which preserved cultural traditions from the past and held out both cultural goals and models. It is less the power to dictate that has produced a uniform mediocrity in Soviet culture than it is the power literally to do away with the few who had the background for distinction.

The few, of course, in time renew themselves, rising from the mass with an astonishing strength and vitality, considering their numbers and their seeming remoteness from practical concerns. But the new Soviet intelligentsia still bear strongly the marks of their birth. They appear to one American to be preoccupied with form rather than content, and to be motivated chiefly by a sense of competing with the *technical* civilization of the West. They are interested in the application rather than in the discovery of principles, in skills rather than ideas. They adapt themselves to the new conditions, but everywhere betray the prejudices and predilections of their upbringing.

The younger generation is characteristically a generation of technicians. They regard with disdain their immediate predecessors, the middle generation, who were recruited directly from the peasantry in the Stalinist era and who represent not so much a bridge from the historical past as a break. The middle generation, now in their fifties and sixties, were literally and self-consciously the destroyers. Although they expressed their mission as the creation of a new culture, they could in fact neither create nor pass on, for they "entered Russian intellectual life as outsiders with no backing of intellectual traditions or experience to guide them. The official ideology and cosmogony provided literally their only intellectual frame of reference; the role defined for them by the Party provided their only

[19] Seton-Watson (247).

100

conception of proper activity in the development of Russian culture."[20]

The current "cultural" awakening in the Soviet Union, for all its stultifying absorption in material things and techniques, can be regarded as a cutting loose from the still more stultifying Stalinist period, when there was nothing at all but the Party word. More fundamentally, it represents a new beginning—really the first reaching of the newly citified peasants for the cultural heritage which they all but destroyed and now must reconstruct from the bits around them. Extensive restoration at least of historical monuments has been carried out in the postwar period. Yet, an assessment of the hierarchy of the Soviet cultured still sets "bullying and half-cynical, semi-Marxist philistines at the top; a thin line of genuinely civilized, perceptive, morally alive and often gifted but deeply intimidated and politically passive 'specialists' in the middle; honest, impressionable, touchingly naïve, pure-hearted, intellectually starved, non-Marxist semi-literates, consumed with unquenchable curiosity below."[21] Below them further the people also stirs, not from intellectual hunger but from that curious indiscriminate upwardness of people who seem created to want and endowed with the power endlessly to discover new necessities.

Women in shawls and boots attend daily fashion shows in Moscow, where stocky models—the rural feminine ideal—promote the current good taste, drab styles lacking color or distinction. In 1957, however, decolletage returned to Moscow for the first time since the peasant revolution. Edward Crankshaw, revisiting the Soviet Union in 1959, remarked a new brightness everywhere and was startled by the suddenness with which it had appeared. "A few years ago," he writes, "the shelves of the suburban shops were bare. Today, these outlying shops are often more reliably stocked than the central ones and a good deal easier to get about in. Again, a new race of shop girls has sprung (there is no other word) into being: charming, kind, neatly dressed, helpful . . ." In the upsurge of civilization, the state has come to manufacture fourteen shades of lipstick. Correspondents find a flirtatiousness in public places that

[20] Haimson (98).
[21] L. (152), pp. 126-129. As to the intellectual awakening of the young, however, there are some solidly based skeptical views; see below, Chapter 9.

101

in grimmer, primmer days would have been an offense against socialist seriousness, punishable by time in a labor camp.[22]

The Soviet road back toward civilization has been long and painful for those who traveled it. The goal is still distant, yet already three distinct turnings can be described, corresponding to the three political upheavals—Leninist, Stalinist, and post-Stalinist.

In the cultural desert made by the civil war and by the consolidation of the Communist power, the ruins were not merely physical or social. Most unbearably, they were psychological. The final effect of the Soviet Revolution was a massive displacement of people out of their familiar relationships with each other, with their traditions, and with their futures. No one knew any longer where he stood, or what was expected of him, or how he should regard himself. The sensitive and thoughtful at least were possessed with a sense of unreality, whether they were among the invaders or the defenders.

Early Soviet literature is pervaded with the feeling that all men were impostors, living a lie or acting a part in a fantastic play. In a novel published in 1922—when writers were not yet entirely under the government thumb—a foreign visitor is made to sum up his impressions of Moscow thus: "Pretense is everywhere, in work, in public life, in family relations. Everybody is lying to everybody—the communists, the bourgeois, the workers, even the enemies of the revolution—the whole Russian nation is lying."[23] They lied because they had decided that they must. The visitor wonders whether they closed their eyes because reality would upset their plans or simply because reality was too frightful to be faced. A character in another novel comes to the conclusion that "The insane asylum is the only place where a normal man can live. Everything else is super-bedlam. I prefer to live with genuine madmen. At least they are not building socialism . . ."[24]

"Russia has always been a land of impostors," another writer observes. One of his characters discovers that a Soviet official has

[22] Cf. Cyril Bay, "Return to Moscow," *Spectator*, 3 April 1959.
[23] Pilniak (218).
[24] Ilf and Petrov (113).

faked his past in order to keep his job. But, of course, does not everyone do it? "Listen, Alexei Ivanovich," says the official, "no one is genuine nowadays. Not I alone, all Russia is a fake. The professor is not a professor, the writer is not really a writer but just happened to write a story while waiting for a better position. Our bookkeeper . . . no, the cashier, he used to be a priest who was going to be shot, but after having typhoid fever he cut his hair, put on civilian pants, and went in for handling money. Or take the caretaker at this office. Do you think she is a caretaker? She is a landowner in Barnaul. And the actor Varnatski? He is not an actor, he is a midshipman, that's what he is. Look around yourself—everybody is acting a part. They're not real; they are counterfeiters . . . And how about THEM? Tell me, what kind of proletarians are they?"[25] In the year before his forcible exile Nikolai Berdiaev, the philosopher, wrote: "Masks and doubles everywhere, fragments and grimaces of men . . . Life belied by the revolution. Everything is unreal. Phantasmic the political parties, phantasmic the authorities, phantasmic all the heroes of the revolution. Nowhere is the sense of reality found, nowhere is the image of man clearly seen . . ."[26]

The point was certainly not that the Russians as a people were more disposed to masquerades than any other people. Calculation —a desire to get ahead or to escape notice—could account for individual subterfuge. But the spirit of play infecting the society generally was something else. A historian of the Soviet theater, Nikolai Gorchakov, describes an extraordinary mass craze for putting on shows of all kinds, an infatuation with amateur dramatics that swept even the remote villages in the first years of the Soviet regime. He calls the phenomenon "unique in human history," but does not try to account for it.[27] Pasternak tells of the succession of revolutionary offices to which Dr. Zhivago, nurse Antipova, and Lieutenant Galiullin were elected; they regarded these "as an outdoor sport, a diversion, a game of blindman's buff"; and they tired of playing and wished to "get back to their ordinary occupations and their homes."[28] Reality, Zhivago muses, had been terrorized into hiding. Make-believe took over.

[25] Chetverikov (44).
[26] Berdiaev (18).
[27] Gorchakov (90).
[28] Pasternak (215).

The impulse to play, Johan Huizinga believes,[29] is one of the fundamental life drives of animals as well as of people. Characteristics of play are that it is voluntary, that it is circumscribed by rules voluntarily accepted but rigidly adhered to, that it has clear boundaries in space and time, and that it is pursued only for its own sake, without ulterior purpose. It contrasts, as Dr. Zhivago observed, with "ordinary life," which one does not choose but accepts, which is not governed by predictable rules but by fortune or by God, without prior notice of what to expect, which has none but the externally imposed limits of physical existence, and which seems constantly to justify itself in terms of something else, ranging from a laugh to the kingdom of heaven.

Play and ordinary life normally exist together in intimate association. The play element—that is to say, the spontaneous creation of games—enters into all human pursuits and leavens them. It is in play, Huizinga argues, that civilization begins and as play that it develops. In archaic societies, in particular, "the play-element is seen everywhere: order, tension, movement, transfer, formality, rhythm, enthusiasm"—precisely the characteristics of children's games or, for that matter, of the play of animals. But play is not something men or societies outgrow—not, at least, until they cease growing altogether. The forms and the rules change, but "at any moment, and even in higher civilizations, the play instinct may awaken in all its vigor, sweeping the individual and the masses in the whirlwind of a grandiose game."

The Soviet Revolution in effect suddenly and violently changed the character and the rules of a game. It was the giant spoilsport. At the same time it all but destroyed ordinary life. One could no longer distinguish between real and unreal. The play instinct not surprisingly resurged to transform all life into a game. Perhaps in this there was a subconscious effort to impose a fictitious order on the chaos. Perhaps, too, the sense of unreality of which the masquerade was born was itself exploited deliberately to make disorder and uncertainty more bearable.

Worse than the game started by Lenin, in any event, was its ending under Stalin. In *Dr. Zhivago*, an enslaved intellectual, Dudorov, describes his arrest and imprisonment. With others he was brought into a forest where there was only a post with a sign,

[29] Huizinga (108); cf. Ortega y Gasset (208).

Camp 92. "They told us, 'Here is your camp. Settle down as best you can!' We cut down saplings with our bare hands in the frost to built huts. And would you believe it, we gradually built our own camp. We cut down the wood to build our own dungeons, we surrounded ourselves with a stockade, we equipped ourselves with prison-cells and watchtowers—we did it all by ourselves . . ."[30] It sounds like a backyard game of Indians, complete with war paint, captives, and torture stake. But Stalin's game had no limits in time and space. Called "Socialism in One Country," it was to be played with millions of lives for as long as the tyrants chose and according to such rules as pleased them. The game engrossed and destroyed life, and the sense of unreality persisted. It even intensi- fied as the gulf between official fictions and observed facts grew steadily more grotesque.

The play, proceeding only at the top, proved sterile. Rules were dictated, not voluntarily adopted. Instead of developing a new life, they stifled it. The most obvious evidence is in the most obvious expressions—the total failure of Soviet art and literature to rise above a dull, imitative mediocrity. But repression hardly less signif- icantly stultified also the development of law and political institu- tions out of the archaic forms carried forward, under new names, by the medieval peasant tradition into the twentieth century. The repressor was not Marxism—not the dogma that art is propaganda or the communist concept of the subordination of the individual to the mass. It was the lid of barbarism that was clamped tightly over the free play-elements, which might otherwise have bubbled up from the masses and, in escaping from the humdrum, have permitted civilization to resume its growth.

World War II lifted the lid temporarily and loosed an almost universal sigh of relief. "When the war broke out," Pasternak writes, "its real horrors, its real dangers and threat of real death were bliss compared with the inhuman reign of fiction. They brought relief because they broke the spell of the dead letter."[31] A Soviet defector tells an ostensibly true story of how a truck loaded with furniture belonging to party bigwigs, and guarded by an NKVD man, was halted near the front by an army lieutenant who wished to commandeer transportation for the wounded. When the guard

[30] Pasternak (215).
[31] Ibid.

protested, the lieutenant shot him dead. One soldier standing by remarked, "Times have changed! He forgot where he was." And another replied, "We'll see better times yet."[32]

The vision of better days was general and made each man dream of the end of what he most disliked in the socialist masquerade. So peasants, encouraged by wartime tolerance of individual garden plots, thought the collective farms would surely be abolished. Intellectuals anticipated a new freedom. Indeed, immediately after the war writers did enjoy some independence and seemed to be developing a more civilized view of the value of human life. Perhaps the fresh appreciation of reality brought by the war could not be crushed all at once, or perhaps the regime was so impressed with the unity of the nation in defense of the homeland that it felt it could relax without relinquishing any real power. In any event, the new day was brutally cut short by literary purges between 1946 and 1948. Alexei Zhdanov, member of the Politbureau, was set up as czar over the realms of mind. And in this way notice was served that the old absolutism was to be restored.

Nevertheless, there had been a change—or rather a complex of changes—which political reaction could not wipe out. Not only had the war opened some cultural doors that could not be slammed shut, but the generations were shifting, as in time and despite tyranny they inexorably do. Since Stalin's death his successors have vacillated, unable to crack the whips that Stalin left, unwilling to push forward into a new freedom. The period of leniency in which Vladimir Dudintsev's mildly critical novel,[33] along with some more daring poems and short stories, were published, and Pasternak was able to deliver *Dr. Zhivago* to the world outside, ended quickly in a new campaign for uniform compliance. Yet this time the reversal was made without major purges or any of the disciplinary actions that were routinely administered to deviants in Stalin's day. Pasternak transparently repudiated his apologies in the act of making them. That he remained in the Soviet Union unrepentant and undisturbed did not, of course, open up immediate freedom to other artists, but it does suggest that the regime was no longer

[32] Voinov (301), p. 244.
[33] *Not By Bread Alone* (Moscow, 1956).

106

able or willing to crush the dissidents; it was content at best to mute them. The subsequent persecution and imprisonment of Pasternak's close friend—and her daughter—suggests that the regime may be preparing Pasternak's apotheosis by shifting to others the blame for his rebelliousness. It would not be surprising to see such barbaric methods employed in the interests of a cultural conquest. So the savage may murder, and adorn himself with his enemy's necklace.

In the fall of 1958, at the height of the Pasternak controversy, a new novel by Vsevolod Kochetov, *The Yershov Brothers*, highly praised by the party critics, raised the banner of reaction, satirizing the literary liberals and appealing to writers to resist the influences of the West. But within a few months the banner had quietly been lowered. In a dramatic version of the novel, which had been clearly repudiated by the public, the satire was altogether removed. Meanwhile, the author was dropped from the editorship of the Writers' Union paper, *Literaturnaia Gazeta*.

Alexei Adzhubei, son-in-law of Khrushchev and the editor who made the Communist Youth paper *Komsomolskaia Pravda* somewhat more readable than the others, had taken over *Izvestia*, the central organ of the Soviet government, promising to breathe into that, too, a spark of life. It was Adzhubei who told the 1959 Congress of Writers that they ought not to construct novels by formula, that one cannot create life as one does buildings, according to mathematical laws.[34] His was by no means an invitation to escape official control but a plea to exercise more imagination in meeting the wishes of the government without alienating the public.

A good deal of uncertainty remains while the leadership tries to seize the best of two worlds. In the fall of 1957, Chairman Khrushchev appealed for public support for himself and the party as arbiters of culture, and warned against flirtations with alien ideas of "artistic freedom." *Izvestia* at that time appealed for voluntary conformity. "Certainly," the paper wrote, "everyone has a right to write how he wants about what he wants. But does everything that is written have to be printed? A magazine is not a mailbox." The freedom to write is thus conceded tongue in cheek, only to be taken away in practice. Nevertheless, the concession remains significant: The party will control publication, but it does not even

[34] *The New York Times*, 18 May 1959.

believe itself that Soviet writers are spontaneously dedicated to the party line. However rudimentary and ineffectual that recognition of individual rights, it is a long way from the insistence that all members of the Soviet family think the same.

Party culture as conceived and propagated by the new leadership is not in any meaningful sense socialist, propagandist, or even political. It is old-fashioned, uncomplicated, soothing, pragmatic; in a word, naïve. It protests the complexities and distortions introduced by the mature, civilized awareness of men. It still expresses the rustic revulsion to city slickness, the older generation's nostalgic memory of rural landscapes. "Our people want works of literature, painting and music that they can understand," is the way Chairman Khrushchev puts it. The standard is the untutored taste of men who have only begun to consider art. Commenting on the Bolshoi Ballet, an American critic writes: ". . . And what strange, powerful, battering-ram techniques they are, especially in the character dances on the first half of the program! . . . The men hurl themselves into action like athletes. The girls dance with what used to be called 'abandon,' double strength. All are fearless, almost reckless, in their attacks. They leap as if they were launching into outer space—and this before the sputnik era. . . . What is most missing is lightness, ethereality, poetry."

Khrushchev, himself in his late sixties, belongs to the generation of Soviet citizens who emerged from peasant boyhood into the new world of the Communist Party, and there spent their entire working life. They have no reason to question its values and no standards by which to do so. Quite apart from rational conviction of policy, they must resist criticism that doubts the all-sufficiency of the party world, because such criticism would call into question their own dedication. But this is at bottom the almost instinctive and self-serving conservatism of self-made men, particularly those—surely the majority—who never quite outlive the sense of inferiority with which they began.[35]

Although that conservatism may be at the moment effective in

[35] Senator Hubert H. Humphrey, a self-made man himself, remarked after a long interview with Khrushchev: "[He] reminded me of somebody who has risen from poverty and weakness to wealth and power but is never wholly confident of himself and his new status"; *Life,* 12 January 1959.

continuing to stifle the development of Soviet civilization, it has the look now of a rear guard defense, touched rather with nostalgia than evangelism. The new, charming shop girls in Moscow along with small but significant literary unrest, the zoot-suiters (*styliagi*) in Mocow along with the suaver diplomatic manners abroad, the willingness to send ballet troupes abroad and receive western musical shows in return, Khrushchev's extensive travels to the world capitals, the new interest in good clothes and good taste, the more frequent and more casual contacts of the Soviet man with civilized foreigners, the troubles getting the younger generation to admire hard work as their fathers did—all these are signs of the irreversible onset of social maturity.

Where the growing-up may lead is not a simple question. Still ruled by ex-peasants, Soviet society is no longer composed predominantly of peasants.[36] Culturally, it has stepped, uncertainly as yet, into a transition period—moving from the game of the revolutionary fathers into the "ordinary life" of the sons. That succession is the gift of time, but genuine progress remains difficult. As Auguste Comte remarked a century ago: "It becomes every day more evident how hopeless is the task of reconstructing . . . institutions without a previous remodeling of opinion and life."[37]

Technical skills acquired and exhibited in the Soviet state are impressive, particularly to a world that has come to have an exaggerated regard for technology. But selective technical achievements, however spectacular, are no true measure of the nation's cultural development. For one thing, these owe much to scientists and technicians brought up in pre-Soviet Russian (like Andrei Tupolev) or in foreign schools (like Peter Kapitsa).[38] To say this is not, of course, to imply that the Soviet human material is in any sense inferior to any other. It is only to indicate the still narrow and shallow cultural base on which the Soviets build. And they build still under serious ideological and psychological restraints.

[36] For the party brass, see the "Biographical Dictionary" in *Ezhegodnik* (71), pp. 625-646. According to the last Soviet general census (January 1959), the urban population had grown from 18 per cent in 1913 to 48 per cent in 1959; cf. 1960 *Ezhegodnik* (71), p. 6. Only three years before it was estimated at 43.4 per cent; cf. *Narodnoe Khoziaistvo* (199), p. 19.

[37] Auguste Comte, *System of Positive Policy* (London, 1875-79), Vol. I, p. 2.

[38] Cf. the firsthand survey of the Soviet world of science and technology by Turkevich (288, 289).

8

CREEDS AND CREDENTIALS

IN THE USHAKOV RUSSIAN DICTIONARY, PUBLISHED BY THE SOVIETS IN 1935, the word "communist" had two definitions: "1. A member of the Communist party; 2. An advocate or supporter of communism." The second meaning was already tagged "obsolete," and in later dictionaries it has been omitted.[1] A Communist in the Soviet Union is a member of an organization, not a believer.[2]

Yet the organization does profess a creed, which at the very least occupies an important place in Party ritual. Communist leaders tirelessly insist that their creed is in fact a complete philosophy, the conceptual instrument by which all life and history are ordered. They pretend that they are not only guided by it but compelled to act in various ways because they must remain faithful to the dictates of Marxism-Leninism.

Now, quite apart from whether they mean what they say, it is apparent that they could not say otherwise. Their own title depends on their seeming orthodoxy. Collectively, their right to rule rests on the Marxist interpretation of history, which makes them not revolutionary upstarts but agents of historical inevitability. Individually, the mark of each new boss's legitimacy is his possession of the right keys to the inherited dogma. He is superior to his rivals for office in that he is believed to be more perfectly the disciple and the performer. As the head of the organization, it is his understanding of the texts which is correct and, therefore, his leadership which is on course.

To agree, however, that the alleged ideology of Soviet leaders

[1] Ushakov (292), Vol. I, p. 1425; *Slovar* (258), Vol. V, p. 1247; later dictionaries, Lekhin and Petrov (162), p. 341; *Slovar* (259), Vol. II, p. 108.

[2] Something like defining "Christian" as a member of one particular church and excluding all others who may believe in Christ.

is really effective one needs evidence that they act as they do because of what they profess. Assuming that their ideas are, indeed, relevant to their conduct, one must still ask whether the ideas are in any sense a mold or are merely a dress tailored to a body that takes shape from quite different facts of ancestry, meat and drink, and exercise. Would the bosses of the Soviet Union act differently if their justification were, for instance, nationalist, or fascist, or religious, instead of Marxist?

The question is historical, geographical, and relative. Marxist theory could not mean the same thing to Lenin and to Khrushchev. It had not the same significance for Stalin in 1918 and in 1940. Clearly it has vastly different meanings for the Chinese, the Czechs, the Poles, the East Germans, and the Yugoslavs. The differences, indeed, are officially recognized as making separate "roads to Socialism." There is no Red monolith except in the affrighted imagination of some outsiders. Travelers constantly testify to the divergencies among Communists. So does history.

In the early days of the Soviet Revolution one met both idealists and practical men, among whom the Marxist philosophy had a strong hold. Some were intellectuals, moving, at least in part, from idea to deed. Others were adventurers, who were nevertheless convinced that the doctrine offered important sustenance, even if it were not the touchstone to revolutionary success. For still others, the Marxist book of knowledge was their window on the larger world into which they stepped and the still larger one to which they aspired. Near the beginning it was possible to believe the largely untested body of dogma and act as though one had only to bring into being a destiny already written. Contradictions between theory and fact, when observed, could still be thought minor or temporary. Yet even so near the beginning there were few leaders, if any, who did not put first the practical demands of power, using Marxism in two ways: to justify what they did and to provide them with ways of thinking about new situations.

Regardless of whether they believed what they said, time could not fail to alter their perspective. As they acted, they had to cover their actions with appropriate citations of the text. Theory in this way was not so much tested by practice as stretched by it. If the

111

book were not to be thrown away, it had to be more and more loosely interpreted. While doctrine was plied and thinned to make woof for all the interweaving facts of experience, experience also grew at the expense of the unknown—the one realm where Marxism could remain perfectly applicable and, for the intellectually timid, indispensable. As the Communists learned more completely and precisely what they were after and how to get it, they had ever less need for a guide. In fact, they came to know a good deal more about their own world than did Marx or even Lenin.

Forty years ago, ambitious rustics in Russia burst onto the great stage of twentieth-century civilization, as strange to them as it was obviously fascinating. "Marxism-Leninism" was their only map of the new reality remote from the experience of the village and the city slum. They had, in effect, a choice between Marxist knowledge and ignorance. Of course, they accepted the keys even before they knew what doors were to be opened. They were also pragmatists, commanded to act, not to think. Theirs was not to question theory, but to make it work.

So at about the same time and under the same historical compulsion, Marxism as theory was removed from creative doubts and debate, while the practical men set about altering it to fit their needs. As under varying but generally acute pressures they solved problems, Marxism-Lininism became increasingly more useful as a rationalization of what they did, steadily less convincing as a reason for doing it.

Nikita Khrushchev, forty years after the apocalyptic vision of November, was under no delusion as to which came first. In an extemporaneous speech in 1957 in Czechoslovakia—one of the few to reach the West in unedited form[3]—he put theory in its place in language of his own that reveals much of the man. "You know," he said to workers at a Pilsen factory, "we have certain kinds of people who think they're theoretical Marxists, bookworms you know, and they say how can such a simplification be allowed which mixes up the solution of theoretical questions and such commonplace questions as, for instance, the production of meat, butter and milk. Comrades, I say to these scholars that if they really consider

[3] Monitored by Radio Liberation, Munich, the transcript was published in *Novoe Russkoe Slovo* (9 August 1957), whose editors vouch for its authenticity. The translation, which tries so far as possible to convey the slanginess and awkwardness of the original, is by John M. Francis.

themselves Marxists they mustn't just read Marx but they also got to get to understand him . . . Comrades, would it be a bad thing for the working class of the Soviet Union and for all its peoples in general and for the countries in the socialist camp, if to the good Marxist-Leninist theory we stuck on a good little hunk of meat, and a good slab of butter and plenty of milk? Why, then even the most obstinate blockhead would have trouble resisting Marxist-Leninist teachings. Because the ideas of Marxism-Leninism when they are well lubricated, you know, will bore into his brains. On an empty stomach, you have to be too . . . you have to make an effort to understand ideologically the revolutionary meaning of Marxist-Leninist teaching, but . . . and that's exactly what I want to say, with some nice butter on your bread, and a cozy little flat, with a good life, just what a person needs, then it is easier to understand this here Marxism-Leninism, too, and, of course, for that kind of life, why, everybody will say, 'I, too, am for socialism and I, too, am for communism.' . . ."

Later that same month he, or his writers, framed substantially the same thought in formal language. Marxism-Leninism, he said (as quoted in *Pravda*), "is not a dogma but a guide to practical revolutionary action. At every stage of historical development life poses its tasks, which stem from the requirements of society. A creative approach to theory, the ability to develop and advance the science of Marxism-Leninism, *consists in correctly understanding the new urgent tasks of social development on the basis of scientific generalization of the experience of life, and in outlining ways for practical accomplishment of these tasks.*"[4]

Few men, of course, yield allegiance to an idea so steadfastly that they don't feel free to defend their interests in spite of it. But Khrushchev says something more than that practical considerations come first. He talks of both following and remaking doctrine in action. His object is not only to be free but to seem compelled. He must find the expedient solutions to all practical problems while seeming to act as the agent of an idea.

So the distinction has been drawn between "practical" and "theoretical" Marxism. Practical Marxism consists quite simply in doing whatever one must do to succeed. The solution then becomes dogma if it works and for so long as it works. A live Soviet leader

[4] *Pravda,* 20 August 1957. Emphasis added.

113

need never make an exception to the rules: He changes the rules to include the exception, avoiding the imputation of opportunism by making expediency (i.e. practicality) the greatest of principles. Any solution can be stated in the language of Marxism and thus called Marxist because the language, long ago emptied of rational meaning, has become, like any official piety, perfectly adaptable. Marxist-Leninist ideology encompasses thought and action as restlessly amorphous as the perimeter of an amoeba, but as all-embracing.

No doubt the rationale is often mere verbal hocus-pocus and no doubt the leaders at least dimly know it. But it is hocus-pocus with serious consequences. They have in forty years explored in rich and probably almost complete detail the discrepancies between Marxist theory and the facts of Soviet experience. As practical men, they have respected the facts and acted accordingly, discovering in the process that no contradiction between Marx and reality is too large to be repaired verbally. Their experience now is so great within their own country, and the adjustments they have made are so numerous and profound, that it would be absurd any longer to suppose that the theories of Marx and Lenin guide the course of the Soviet experiment.

Theory, however, has been manipulated only to fit the needs of action. The ideas are not rethought. Theoretical "revisionism" is severely condemned. There is no wish logically to correct the Marxist world view to accord with observed reality. On the contrary, Soviet leaders insist on maintaining the fiction, "guarding the purity of the Marxist-Leninist theory like the apple of our eye."[5] If there may be something here of the primitive "religious fear of departing even by an iota from the traditional customs and beliefs of the group,"[6] there are also sufficient reasons of policy.

One big and obvious reason is that the universal precepts of Marxism—such as the inevitability of capitalist decay—serve to justify and even partly conceal Soviet imperialism. The common

[5] *Ibid.*, 5 April 1956; emphasis on strong party indoctrination was renewed in 1959 and in 1961.

[6] Noss (203), p. 11.

114

language, however empty of rational meaning, serves, too, as a sort of fraternal jargon to link various national Communist parties, at least in the common rejection of non-Communists, much as teenage slang joins the high school set in a comforting sense of solidarity against adult outsiders. The most important reason, however, for continuing to interpret the capitalist world by Marxist dogmas is that the Soviet leaders still have insufficient data to form any other view. Their personal experience abroad, though growing spectacularly as compared with the Stalinist era, is still too small and spotty to break the cast of prejudice, particularly when the prejudice is so much more obviously useful.

Finally, it is not in the nature of practical men to generalize. A peasant does not. He knows intimately the environment in which he must live and he knows in detail what works in that environment. Reality is for him whatever impinges directly on his senses. Beyond the range of sensory impression lies the world of hearsay with which he has little to do—the less the better. Having, for the most part, no business with it and not knowing it, he feels neither capacity nor compulsion to think about it. What goes on beyond his ken is to be accepted on faith, and in matters of faith he is prepared to be coached by his father, his priest, his traditions, or his fears, but not by reason.

Khrushchev is strikingly the practical man of rural upbringing. "To read Khrushchev's speeches to the builders, the brickmakers, the peasants, the textile workers and all the rest," writes one of the wisest foreign observers, "is an education. No doubt he talks to the atomic scientists in the same way. These speeches are not concerned with building communism. They are concerned, and with minute attention to the most trivial detail, with how to make things work— for the ultimate glory of Russia."[7] Senator Humphrey, in a long interview with Khrushchev, in 1958, was impressed by his "headful of facts on the most diverse matters of concern to one whose nation is his household."[8] No one, on the other hand, ever suggested that Khrushchev, any more than Stalin, had any interest in, or any talent for, abstract speculation. In all practical dealings both have been

[7] Edward Crankshaw, *Life,* 2 December 1958; cf. speech at Pilsen, quoted above.
[8] *Life,* 12 January 1959.

flexible and undogmatic. By the same token, their general notions—on which they are not called to act—remain unexamined, as rigid and impervious to debate as incantations.

Khrushchev told Eleanor Roosevelt: "Communism will win the whole world. Your people in the United States are cultured people, so you know that all kinds of change take place in economics and how the relations between nations change—feudalism, capitalism, then socialism. And the highest state will be communism. It is well known—this is the meaning of history."[9] Yet it is not, demonstrably, the meaning of anything that Khrushchev himself does. What he states as philosophic conviction is actually faith and nearly as remote from action as the creed of the ordinary nonpracticing Christian. It does not even provide an effective goal. As Crankshaw observed, the Soviet leader is willing to try almost anything but "there is very little to suggest that he knows exactly where he is going."[10]

Inside the Soviet Union the constant concern of the leadership with the purity of doctrine appears to be not an ideological exercise but a quasi-religious one. The fact that Nikita Khrushchev, with or without the assistance of the Central Committee, must have an orthodox opinion before making a state decision no more makes communism an ideology than saying a prayer before setting out to sea makes seafaring a holy crusade. The ritual in each case has a more or less fortuitous relation to the action it is supposed to serve, though it may bear a deep relation to the psychological needs of communists and seamen respectively.

That communism has many of the marks of a religion has been often observed.[11] Jules Monnerot calls it a "secular religion of the Islamic type." Arnold Toynbee sees communism and nationalism as newer religions which are basically "man's self-centered worship of himself." Bertrand Russell has written that he thinks "all the great religions of the world—Buddhism, Hinduism, Christianity, Islam and Communism—both untrue and harmful." Henri Barbusse believed that "in the Communist Party you will find the modern

[9] As reported in her weekly column, 6 October 1957.
[10] *Observer* (London), 12 April 1958.
[11] See Bibliographical Notes.

116

counterpart of the faith of the medieval mystics, the self-sacrifice of the Christian martyrs, the fierce spirit of the Jacobins of the French Revolution." A good many Protestant theologians have been impressed (and confused) by parallels they thought they found between communist and Christian purposes. At one time Reinhold Niebuhr regarded the "proletarian state of mind as both tragic and helpful." Paul Tillich found resemblances between Marxist and Christian analyses of the opportunity presented by the crisis of capitalism. Karl Barth, who denounced Nazism as demoniac, the politics of Antichrist, takes a much more conciliatory view of communism.[12] The most systematic parallelism has been drawn by Paul Hutchinson, who says: "Communism reproduces the characteristic marks of organized religion more faithfully than do many of the churches. It has its sacred scriptures, its inspired revelators, its dogma, its heresy trials, its demonology, its missionaries, its proselyting passion, its initiatory vows, it sacred shrines, its apocalyptic future to compensate for a grim present. . . . And in the spirit which inspired Communism there is limitless devotion and often concern for human salvation that can hardly be understood except as the oblation of a religious zealot."[13]

In ways easily demonstrable these observations are true, but none of the parallels on closer look are exactly parallel. For instance, there seem to be unusual limitations to a "proselyting passion" which, in fact, does not seek converts within communist countries, but rather holds exclusive party rolls closed to the uninitiated multitude. Communism's "inspired revelators" also are abnormally subject to change on such short and violent notice that the faithful by this time must have learned to heed no prophet but the living Caesar himself. No First Secretary, the high priest of communism, confesses an invisible power, whether deity or idea or primal force, to which he must answer. Such power as he recognizes he also controls. Even the Party great speak only through him and in such fashion and to such purpose as he chooses. As to the "spirit of communism" which allegedly inspires it with concern for

[12] The theologians' views are summed up in West (306); for the "Christian progressives" in France, see Aron (8). *Terre Nouvelle*, a magazine for "revolutionary Christians" published in France before World War II, expressed its dual faith by printing on the cover a cross with hammer and sickle superimposed.

[13] *Life*, 10 March 1947.

human salvation, where among practicing Communists is it to be found? In Siberian labor camps? In Chinese communes? So to the other at first impressive resemblances between communism and religious systems important reservations need to be entered. When added together they call into question the notion as a whole—that communism may usefully be regarded as religion and illuminated by the application of religious concepts.

In any event, the point of view leads to abstract analysis as likely to carry one far from the Soviet scene as the attempt to find Kremlin actions blueprinted in the pages of Karl Marx. More interesting and far more meaningful are the needs that Communist ritual proposes to serve—needs which unquestionably belong partly to spiritual yearnings normally answered by religion. The question then becomes not whether communism is a religion or even resembles a religion in itself, but to what extent it has been able to function as one in the Soviet Union.

Christianity in ancient Russia was grafted onto a set of loosely organized animistic beliefs. The heads of the households, accepting conversion to the new faith, had still to make their peace with the old gods and evil spirits among whom they and their families continued to live. Old gods might be demoted, but they did not disappear. A Christian's duty was to struggle against them, and Christian ritual provided some powerful magic to help. But it was safer, after all, not to assume a victory that might not have been won.

"After prayer in the Christian church, the Slav went into a sacred wood, or to a river, lake or stream, or under an old oak or birch tree, or to a sacred stone, or simply behind his barn, and performed the simple ancient rite as his forefathers taught him. . . . He sang the old hymns praising the beautiful sun, the bright young moon, and the sparkling stars. Little pagan gods still stayed near the ikons in his home. His family prepared food for domestic deities. . . . At times people would gather at the tombs of their fathers to perform traditional rites in common, and festivals among the villages were organized."[14]

Of course, this is the typical reaction of primitive minds which, having peopled the world with hobgoblins from the need somehow

[14] Khlebnikov (128).

118

to explain and control nature, cannot banish the spirits until the need is otherwise filled. Among the peasantry the primitive religious needs long endured. Christian prayers were easily transformed into magic incantations, the more powerful in protecting the believer the less the Church Slavonic words were understood. Chekhov tells the story of peasant women who wept with ecstasy every time the priest at mass uttered the old Slavonic words, *ashche* and *dondezhe,* meaning "if" and "until."[15] Priests of all lands and times have known the efficacy of a ritual language mysterious and impressive to the ignorant. Polish and Hungarian peasants listen piously to Latin, convinced that only the initiate are given the grace to understand the divine tongue.

Christian sacraments were also generally regarded as devices by which a prudent man kept in with gods, safeguarding his fortunes on earth and his chances in the hereafter. Priests, who had the exclusive knowledge to handle these mysteries, appeared to the peasants as species of "tradesmen who have wholesale and retail dealing in sacraments."[16] In many villages, a witch or wizard often worked the other side of the street among the pagan spirits, wooing the favor of the good, scaring off the bad. These religious technicians were seldom looked upon as holy men and, indeed, seldom deserved to be. Village priests quite commonly abused their power by extracting tribute from the superstitious of their flock. As for the peasant, he paid, but retaliated with a contempt that is eloquent in his folklore. He was apt to hold the local wizard in higher esteem because the wizard was a peasant like himself, and worked more familiarly among the more familiar demons of ordinary life.

That curious mixture of awe and contempt was, indeed, characteristic of the religious attitudes of the Russian village. The saints, to whom the ordinary peasant prayed not only for his immortal soul but for his harvest, themselves led rather disreputable lives in heaven where, according to the folklore, they quarreled among themselves, boasted of their prowess, cheated each other, played tricks, and even lied. They behaved, in short, like the heroes of pagan mythology and legend. By thus "humanizing" his divinities the peasant was able to live intimately among them as the Greeks

[15] Chekhov (42).
[16] Stepniak (265).

119

had lived among their gods. The result was that if his worship was theologically shapeless and his piety ambiguous, his religion as a whole was entwined inseparably with his culture. "The nation," concluded a French ambassador to Russia before the Revolution, "is more religious than its Church."[17]

But others, on the same evidence, have come to the opposite conclusion. Belinsky, writing to Nikolai Gogol in 1847, said: "Look a little more intently and you will see that [the Russian] is a profoundly atheistic folk. There is still a great deal of superstition in it but there isn't even a trace of religiousness. . . . The majority of our clergy has always been distinguished solely for potbellies, scholastic pedantry, and savage ignorance. . . . About whom is it the Russian folk tell a filthy story? About the priest, the priest's wife, the priest's daughter. . . . According to you the Russian folk is the most religious in the world. This is a lie. The basis of religiousness is piety, reverence, fear of God. But the Russian utters the name of God even as he scratches himself. . . . He says of a holy image: If it works, pray before it; if it doesn't work, use it for a pot cover."[18] This is all true but largely irrelevant. The standard of sophisticated piety applied to primitive rural societies has no meaning. Nor does the allegation of atheism, against a people who have never been moved to consider the existence of God theologically at all, but live at a cultural level below such perceptions and equally below such doubts.

In our day, Mikhail Boykov, former inmate of Soviet prisons, recalls how he was brought to a NKVD office for interrogation:[19] "The officer in charge was late and the 'bodymechanic' [*telomekhanik*, a Soviet euphemism for torturer] also waited, pacing back and forth in the waiting room. A big black cockroach slowly crawled across the room and each time the man approached it he carefully moved his foot not to crush the insect. 'Why don't you step on it?' I asked him impatiently. . . . Kravtsov stopped, looked at me heavily and said, barely moving his thin lips, 'Crush it? Why, a cockroach wants to live, doesn't he?' Scornfully I replied: 'And how about us? About me? Don't we also want to live? You pity a

[17] Paleologue (211).
[18] Belinsky (16), p. 244.
[19] Boykov (32), pp. 342-344.

cockroach, and for people you have nothing but torture and death. You, murderer!' He took no offense and answered softly: 'It is not my wish to torture you. I have a job, you know.'

" 'The devil with your job!' " I shouted in disgust.

"Kravtsov's face suddenly lost its cool impassiveness and terribly changed; his pale lips and hollow cheeks began to tremble, his eyes opened wide with terror. 'Don't talk about that,' he whispered.

" 'About what?'

" 'That word you used . . .'

"An absurd thought struck me and it was so funny that I laughed: 'Do you believe in devils?' I asked.

" 'Wouldn't you if you had my job?' he said. 'There wouldn't be such jobs if not for them. I know it.'

"I shrugged my shoulders, 'Maybe you believe in God, too?'

" 'No, I don't,' he answered. 'If there were God there wouldn't be any of this. I mean, no NKVD, no prosecution officers, no body-mechanics like me . . .' "

"I have often heard in prison," concludes Mikhail Boykov, "that many NKVD men were highly superstitious and, not believing in God, firmly believed in Satan, the devils, evil spirits, and the like. I had doubted it, but now Kravtsov himself corroborated what other inmates were telling me."

Professor Serge Elisséeff, internationally known orientalist and director of the Yenching Institute in Harvard University before his retirement in 1958, was brought up, as was the custom in well-to-do Russian families, by a peasant woman (*niania*), illiterate but, by her lights, devout. She knew the prayers and holy tales by heart and believed as unshakeably in God as in the good and evil spirits. He learned from her not only the rituals but surely something of the emotion that accompanied them. He writes: "Every time I was about to take an examination, I would hurry into the Cathedral and go to the right side of the altar where there hung a large ikon of the Saints Cyril and Methodius. I put a candle in front of the ikon and prayed to the two scholar saints to help me in my examination. When it was in mathematics or history I bought a fifty-kopeck candle; when it was in Greek or Latin, which I knew better, I considered a twenty-five kopeck candle would be sufficient. On the morning of the French and German examinations I simply kissed the ikon, anticipating no difficulty. This kind of ritual, which I abandoned when I was sixteen years old, gave me a feeling of assurance and tranquillity."[20]

One may endlessly debate the "religiousness" of such use of religious symbols, but hardly question the universal human need which it answers. The need is no less earnest because it may seem to sophisticated observers simple-minded. Professor Elisséeff's remark that he gave up his naïve ritual when he grew older is a reminder that religious observances are more likely to be shaped to the relative maturity of individuals and societies than to some indefinable and inexplicable differences in piety.

Differences in piety, indeed, are and must be individual, not national. So to point out the primitiveness of the religious forms in the peasant world is not to suggest that the religious emotions behind them were necessarily shallow. In old Russia, monasteries and shrines swarmed with pilgrims, simple men and women who were stirred to these expressions of piety by their religious sensibilities. Under the Soviets, millions of peasants continued their worship despite persecution, and thousands accepted martyrdom. In the face of such evidence one cannot doubt that, whatever the cultural meaning of the rituals performed, the peasant faith might be no less worthy of respect than any other.

In all religions, and among all peoples, the borderline between religious devotion and superstition is thin. But, however difficult in practice, the distinction in theory is simple enough: What for the worshipper makes his prayer effective? Is it the ritual act or the attitude of devotion? What is required for salvation, obedience or love? If the relation between man and God demands the exercise of love, the rite expressing it is symbolic but otherwise immaterial. But if the relation is between ruler and ruled, then the chief religious requirement is obedience, and the performance of prescribed ritual becomes the worshipper's essential act of submission and service. When obedience is enforced from without it does not matter what a man may think so long as he observes the rules, or at least is not caught breaking them.

Paradoxically, a ritual thus void of inner meaning, performed

[20] Elisséeff (69).

mechanically without any effort to understand, is more exigent than if it sprang from religious passion. If the substance of a prayer be not understood then it can exist only as form, and every part of the form must be considered equally important, since none may be rationally weighed. If all is pronounced by rote without thinking, then all must be trivial or all vital. To alter is to damage in ways and to degrees the transgressor has no means of judging. All he can be sure of is that he has broken a rule governing his relation with the Almighty, by which he had been assured a certain place in the scheme of things. That fact of disobedience exposes him to divine punishment and, worse, may remove him from divine protection. Hence the terrible passions on both sides of the great seventeenth-century Russian schism (*raskol*), when the orthodox and the dissenters disagreed over religious forms, but agreed perfectly on their absolute importance.

The old warrior Eroshka, in Leo Tolstoy's *The Cossacks,* used to repeat every time he mounted his horse a nonsensical rhyme that went like this:

> Hail ye living in Sion,
> This is your King,
> Our steeds we shall sit on,
> Sophonius is weeping,
> Zacharias is speaking,
> Father Pilgrim,
> Mankind is ever loving.

It was his own charm, he said, and of course it worked, for "no one ever killed me!" Between the nonsensical verse for good luck and the full panoply of ecclesiastical ritual there lies no doubt a very wide emotional gulf. But as devices to relate man to the universe they are of the same essential character. Both belong to the sorcery by which primitives try to persuade their gods to be kind. They are attempts to influence the attitudes of divinity, rather than the attitudes of the worshipper. Since they are believed to operate on the inscrutable powers outside, they do not have to be comprehensible to men. For the same reason, the only possible test of their value is their effectiveness.

Marxism-Leninism fits easily into the primitive pattern of superstition and ritual. That context makes irrelevant the objections most

123

commonly raised by sophisticated critics, that the doctrine is false philosophy, immoral and atheistic. For the shrewd peasant who found communism thrust upon him and who as usual preferred to make his peace, the question was not whether he could believe the dogmas but only whether they were useful—not whether they appealed to *him* but whether they might dispose the powers governing this world in his favor.

Like most missionaries with power, the Communists at first bid for too much and failed. When they tried to drive out all earlier, logically competitive, beliefs the peasants resisted with such stubbornness that within twenty years militant atheism had to be abandoned as state policy, even though it has remained the policy of the Communist Party. In 1937, the Soviets found that "more than half, perhaps two-thirds," of the rural population still "believed in God," while nearly all of them "also believed in the devil."[21] Today, Church authorities estimate the number of communicants in the U.S.S.R. at 50 million—a proportion of the whole population that compares favorably with the churchliness of other Christian nations.[22] Communicants are not confined to the elderly. *Komsomolskaia Pravda* frequently reports on young Communists reprimanded, or even expelled from the Communist Youth (Komsomol) for having a church wedding or baptizing their children.[23] It is hard to believe that the younger people do this "merely from curiosity," as Chairman Khrushchev insisted when questioned during his visit to the United States.

The durability of the old faiths, however, is not an exact measure of resistance to the new. The habit of regarding religion and Marxism as implacable foes and the insistence that godliness must war

[21] A statement by Emelian Yaroslavsky, President of the Union of the Godless, as quoted by Timasheff (274).

[22] Cf. Timasheff (275), p. 329. According to French sources there were 20,000 Orthodox parishes and 35,000 clergy in the U.S.S.R. in 1957, as well as 50 monasteries with 8,000 monks and nuns, 8 theological seminaries and 2 graduate schools, or academies; *Le Monde* (Paris), 2 August 1957. Statistics concerning other religious bodies in the Soviet Union can be found in various sources, but their reliability is difficult to ascertain. In the *Journal* published by the Moscow Patriarchate, information is confined to current affairs of church administration.

[23] Timasheff (275), p. 335. For data more recently gleaned from the Soviet press, see *Religion in the U.S.S.R.* (Munich Institute, 1960), as well as articles in *Novoe Russkoe Slovo* (1960-1961).

to the death with godlessness are sophisticated notions—or one might almost say, sectarian notions. In the village, there was no such exclusiveness. Coexistence was the rule. In Ukrainian and Belorussian schools in Stalinist times, the crucifix often hung between portraits of Lenin and Stalin. All were talismans worthy of obeisance for different purposes on different occasions.

In slightly more sophisticated Soviet circles the mixture also persisted. Khrushchev, a declared atheist, nevertheless "invokes the name of God in every other breath as the passionate words come tumbling out to jerk the clumsy, slovenly Russian into some sort of efficiency."[24] Quentin Reynolds was once startled to hear Stalin say: "May God help your President," in proposing a toast. "Stalin was quite serious and not aware of any incongruity," Reynolds recalls. "I spoke to Lozovsky, Litvinov and Oumansky about it afterward and they . . . were puzzled at our surprise."[25] Thomas Preston, a former member of the British Foreign Office, recalls that Andrei Vyshinsky, Stalin's Deputy Foreign Minister at that time, before taking off from Cairo, "performed the old superstitious ceremony (a religious relic of Tsarist days) of sitting down in silence for a few minutes in order to receive 'the Lord's blessing for a safe journey.' To complete the picture, Vyshinsky's police escort and I sat down, too."[26]

The campaign for atheism simply missed its mark. It could only succeed among the intelligentsia, and only among the intelligentsia was it needed. No others demanded the emotional consistency of adoring one God or none, or the intellectual consistency of an all-embracing dogma, or the excitement of total dedication to a new idea. No others were prepared to abandon traditional faiths and customs. The ex-peasant Communist bosses themselves took their "atheism" as pragmatically as they had taken their "religion" in the past.

For the mass of peasant converts to Communism the new slogans and rituals answered psychological and sociological needs of a

[24] Edward Crankshaw, Life, 2 December 1957.
[25] Reynolds (236).
[26] The Boston Daily Globe, 28 November 1954.

simple people. Like primitive religious systems, the new forms were "adaptable in nature, unifying, comfortable, and sacred."[27] Primitives, according to one student, characteristically share "a very deep feeling that man depends for life and fullness of being on forces outside himself."[28] So do Soviet citizens, if their literature truly reflects them. The novel shows them constantly seeking out correct ways of behaving toward "the realities apprehended immediately around" them. The unending stream of Communist rules of behavior seems aimed quite as much at assisting that process of individual adaptation as at maintaining group discipline.

Party creeds, regulations, and the pretentious Marxist jargon all serve also as the means by which unanimity in action is achieved and unanimity in opinion may be compelled or dissembled. On the eve of the purge that dismissed Molotov, Malenkov, and company from the top councils of the party, a *Pravda* editorial headed, "The Leninist Unity of the Party—The Source of Its Unconquerable Power," affirmed that "Marxism-Leninism, in all its totality and fullness, is the basis of the unity of views and actions of Communists."[29] The formula conveniently makes intraparty quarrels among equals impossible, since the losers are automatically tagged with heresy. A magic unity is plucked from a real disunity in precisely the way it has always been by all priesthoods everywhere so long as they remained in possession of the true church.

Party creeds, regulations, and the established jargon are comfortable because they mark out for an individual a ready-made and not too exacting life pattern that suits his status and is stamped with social approval in advance. They are sacred because hallowed by the quasi-gods of the Communist community—Marx, Engels, Lenin, Stalin—whose very names work miracles.[30]

"For archaic man doing and daring are power, but knowing is magical power."[31] Marxism for the peasant convert was a kind of

[27] Noss (203), pp. 10-11.
[28] *Loc. cit.*
[29] *Pravda,* 3 July 1957.
[30] Cf. *Bolshevik* (later renamed *Kommunist*): "The way indicated by Lenin and Stalin is the only true one for all" (October 1948). Leon Trotsky once took part in a discussion of whether the Party was infallible when it made a pronouncement after full consideration, "and they discussed it gravely and in good faith"; Maynard (181), p. 376.
[31] Huizinga (108), p. 105.

touchstone of magical knowledge.[32] An American enlisted man recalls a conversation with a young Soviet soldier over a bottle of wine in Berlin after World War II. " 'I am a Marxist,' said the Russian, 'and I cannot admit the existence of two truths. It would be futile always to argue about problems which separate us. We are positive that there is only one truth and only one way of solving each separate problem. In order to know how you must use the principles of Marxism. There cannot be any error or mistake.' "[33] Since the principles are embodied in words and rites, it is sufficient to know the "word" and the "rite" to master the principles. Knowledge, in short, comes not from investigating reality but from unlocking secret doors with the specially made key that one is assured in advance opens them all.

The attitude is strikingly like that of ancient man toward riddle-solving, which Johan Huizinga describes as a kind of playing with knowledge. He has this to say about it: "The answer to an enigmatic question is not found by reflection or logical reasoning. It comes quite literally as a sudden *solution*—a loosening of the tie by which the questioner holds you bound. The corollary of this is that by giving the correct answer you strike him powerless. In principle there is only one answer to every question. It can be found if you know the rules of the game. These are grammatical, poetical, or ritualistic as the case may be. You have to know the secret language of the adepts . . ."[34]

The Marxist-Leninist game is perhaps less playful and a good deal less fair, since the rules may be changed almost at will by the leader. Yet the fact that there are rules, that every deflection in policy however obviously at odds with the past must be justified as the true orthodoxy, does impose restraints. Khrushchev discovered sharply during the smashing of the Stalin idol that they were greater than even he had supposed. But as a practical man he must long have realized that in some degree—varying with circumstances—he had to share power with the party shamans.

One of the most powerful men in the Kremlin hierarchy at this

---

[32] An anthropologist describes magic as "an endeavor through utterance of set words, or the performance of set acts, to control or bend the powers of the world to man's will"; Radin (229), p. 15.

[33] *Novoe Russkoe Slovo*, 2 October 1950.

[34] Huizinga (108), p. 110.

writing is Mikhail Suslov, one-time editor of *Pravda* and professional interpreter of Marxist-Leninist texts. For many years a top party leader, he notably survived the purges to stand at the boss's right hand, too useful or too dangerous to dismiss—or both. Suslov, about ten years younger than Khrushchev and also born and reared in a village, is one of those peasants (*nachetchiki*) who in old Russia, especially among the Old Believers, would have known the sacred texts by heart. He is, indeed, reputed to have committed to memory every word of Marx, Lenin, and Stalin. He is said to edit—sometimes drastically—the speeches of Khrushchev before publication. Often referred to in the American press as a strict Stalinist, his real power lies in the fact that he is not just the guardian but the creator of orthodoxy. Significantly, it was he who was sent out first to Peiping in 1959, then to Peiping again and to Delhi in 1961, when "ideological differences" with Chinese and Indian leaders seemed publicly to weaken Communist solidarity. If he can be considered as a threat to Khrushchev's position it is not as a Stalinist—whatever that may mean—but rather as a medicine man, whose special powers necessarily both complement and challenge the powers of the chief.

On the other hand, the medicine man himself of course has rivals and can oppose his chief only at the risk of his own power. That became apparent not long ago when Khrushchev decided to sell the MTS (motor tractor station) equipment to individual kolkhozes—a drastic reversal of Stalin's formula that had been officially defended as Marxist-Leninist orthodoxy. Suslov apparently opposed the measure and kept silent while Khrushchev was praised by such party theoreticians as Mitin for "creative development of the Marxist-Leninist theory," and Fedoseyev for "concentration of the Marxist-Leninist teaching about the forms and methods of graduate transition from socialism to communism." In the end, Suslov was still chief augur, but the point had been made that he was not to be considered irreplaceable.

Cicero more than 2,000 years ago wrote: "Experience, education and the lapse of time have wrought changes in the art of augury; but with an eye to the opinion of the masses the practices, rites, discipline, and the laws of augury and the authority of the college of augurs have been maintained for their great political usefulness."[35]

No one knows how much Soviet leaders believe of what they say; there can be no doubt that they believe in the value of saying it. Marxism-Leninism, which began partly as *ideology,* appealed to religious hungers and seemed to work as *magic,* is finally and transcendently a governing *technique.* That is not to say that Soviet leaders, talking the jargon of communism, have nothing more in mind than the deception of the people. These leaders have, after all, been brought up themselves on the jargon and could not escape its shackles on their minds if they wanted to. They cannot manipulate words and symbols like an advertising man, because unlike him they do not live in one world and dream another. The fact is rather that forty years of squeezing the language of Marxist-Leninist idealism to fit the brutal realities of the peasant revolution has produced a vocabulary, even a syntax, with meanings all their own. The sincerity or hypocrisy of Khrushchev's use of the official cant is not discoverable directly by comparing what he says with what he does; one must also know what he means.

When the Soviet leader stirs up war out of his love for peace, or enslaves Hungary in order to liberate it, he has the outward look of a hypocrite. When the Communists habitually use "democracy" to denote dictatorship, "freedom" to describe life in a prison camp, and "treason" to cover nearly every normal instinct and aspiration of the independent soul, they appear to have worked out a technique of the big lie; if not new in human affairs, at least it seems more flagrant and systematic than the propaganda of any governing class before them. George Orwell, with a good deal more poetry than truth, called it "doublethink" and envisaged it as a calculated perversion not just of language but of the whole process by which human beings make contact with reality—a kind of official mirror forced between people and life to persuade them that right really *is* left.[36] The notion—with all respect for the brilliant imagination that evoked it—is nonsense. It omits the simplest of all reckonings, that words not only have different meanings, but may have no rational meaning at all. It ignores a scarcely less basic appreciation of how all governments and all people in fact adjust language to action.

[35] *On Divination,* II, XXXIII, 70.
[36] Orwell (209).

The Kremlin acts, like other governments, in what it conceives to be its self-interest. It puts down a revolt in Hungary because not to do so would be to risk the loss of the Eastern European empire. After acting, it must justify what it has done, again like every other government. "Now, in the row that blew up over the Hungarian question," Khrushchev said, "what did we get? The absolute unity and solidarity of the Communist ranks in the entire world, that's what we got."[37] Words are used neither to reveal nor to conceal reality, but to rationalize it, that is to say, to make it fit the preconceived scheme of things. The process is absolutely normal, not peculiarly primitive nor Russian nor Communist. For contradictions between word and meaning hardly less striking than those developed behind the Iron Curtain, consider the United States's justification for dropping the atomic bomb as essentially an act of humanity, to save lives, or the almost daily paradox by which we threaten to annihilate the Soviet Union in the adamant defense of peace.

Yet while these are examples of the same sort of thing—close enough to forbid us to believe the Communists have invented a kind of double talk all their own—nevertheless they are not just the same. Communist words are not merely twisted into new meanings, they are wrenched out of any meaning whatsoever. That was the inevitable result of clinging to Marxist-Leninist theories while the Soviet reality developed in flagrant opposition. The promotion of a purer democracy, for instance, was a basic objective of Marxist theory; it was, therefore, also an objective of the Soviet state. Since the Communists have succeeded in the U.S.S.R., it must follow that they have created a purer democracy. "Democracy" must, therefore, mean the political system which exists under Communist rule —and that is exactly how the Soviet dictionaries define it.[38] According to Leninist theory, the rule of the Communist party is also the "dictatorship of the proletariat." Democracy and dictatorship of the proletariat, therefore, must be synonymous and are so treated in Soviet writings.[39] Clearly, words in such usage have not just

[37] Speech in Pilsen; cf. note [8], above.
[38] Cf. Ushakov (292), *Slovar* (258, 259), and Rozental (238).
[39] "The dictatorship of the working class is genuinely a whole-nation socialist democracy"; Aleksandrov (3), p. 175; also Ponomarev (222), pp. 163-164. The platform of the Communist Party of the Soviet Union, adopted by the 22nd Party Congress (October 1961), explains the contradiction by pretending that "The state, which arose as a dictatorship of the proletariat, has developed into

been emptied of their usual denotation and filled with a new one; they have been crushed into nonsense. It is notable that Soviet defectors, though bitterly anti-Communist, nevertheless seldom express admiration for "democracy" until they have relearned its meaning in democratic society.[40]

The Marxist-Leninist jargon as a whole no longer serves as a vehicle for thought, but as incantation in the ceremonies of headship. It sanctifies many tyrannical and opportunistic actions. It supplies also a kind of unction of orthodoxy for the usurpers. These are the external uses of power politics. An internal usefulness may be hardly less compelling. The leaders at least act as though they derived assurance themselves from the magic verbal coating they lay over their policies.

Language even to the most sophisticated never quite loses its power magically to transmute the fact into something a little larger and better than the fact. Congress not long ago solemnly added "under God" to the oath of allegiance, after a considerable discussion over what effect the phrase might have in mingling church and state and contaminating both. No one could observe publicly that since nothing was being said with any definable rational meaning, no significance at all could attach to whether it was said or not. The words themselves were conceived to be touched with the divinity; one did not lightly risk treating them lightly. "In the same way as the savage adorns himself with shells and fish-teeth," Maxim Gorky observed after the Revolution, "the Russian puts on the showy trappings of cheap bookish words."[41]

But for the outsider the words exasperatingly remain words, however absurd their application. He is fatally tempted either to argue against their assumed meaning or to pry into them for some other meaning. The Kremlin talks incessantly, for instance, of the inevitability of the victory of communism throughout the world. At the same time, Soviet power pushes restlessly into the rim of the encircling capitalist world. Here would seem to be some obvious connection between Marxist doctrine and Soviet policy.[42] No doubt

---

a state of the entire people, an organ for expressing the interests and will of the people as a whole," that is, into a "socialist democracy."

[40] Cf. Bauer (15) and Inkeles (116).
[41] Gorky (92, 93).
[42] Cf. Leites (160).

131

the connection is not that pretended by the Communists: that they act merely as agents of the proletarian revolution. But might they not really believe that they must continue their hostile thrusts and finally succeed in them because Marx said so? A fanatic faith in their mission could certainly be a motivation of Soviet policy. But on examination it does not seem to be.

The Soviet Union has not acted in the least like a fanatic. Quite the reverse. What has really happened is that Soviet power has patiently and cautiously sought out softness in the enemies around it. Wherever it found hardness it has recoiled. This is the method of expediency, the way of men out for whatever they can get, not the course of the dedicated, driven by the itch of destiny. It is precisely the behavior one would expect of a covetous and unscrupulous peasant neighbor.

True—it is commonly said in rejoinder—but one must distinguish between communist tactics, which are opportunistic, and communist strategy, which is firm and consistent. What strategy? Strategy must lay out some sort of pattern of action. It cannot consist simply in a command: "Conquer the world." Nor can it be defined as a prescription to exploit opportunities, which is opportunism and the antithesis of strategy. What strategy, then? The sum total of communist action, in fact, is *tactical*. Soviet leaders do not act as though they pursued a goal; they only talk that way. The goal they talk about exerts no perceptible attractive or compulsive force on them as practical politicians. It prods them into no risks that they would not otherwise take. It points them in no direction that they would not otherwise choose. They behave as though they ignored their own crusade, indeed, as though they made a virtue of ignoring it in order to be good Marxist realists. They respond, in short, to the impulsion of *power* rather than to the compulsion of *ideas*.

There is nothing to indicate that Soviet tactics will not indefinitely continue to be shaped by the calculus of power without the slightest practical regard for the ultimate Marxist future. Unlike the fanatic they will take only what they can get (or think they can get) without the risk of self-sacrifice. They will, in short, never act like communists except when acting also like Russian expansionists. To paraphrase Stalin, their creed is "socialist in form, nationalist in content"; they no longer even claim to hold credentials from world

132

communism. Can one imagine Khrushchev, Mikoyan, Kozlov, or Brezhnev struggling in exile to make the Communist ideal prevail, as Trotsky did?

In the earlier period of Soviet history, the rulers insisted and perhaps believed that their acts were motivated by the ideals they professed, although it was Lenin himself who turned Marxism into an infinitely flexible philosophy of party tyranny. In any case, since Lenin, the leaders have been eager only to show that their acts can be justified by the sacred texts. Modern Soviet dialectics is, in fact, a revival of the ancient art of accommodating the Bible to daily life—in which rural readers (*nachetchiki*) in Russia always excelled. Official jargon has become as stereotyped as Church Slavonic in homilies and prayers.[43] It is in fact a kind of dead ritual language, stuffed with words of foreign origin and obscure meaning. People do not talk it. It sounds only when authority speaks.

[43] Cf. Fesenko (78) and Vakar (297).

9

THE MARCH OF THE GENERATIONS

IF COMMUNISM IS THE ARTICULATION OF *ideas*, THEN IT WILL CHANGE only as the ideas may change when demonstrated to be unworkable. An outsider might try to help transform it by challenging with better ideas, both in precept and example. But if Communism is a political *form* under which a backward society has seized power, and under which it tries to live and flourish, then it can be expected to change not by conversion but only by growth.

Hatred of the word communism, which appears to stand for an entity indivisible, static, and forever unforgivable, ought not to becloud the fact that we actually confront a society neither static nor monolithic, and hateful only for its malefactions. To be sure, time may compound these. The guarantee of change does not also guarantee progress. But whatever the direction of evolution, it takes time, and in human affairs time gives effect to mortality. Men get old and die; others take their places.

As ordinary as that observation is, much that is said about communism has ignored it. Soviet behavior during forty years is more often than not considered as if a single personality were being described. For instance, a contemporary restraint in liquidating political enemies is skeptically noted as perhaps signifying improvement in the character or manners of communism. Or it is attributed still more skeptically to the accident of Nikita Khrushchev's personality or his immediate difficulties in grasping the whole power. But the more obvious fact is that exile for the political losers, instead of murder, is part of a policy exercised by a new generation of leaders over a new generation of people.

The movement of generations in the Soviet Union has been partly masked from outside view by the aging of the leadership. At the eighteenth Party Congress in 1939 only 3 per cent of the delegates were over fifty years old. At the twentieth Party Congress in 1956, nearly a quarter were that old. Still more strikingly, the commanding positions in the Party are almost exclusively held by men in their fifties and sixties, nearly all of them of rural background. Though not the leaders of the Revolution, they belong to the revolutionary generation in the literal meaning of those born into the old order who survived to make their career in the new. They are a generation distinct from the next younger age group, who were inarticulate children or not yet born when the Soviet Revolution broke their homes and altered their heritage. Men and women over fifty years of age at this writing and counted only in the thousands, they rule as seniors over a Party more than eight million strong.[1] Although not necessarily ever moved by revolutionary ideas, they are those for whom the Communist way was their fighting chance to make good. They are the last of the Revolution's bootstrap self-made men, whose basic view of the world was formed from the village enviously looking out, whose emotional poles have been hatred for the world in which they were born and passion for power in the world they helped to make.

These two attitudes—strong repulsion from the old, strong attraction to the new—together constitute the characteristic revolutionary drive. Communist propaganda has made unsparing efforts to keep both alive. Forty years after the liquidation of landlords, capitalists, and the bourgeoisie in Russia, the Soviet press still belabors them as furiously as ever. If one accepted the propagandists' fury as a rational reaction to the Soviet scene one would have to conclude that forty years of the most rigorous and ruthless despotism ever practiced has failed even in its minimal goal of extinguishing the former ruling classes. But the exercise is not rational. The conclusion it leads to is rather that the present Communist leaders still need to see themselves in hostile relation to old enemies. Despite success, psychologically they remain rebels whose primary justification is in what they oppose. Their first and indispensable

[1] As stated before the Twenty-first Party Congress in 1959, the Communist Party of the Soviet Union had 7,622,356 members and 616,775 candidate members, a total of 8,239,131 at that time, that is, 1,023,626 more than at the time of the Twentieth Party Congress three years before. In the course of 1959, 579,000 more members were admitted. The total, as of January 1, 1960, was 8,708,000 members and candidates; cf. *Ezhegodnik* (71) for 1960, p. 11.

virtue was that they destroyed a bad world—bad because it made no suitable place for them. Hostility was the first and main source of their energies and was the instrument of their ambition. They throve psychologically and materially on aggression. Thereafter, the emotional pattern was bound to continue of its own momentum, like any addiction, regardless of external stimulus. The world they hated has long since been destroyed and a new one made in which they have their place, but the inner need for enemies has not lessened. So enemies must be manufactured and kept fierce. The world view of the Soviet leaders is still shaped by sensory experiences of the past.

Younger men, from whom new leaders will in time be drawn, have not shared those experiences. Daily fulminations against the capitalist enemy may keep alive memories of the old fight among old fighters; it cannot stir those who were not there. The pretence of Soviet propaganda is that it conditions youth to unquestioning devotion to the Communist state along with absolute repugnance for the capitalist foe. But this is to mistake words for things. What does the symbol "capitalist enemy" bring to mind among persons who have never known a capitalist? The revolutionary contrast between capitalism and the new communism, or socialism, which may serve to polarize the emotions of the older generation, does not exist for those who came to conscious maturity only after 1917.

For the elders a landlord may have been a terrible reality, a real devil responsible for real misery, as well as a symbol of a way of life associated forever with feelings of frustration and injustice. For Soviet youth "landlord" is an abstraction; the experiences connoted are only literary. The young can be taught bad words and induced to attach them indiscriminately to persons they are conditioned to distrust. But the enemies so stigmatized do not thereby become objects of personal hatred. Rather, they find a place in legend and imagination as bogeymen who frighten but also fascinate. Those whose whole experience lies with the Soviet era must obviously also find their scale of values within it. What they personally dislike must be as communistic as what they like. Their enemies as well as their friends must be *inside* the system. Their overwhelming emotion when they first see a foreigner—or a former landlord—is neither hatred nor friendship but curiosity.

136

The ex-peasant leaders have been building communism in their own image. But in so doing they cracked the mold. Paternalistic relationships, which they borrowed from the traditional village and applied to the nation, enabled them to continue the patterns of authority with which they were familiar, the only ones they knew. Those patterns, however, have no spontaneous appeal for the generation that grew up not in patriarchal families but in the cultural and social wilderness of the civil war, often without knowing any kind of father.

The senior group who share formative experiences in prerevolutionary Russia cannot much longer monopolize the positions of power, if only because they are not immortal. As they drop out, their places will be taken by the middle group, now aged thirty to fifty plus, who have undergone different life experiences and may be expected to constitute a somewhat different human breed.

In that age group are the waifs of the Soviet Revolution—the *besprizornye*—an extraordinary host of orphans and homeless children whom the nation, spinning into barbarism, cast off altogether, as by the snap of a whip, into the jungle. They were the children of parents who were arrested, deported, or shot as enemies of the people, or who died in the civil war or from starvation during the great famines of 1921-1922 and 1930-1932. Nadezhda Krupskaia, Lenin's wife, wrote in the spring of 1923: "We have registered seven million waifs, and have room for at most 800,000 in our children's homes. What shall we do with all others?"[2] Anatoly Lunarcharsky, People's Commissar of Education, estimated the number of homeless children at 9 million at that time.[3] Their number was even greater in the 1930's, when over 5 million peasants were uprooted by collectivization, and the great famine struck both village and city. The besprizornye roamed in packs all over the Russian empire, hunting like animals for food and shelter, living by thievery. Citizens found it generally healthy to stay out of their way. Authorities found it useless to round them up. Without resources of trained people, the hastily organized "children's homes" (*detdomy*) or detention camps were useless. The inmates could

[2] *Pravda*, 1923; quoted in Zenzinov (321), pp. 114-115.
[3] *Izvestia*, 20 February 1928; quoted in Zenzinov, *loc. cit.;* cf. there estimates based on other sources.

scarcely be fed, much less cared for. From abuse and neglect the waifs learned to hate an authority whose guardianship meant only privation and maltreatment. They learned to run away, to lie, steal, beg, kill. They learned that all they could expect from the world was what they themselves could take.[4]

Although most of the besprizornye were the children of ruined peasants, displaced workers, unmarried women, and war casualties,[5] to the Party, which could scarcely be bothered with them, they were conveniently the spawn of the enemy. In theory, they became wards of the state, which was to be their socialist father, mother, brother, and sister. In practice, they were more likely to be treated as the offscourings of sin. Of course, they retaliated by hating their world and sought in their own gangs the loyalty and sense of belonging denied them in the larger society.

Waifs in the pack learned to hate not just an upper class but all outsiders, including the Communist above all, for the Communists were authority and the proximate cause of their misery.[6] Such security and happiness as the unfortunate youth could find in the hostile world around them they gathered from the intense fellowship of the gang and from the strength of the leader, who was usually an older underworld professional. The gang was home, family, nation—all of the world that mattered. The intolerable fate was to be left out.

The Soviet press in the 1920's frankly described the inhuman life of the group and probed in public discussion for solutions to the problem.[7] In the 1930's, while the situation grew worse, press discussion of it was forbidden. Novelists were a little freer.[8] But perhaps the most eloquent commentary of all was the amendment, on April 7, 1935, of the Soviet criminal code to extend capital punishment to minors.[9] Much later, Soviet citizens would recall those

---

[4] Cf. Makarenko (175), Voinov (301), and Zenzinov (321).

[5] For 1921, Soviet authorities analyzed the parentage of the waifs as follows: 54.5 per cent peasant; 24.3 per cent workers; 5.5 per cent white-collar; 3.3 per cent Red Army; 5.5 per cent artisan; cf. *Pravda*, 20 February 1926, as quoted by Zenzinov (321), p. 121.

[6] Cf. Voinov (301).

[7] For abundant documentation, see Zenzinov (321).

[8] Cf., for instance, Gladkov (88), Leonov (163), and Pogodin (225).

[9] Criminal Code (51), Art. 12.

years with even greater horror than the chaos and famine of the twenties.[10]

In the rigors of the human jungle hundreds of thousands, perhaps millions of Soviet children perished. Most of the survivors were those who, in their teens, discovered the advantages of running with the hunters instead of the hunted. They transferred their gang loyalty to the Communist Youth League (Komsomol) as to a larger, legal gang, in exchange for better living and greater security. More importantly, from the bargain they received skills, education, and opportunity.[11] If not necessarily the strongest and the ablest they were the most adaptive of the breed. Several now hold high Party or government positions: Some have even qualified to direct the cultural life of Soviet society—like Georgi Aleksandrov, Minister of Culture in 1954-1955, and his successor Nikolai Mikhailov, in 1955-1960, known as former waifs and as members of the Komsomol in the twenties.

What either culture or communism can mean to these men is hard to imagine. Their points of departure at least are quite different from those of their elders. Different, too, must be the conditioning of others of this generation who may not have been waifs, but felt the impact of revolution in their most impressionable years in the savage struggle for survival.

The middle-aged group no doubt is transitional and mixed. Village Russia was not wiped out or wholly bolshevized at once. Even in the 1930's in many areas traditional rural ways persisted. They have not entirely disappeared today. There are certainly Soviet citizens in their forties at present who despite the Revolution were reared in the old peasant culture. One of those in their early fifties is Frol R. Kozlov, Deputy Premier (since March 1958) and Secretary to the Central Committee (since May 1960), widely regarded as heir presumptive, who was born a peasant in 1908. The similarity of his background to Khrushchev's may help endear him to the boss. Whether it will stand him in as good stead in the struggle for the succession seems more doubtful. His breed, though far from extinct, is already old-fashioned.

[10] Cf. Luke (172), p. 38.
[11] Cf. Makarenko (175).

139

At this writing, the average age of the Presidium members is 59.0 (median 58); of the alternate members, 59.4 (median 59); and of the five Secretaries, 60.6 (median 59).[12] Among the fourteen full members only two, and among the seven alternates only one, are under 50 years of age, while five in the first group and three in the second are over 60. The head, Nikita S. Khrushchev, was 67 on April 17, 1961. Only three members and one alternate survived from the period before 1917, and seven others joined the party while Lenin was still alive. All the rest are of Stalinist vintage.

The Party thus remains firmly in the hands of the elder brothers. But some of their juniors have already cut in, and the pressures from below must be strong. Among the 1,355 delegates to the Twentieth Party Congress in 1956, who represented the Communist governing élite,[13] only 22 were survivors from the period before 1917, only 60 from the period before 1921.[14] The weight of the Party is settling on those who were born into prerevolutionary peasant homes, but were small children when the Soviet Revolution changed the course of their life. Today, they vote for their seniors obediently but not—one may surmise—without impatience.

The generation that includes the waifs thus dominates numerically the Party and the state machines, duly commanded by the dwindling minority of elders, who are subjected to increasing pressure from below. The middle group suffers the squeeze and, no doubt, the anxieties of the vice-presidential level of organization men everywhere. They have, of course, more to gain and much less to lose by waiting for the succession than by bidding for it in an open revolt. That means effectively a kind of alliance with the elders, which, in any case, is natural to them, since they are necessarily more afraid of the better educated young who are pushing up.

The alliance is conditional, however. The father-figure which

[12] As of January 1, 1961.

[13] According to Averky B. Aristov, member of the Presidium, 1, 141 delegates, or 84 per cent, were Party or state officials; 116 were military men, and 98 others had miscellaneous designations. For details, see *Pravda*, 17 February 1956, and *Krasnaia Gazeta*, 24 February 1956.

[14] The others joined the Party in the following years: 1921-1930, 24.9 per cent; 1931-1940, 34 per cent; 1941-1945, 21.6 per cent; 1946-1955, 13.4 per cent. At the Twenty-first Party Congress, three years later, the proportion of delegates who joined the Party since 1941 increased from 35 to 41 per cent; cf. *Pravda*, 5 February 1956 and 30 January 1959.

140

kept the older peasant generation in line can have little meaning to former waifs. Those whose image of security was shaped in the gang can respect a leader only as long as he is successful in providing spoils. Khrushchev knows that. "If leaders are no good," he said in 1959, "if they've reached their ceilings and cannot do more, others should be boldly put forward." That is, of course, a principle of efficient government, but the bloodless purges seem to have outrun demands for efficiency. In the course of a few years, nearly one-third of the 133 members of the Central Committee elected at the Twentieth Party Congress have been quietly dropped. All secretaries of Central Committees, chairmen of governments and chairmen of Supreme Soviets of the Union Republics and, in two cases, more than half of their Central Committee memberships have been replaced.[15] In distributing patronage[16] Khrushchev has not hesitated to sacrifice an old crony to strengthen his hold on those coming up. He can play the benevolent father, but he can also speak to former waifs as if he were one of them. With them he must not only succeed, but seem always to be tough, vigilant, and in command. That requirement may well be sufficient to account for his outburst at the Paris news conference in May 1960, marking the final collapse of the scheduled summit conference. The tough-guy showmanship, the underworld language, were perhaps calculated to retrieve in the eyes of the gang a previous appearance of softness, the more necessary since softness had so evidently failed.

[15] A. Avtorkhanov has compiled the following table of "bloodless purges" of the Party Central Committees for six Union Republics:

Republics	Members in 1958	Purged by 1960	% of the Purged
Tadzhik	120	34	28.0
Ukrainian	111	36	32.0
Lithuanian	120	40	33.0
Latvian	80	38	44.0
Turkmen	100	53	53.0
Azerbaidzhan	93	53	57.0

(Source: *Nashe Obshchee Delo*, No. 1 (113), January 1961.)

[16] The latest published data of the 1959 general census show that approximately 1,347,000 persons hold leading positions in the Party and state machines: 392,000 in the Party and government administration; 852,000 in industry, trade, transport, etc., and 103,000 in the collective farms. Cf. *Vestnik Statistiki* [Messenger of Statistics], No. 12, Moscow, 1960.

Changes effected by time are easier to describe than interpret. Younger ex-peasants, if they should continue on top in the struggle for survival, may blur the shift of generations. Since men are never determined by background alone, a leader may quite unpredictably arise from a group from which he is alienated, and may direct his fellows and his nation along a course they could not otherwise have taken. Prophecy is foolhardy. Nevertheless, the kind of human material observably at hand for leadership establishes probabilities at least as worthy of consideration in calculating policy as in playing poker.

On the whole, it is more reasonable to expect a lower than a higher order of statesmanship from the waif generation. Paternalism, even if practiced only as a pose, tends to force attention to the general good and keep the tyrant conversant with his responsibilities even when he does not discharge them. The new focus is on the well-being of the ruling group itself. The crime of which the party leaders are accused to justify their demotion or expulsion is no longer "deviation" as in the twenties, nor even "treason" or "spying for capitalists" as in the thirties, but displaying an *antiparty* attitude."[17]

When, in October 1956, Vladimir Dudintsev was called publicly to account for mirroring Soviet officialdom in his novel, *Not By Bread Alone*,[18] Konstantin Paustovsky, a survivor of the old intelligentsia, was one of the few who found courage to defend him. "Why," Paustovsky asked members of the Soviet Writers' Union, "is Dudintsev, a courageous and honest man, thus disturbed? Because [the story] is not simply a case of a few Soviet careerists. All this is much deeper and much more important. The point is that in our country a new social stratum—a new petty bourgeois caste—is not only allowed to exist but flourishes. It is a caste of rapacious mercenaries that has nothing in common with the Revolution, nor with our regime, nor with Socialism. They regard the people as dirt and have developed the lowest human instincts. Treachery, slander, moral assassination and plain murder are their weapons. . . . We see these people, the Drozdovs [party bureaucrats in the novel], every day. They all resemble one another not only in char-

[17] Cf. demotion and expulsion of Malenkov, Molotov, Kaganovich, Shepilov, Marshal Zhukov, and Bulganin from the higher councils of the Party in 1957 and 1958.

[18] Cf. Dudintsev (66).

acter but even in the way they dress and the way they talk, with complete contempt for the Russian language, in an artificially created, dead bureaucratic jargon. Their power lies like a heavy burden on the country. And all this is done to the accompaniment of deceitful talk about the people's happiness! . . . Coming from them such talk is a crime, a sacrilege. They dare to call themselves representatives of the people, they dare to rob the country of its human and material riches, merely to serve their selfish petty interests . . ."[19]

The charge could hardly be more damning, yet neither Dudintsev —reprimanded by Khrushchev for "certain exaggerations"[20]—nor Paustovsky has been punished or silenced.

From the inside view of what they are, the middle generation getting ready to replace their elder brothers does not promise improvement. They will be subject, however, to increasingly severe external restraints. Chief of those is the generation below.[21]

The group now under thirty belongs to a different world. They were born into new Soviet homes. Many now coming up the party ladder are the second generation of a ruling class, the sons of Red Army generals, party bosses, and factory managers. The Soviet Revolution and civil war are history to them. They take the "socialist" system for granted. For them, it is the established order— established and maintained by someone else. They have no responsibility for it, but neither have they any commitment to alternative systems. Root-and-branch rebels are surely as exceptional among Soviet youth as in any other modern state. Devoted Communist idealists among them can hardly be more common. At least they

[19] The text of Paustovsky's speech has never been published in the Soviet Union. Smuggled abroad, it first appeared in a French translation in *L'Express* (Paris), April 1957, and is quoted here as retranslated from the French by *Novoe Russkoe Slovo* (New York) 17 May 1957. Dudintsev's novel was published in installments by the literary magazine *Novy Mir*, "hot copies" of which were soon selling in Moscow "for three times their original value" (see *The New York Times*, 27 January 1957).

[20] In his address to the Third Congress of Soviet Writers (see *Pravda*, 24 May 1959).

[21] Already there were 106 delegates to the Supreme Soviet of the U.S.S.R. in 1958 under 30 years of age: 45, or 6 per cent, in the Soviet of the Union (lower chamber), and 61, or 10 per cent, in the Soviet of Nationalities (upper chamber).

143

do not flourish in contemporary Soviet literature, where they ought to appear larger than life.

The rather meager data available on what goes on in the minds and dreams of young Soviet citizens suggest that their minds and dreams for the most part stay clear of politics altogether. A generation of technicians—who are the new intelligentsia—is absorbed in getting things done as best they can or in getting themselves ahead. Among them is some evident unrest. Foreign travelers have commented on the hunger of Soviet youth for information, which sets them so strikingly apart from their elders. A Soviet member[22] of this generation has acidly rejoined that the hunger in fact is only an appetite for status. So be it. The young stirring and reaching beyond themselves, for whatever reason, are a socially significant force: Their restlessness none denies. Fulminating against various sowings of wild oats, the Soviet press has confessed not only the problem (which of course is hardly unique to the Soviet Union) but, in general, the helplessness of the all-powerful state to do anything more effecitve than preach against it.

Much of this youthful ferment—perhaps most of it (good and bad)—is normal to a maturing society and has little directly to do with political tyranny. Some of the most unruly are the children of the newly privileged, who have had position and comparative affluence without traditions of responsibility. Some unquestionably are victims of the wholesale migration from the country to the city and the consequent weakening of family ties.

But some, important in kind and quality, however small in numbers, are clearly enough responding to the irritations of the system, trying not so much to upset it as to make room for their own needs and aspirations. The most significant contest for possession of the future may well be taking place, quietly for the most part and probably without full awareness on either side, between a new, young, educated élite and the party bosses. The battle is only obliquely joined. The young intelligentsia, even when only technically trained rather than educated, are likely to be culturally superior to the ubiquitous bureaucrats who manage their lives. For that reason alone they must resent continued dictation. It

[22] A. P. K., *Novoe Russkoe Slovo*, February 1961 (several articles); see Bibliographical Notes.

would be wrong, however, to suppose anything like a revolution in the making.

The young élite do not even appear to protest repression or censorship and propaganda as such. They react rather against the intellectual dullness which these have produced. It is improbable that they aspire in large numbers to freedom itself as an ideal. A Soviet girl to whom "freedom" was mentioned said, "What a word . . . as though with wings, vast . . . very big . . ." But when asked whether she understood the notion, she replied: "I do and I don't . . . It must be something like the sea. I saw it once . . . Or like the wind. In nature, I can understand it; but what it may mean for people . . . I really don't know."[23] Boris Pasternak believed (though with him this was a necessary act of faith) that freedom "grows slowly, imperceptibly, like grass. The most significant thing about this era is that liberty is growing."[24] Even so, freedom at most is to be seen in the soft light of a dawn inside, not yet on battle flags in the open.

Meanwhile, the struggle is for the fruits of freedom, and particularly for the variety that freedom alone makes possible. The new intellectuals struggling to be born in the universities scramble not only for knowledge but for the latest rock and roll records which, reproduced on old X-ray plates, have circulated in the dormitories like precious contraband.[25] Recently, in a letter to the editor of *Komsomolskaia Pravda*, a young man, signing himself "Milka" (a Russian equivalent of "Deary"), professed to be worried about the bubbling of vitality and curiosity inside him: "I don't understand the communist terms," he wrote, "I live by several mottoes, 'Everyone is crazy his own way,' 'Do what you like and not what you ought to do.' I like to dance 'rock' and use the hula-hoop, to take a woman with one look, to be the center of attraction and, in general, to stand out above everybody else . . . I like the pictures in the Hermitage but I like Polish abstractionists, too; while [Louis] Armstrong [jazz trumpeter] has the same effect on me as [Fedor] Chaliapin [operatic bass] . . . Tell me please why have I become what I am instead of, at the worst, being a

[23] Krasnov (141), p. 302.
[24] Interview with Herd Rugge of *Die Zeit*, quoted in *Novoe Russkoe Slovo*, 9 February 1958.
[25] *The New York Times*, 3 February 1957.

145

mediocrity."[26] The passionate interest of students in things American has centered on our material gains, and so echoes the official envy. But it goes beyond emulation, all travelers attest, to a wide-ranging curiosity which officialdom would gladly discourage if it could.

Soviet youth finds itself not contradicting its elders so much as straining to push out ahead. Their rebelliousness suggests rather the hot rodder who yearns to step on the gas than the disgruntled idealist who would pull down temple walls. One may guess, in short, that they feel within them capacities that demand not only release but proving. As one observer remarks, "They are trying with everything they do, and with every word they say, to develop a Soviet élite as distinct from a Party élite, for which no model exists."[27]

This, of course, is essentially self-development, social and personal, not political. But the implied political challenge could hardly be ignored by the Party élite, who, while remaining all-powerful in action, are threatened with uncomfortable and finally dangerous ego-shrinkage. The countermeasures suggested and taken, however, are patently either hopeless or likely to speed the process they aim to check. The press asks for more discipline, more rigorous indoctrination in "socialist" standards of behavior, a return generally to the old-fashioned virtues. Khrushchev experiments with reorganization of the educational system, greatly to reduce its already narrow liberal content for most of the students. While his main purpose is apparently to squeeze more workers out of the sparse generation of war babies, he may wish also to get docile workers by withholding from them the glimpses of better things that courses in liberal arts are reputed to provide. At the same time he proposes to expand Soviet boarding schools, chiefly for children of the Party élite. Presumably the object here is to tighten discipline and control over those who with the very rapid development of a caste system are tabbed to inherit the state.

The concern of the older generations does not seem to be primarily with the dangers of political heresy. It bothers them much more that the young no longer admire hard work. The complaint

[26] Quoted by Ralph Parker, "Live Letter-Box," in *New Statesman* (London), 8 August 1959.
[27] Edward Crankshaw, *Detroit News*, 25 February 1959.

is traditional, of course, from fathers to sons, but it comes most poignantly from the self-made man who, as part of his rise in the world, has educated his offspring above him. Learning their lesson his children grow up to despise manual labor and factory work. "Father," says a young loafer satirized in the Communist Youth paper, "you have been a proletarian all your life. At least let your son become cultured!" The paper goes on to describe a "typical day" of this "cultured" scion of a privileged Soviet family that had "just moved into a new apartment": "After an all-night drinking bout he wakes up at eleven, lies long in bed staring at the ceiling, then turns on the radiola . . . He eats at four, then makes a telephone call, 'Hi! . . . Is that you? This is me. Where tonight? Same place? *Okay!* Well, I'd better hang up . . . My proletarian may show up any minute now.'"[28]

Though designed to educate the mass, Soviet schools have kept standards high since the war. Competition for the very limited spaces in the universities at the top has been keen. The contest of course is not wholly one of merit. But whether students deserve university places or get them because of the social and political position of their parents, the gulf between them and their fathers widens.[29]

The dearth of technicians and the need for them in a hurry to build and operate the new society give schooling a seriousness it often lacks in more advanced nations. Since exceptional rewards await the educated few in contrast to the enslaved many, school becomes the initial and critical testing ground for the ambitious, who must succeed in it or lose their chance for success outside it. In these ways mass education in the Soviet Union, while raising slightly the literacy of all, has, even more significantly for the future, selected and trained a new upper class. Khrushchev's reforms seem destined to intensify this process. As the many get less schooling and more job training, the few must come into a greater monopoly of learning, and the gap separating them from the mass must grow.

On the other hand, isolation of the new intelligentsia under more rigorous discipline and indoctrination is unlikely to tame the strays or come any closer to turning out the new Soviet man. The

[28] *Komsomolskaia Pravda,* 4 October 1956.
[29] Cf. Kalb (123).

147

fact that he has not been developed in forty years of the most comprehensive system of mass mind-conditioning ever attempted seems proof that the system is ineffective or the goal unattainable— or both. To cry for more of the same is the last resort of those who don't like what has been wrought, but haven't the slightest idea what to do about it.

Actually, if Soviet leaders were not blinded by the delusion that they are new men working a new scientific Marxist magic, they could easily enough recognize their difficulty as the perennial experience of maturing societies. Their newly educated children get into the same kinds of trouble, demonstrate the same kind of eagerness to learn and to be free (or to get diplomas and run wild), and express the same kind of contempt for their elders as the children of immigrants to the United States so often have for precisely the same reasons. Rebellion in each case has sprung out of the clash of cultures, intensifying the normal passion of the young for independence.

Precise and instructive parallels of the Soviet dilemma can be read in Russian history of a hundred years ago, when the government, similarly obsessed with making autocracy permanent and rebellion impossible, similarly hit upon the idea of putting it up to education. Embracing the primitive notion that minds are shaped like cups, to be filled at will with trash or truth, the Tsarist government early in the nineteenth century began force-feeding religious orthodoxy in the schools and universities. It was supposed that souls bound to the established church would necessarily entail minds devoted to the state.

The lengths to which religious indoctrination was carried then remind one forcefully of the latter-day efforts in behalf of communism. In Kazan University in 1819, for instance, the course in political economy was ordered to be constructed on the fundamental teachings of the Scriptures. The biblical view—whatever that might mean—was made obligatory in physics and medicine. Professors of mathematics were directed to show the symbol of the Trinity in triangles. Students were compelled to read and sing prayers in unison. Transgressors were made to wear a tag inscribed

148

"Sinner" and afterward to do penance. In all schools and universities, students had to take examinations in theology.

At the same time, an increasingly harsh and niggling censorship tried to wipe out hostile thoughts. Under Nicholas I (1825-1855), works on logic and philosophy were prohibited. Newspapers were forbidden to praise new inventions until they had been officially approved. Count Uvarov, later himself a minister of education, in his book on Greek antiquities was not allowed to use the word *demos*. Censors excised from scientific writings such vaguely heretical expressions as "forces of nature." The Tsar's minister of education remarked that, "The population needs just as much education as required by technical needs of the state, and must be carefully guarded against infiltration of pernicious political ideas." Like the Marxists-Leninists today, he thought minds could be controlled by controlling what was put in them.[30]

The most striking consequence of religious indoctrination in old Russia was just what a student of human nature would have expected—the luxuriant growth of atheism among the young who felt that they ought to know more than their fathers knew. The more rigid the government autocracy and the more closely it was identified with churchliness the more clearly the students understood that to begin to think for themselves they must start by denying God. Atheism became for the young Russian intelligentsia "the cornerstone of personal freedom."[31] Similarly, the Communists, by insisting on ready-made answers to all intellectual questions, have made disbelief in Marxism-Leninism an essential first step in individual development.

There has been a significant difference, however. For the nineteenth-century Russian intellectual, atheism took chiefly the form of passionately seeking a substitute for God. Godlessness directed minds as much to otherworldliness as piety and, in fact, fired many with an even greater spiritual energy. But Marxism has no such lively opposite. It is easier to withhold belief than to find a substitute. Indeed, the object of the free mind is not to invent better systems but to learn to do without systems altogether, since all hobble thought. It is because anti-Marxism in the Soviet Union

[30] Cf. Kornilov (139), Pares (214), and Sumner (271).
[31] Cf. Lavrov (156).

149

among those who have never known alternatives must first of all be expressed as general skepticism, that even incipient rebels may seem outwardly blasé rather than passionate.

A former Soviet student has explained what happens when good minds are propagandized instead of taught: "The age of 8 to 20 when the human personality is formed we spent in the Soviet school, that is, in complete isolation from the outside world . . . We were not—and could not be—anti Soviet politically but we had a definite feeling that we were being deceived, and we knew that not one word of the Soviet officials could be trusted." He and his schoolmates learned neither Marxist ideology nor the sort of reflex loyalty to the regime which Soviet propagandists were so sure they could develop. "To assume that my generation believed in Stalin and in communism would be a mistake. At best, we believed in nothing. . . . Others sought answers in religion or in Russia's glorious past. They were patriotic and, as a rule, suspicious of the West, but no one would ever make good Communists of them."[32]

An American who attended a lecture on current events in the Lenin Library, in Moscow, observed that, "Whenever [the speaker] used a typical propaganda phrase like 'the glorious, mighty, genius-full Soviet people,' almost without exception the young listeners around me either yawned loudly or made crude, sarcastic comments, or continued to read books or newspapers. Ninety-five per cent seemed to be bored with such phrases and showed cynical disbelief."[33] European visitors have had the same impression: "The universities are seething, not with revolution, but with cynicism as far as the regime and the Marxist dogma are concerned."[34] Opposition among the young to the Soviet system "often takes the form of debauchery, drinking, vandalism, violence, and the like."[35]

Well attested as the fact of turbulence among Soviet youth is, its significance remains obscure. Foreign observers in general tend to be impressed with the liveliness and ambition of the young and so are inclined to see a society on the move. At least there seems no question that the current Soviet scene presents to outsiders a lively contrast with the gray days of Stalin. The improvement,

[32] O. Gorsky, *Novoe Russkoe Slovo,* 22 December 1950.

[33] Kalb (123).

[34] Raymond Levasseur, a French composer and critic, telling his impressions to Otto Zausmer, *The Boston Daily Globe,* 26 May 1957.

[35] Gorsky, *loc. cit.*

superficial though it may be, inevitably suggests more to come. But how deep can the outsider see? One privileged member of this Soviet generation, who nevertheless defected in revulsion against life in the U.S.S.R., believes that foreigners are misled not by official censorship but by the reluctance of the people themselves to uncover their private lives and expose the "real poverty, vulgarity and bestiality." "In Moscow I was not afraid to talk freely with foreigners," she says. "Was I willing to be honest and frank with them? Yes, I was, but I couldn't bring myself to tell them the whole truth. I was ashamed!" Herself educated in the best Moscow schools as one of the new élite, this witness cites with bitterness the training she says her contemporaries have had since childhood in lying, cheating, betraying, and foul speaking from parents who were children themselves during the Revolution. The dominant characteristic of Soviet young people, she thinks, is not intellectual curiosity, vitality, ambition, or rebelliousness. It is "greed of the hand and hardness of soul." There are in the Soviet press and literature, as we have noted, impressive bits of evidence to support her.[36] Yet another inside observer, seemingly no less qualified to generalize, has written: "Rough and tough as they may appear in their struggle for survival, you still find among the young people many romantic and sensitive souls, human loyalty, unselfishness, humility and sacrifice."[37]

One can multiply but not resolve such contradictory perspectives. The evidence is too fragmentary; a systematic study of the Soviet scene from a cultural point of view remains to be undertaken. To know what these young people are like, and especially what their leadership is like and what they expect of it, would be of inestimable practical value. In a few years these are the men and women who must begin to direct Soviet affairs. Where will they wish to go?

Admittedly, generalization would be difficult even with much fuller information. This is, by all accounts, an apolitical—even anti-political—generation absorbed in the multiplicity of their private

[36] A. P. K., *Novoe Russkoe Slovo*, February-March 1961 (series of articles); see Bibliographical Notes.
[37] P. Uranov, *Novoe Russkoe Slovo*, 29 May 1951.

affairs. Indoctrination, which has backfired in political apathy or cynicism, may also paradoxically have awakened individualism. As propaganda over the years has poisoned the wells of instruction, all who wanted to think have had to start afresh, using their own brains on all subjects. "Independent thinking is concealed," writes an ex-Soviet citizen, "and only among students, curious and eager to learn, can one find persons bold enough to have overt opinions of their own. Generally, free opinion is expressed in 'tendencies' which do not seek to overthrow the regime but to transform it from within."[38]

If he is right, tyranny is being challenged quietly but deeply by alteration of the human material with which it has to work. The young who have learned to think for themselves and insist on doing so may remain outwardly manageable, but they are no longer the docile mass on which slavery counts. And if they are not, then they must either be totally suppressed or accommodated.

But the choice is not really a choice at all. Peasant society was stable because the sons were not taught, and did not ordinarily wish to learn, more than their fathers. The Soviet state, governed by ex-peasants, is no longer peasant. It cannot eliminate the newly educated because they are indispensable to the operation of the increasingly sophisticated, urbanized society. In time, it matters little whether the old guard yields or not; time will carry them off. The Soviet Union will continue to take shape as the upcoming generations determine. The social answer to the war between fathers and sons is that sons at last cannibalize their fathers. Prophecy may safely go that far but hardly any further.

How the Soviet Union may change thereby one cannot rationally predict. On the face of it, there is little reason to expect the development of political democracy soon. Soviet society has shaped itself very rapidly into a caste system in which hereditary status tends to become the rule. The challenge of the young does not now at least seem to attack that basic disposition, since the restive for the most part already belong among the Brahmins. It is the composition of the élite rather than its pre-eminence which appears to be at issue, and the change between generations promises now to be more a change of men than of institutions.

[38] *Ibid.*

Nevertheless, the generation now chafing against controls designed for a nation of peasants, when it comes to power must at least relax the system enough to accommodate its own greater variety of interests and tastes, occupations and perspectives. And that necessarily requires a larger freedom.

10

CULTURE AND COEXISTENCE

WHILE THIS IS NOT THE PLACE TO ATTEMPT SWEEPING CONCLUSIONS OR to embark on a survey of world affairs, it might be useful to recapitulate some of the main ideas, already argued, in the more explicit context of getting along with half a world now emerging more or less explosively from primitivism and poverty.

Our first main point was historical: emphasis on the changes that took place in the Soviet Union after the death of Lenin. The Bolshevik Revolution was carried out according to the Marxist book, extensively revised but nevertheless used as an ideal blueprint. The second revolution, under Stalin, retained Marxism-Leninism as a language and as a rationalization, but reorganized the Soviet Union according to the cultural models and power demands of ex-village bosses. Now, under Khrushchev, the village model is being modified to fit the needs of a maturing society.

While the Soviet pattern is not likely to be exactly repeated elsewhere, it is highly probable that other "Communist" revolutions will also be shaped finally by native culture rather than by Marxist idealism. The economic appeal of communism to underdeveloped nations—its demonstrated capacity to industrialize rural economies fast—is significantly matched by the ethical appeal of Communist political methods, which impose on the nation the controls that universally rule the patriarchal family in pre-industrial societies.[1]

Democracies seeking to prevent the spread of communism face

[1] In 1957, Moscow claimed that the 76 Communist parties throughout the world had a total membership of 33 million (Associated Press, 18 June 1957); of that number only 2.4 million were in Western Europe (Cf. *The World Marxist Review*, November 1959). Eighty-one Communist parties signed the Communist Manifesto in Moscow in 1960, but while new parties have been formed in underdeveloped countries, no increase in membership has been claimed in the industrialized West.

not only an economic challenge—supplying capital for industrialization, so that it does not have to be wrung out of the farmer's livelihood by police state methods—they have also to calculate the possibilities of gaining acceptance for political institutions that to the native tradition must seem less natural and less effective than the Communist ones. There are many places in the world where efforts to promote democracy now are neither hopeful nor relevant, and where to push the cause of attachment to our ways or our camp can only multiply our defeats while distracting us from tasks in which we might succeed.

It is a truism—though one curiously neglected in cold-war strategy—that democratic institutions are the invention of the middle class and remain dependent on its support. In the absence of an economically strong and politically sophisticated middle class, the masses everywhere have always found themselves at the mercy of despots.

All men seem to aspire to freedom by nature. But there is nothing natural, instinctive, or inherently acceptable about the techniques that assure freedom or about the philosophic principles that underlie its defense. The rightness of modern democratic institutions, in fact, never becomes clear even to large numbers who enjoy the benefits of those institutions and are constantly indoctrinated with their virtues.[2] Among newly emergent nations, one cannot expect a love for liberty spontaneously to express itself in democracy, no matter how skillful our diplomacy. The concept of selling democracy abroad is a delusion of those who have forgotten that political systems are a product of culture and that culture is simply not for sale.

Only a few underdeveloped countries in our time have a middle

[2] A recent survey of American teen-agers, for instance, revealed that "only forty-five per cent of the nation's young adults believe that newspapers should be allowed to print anything they want except military secrets. Thirteen per cent believe that religious belief and worship should be restricted by law. Twenty-six per cent believe that the police should be allowed to search a person or his home without a warrant . . . Seventeen per cent say it may be right for police to jail people without naming charges against them. Thirty-three per cent say that people who refuse to testify against themselves should be made to talk or should be severely punished . . . Thirty-seven per cent say that immigration of foreigners should be greatly restricted, since it may mean 'lowering national standards.' Thirty-eight per cent feel that the greatest threat to democracy in the United States comes from foreign ideas and foreign groups"; see Remmers and Radler (234).

class capable of maintaining itself against the pressures from below while providing education and increasing opportunities for the laborer working up out of his age-old bondage. Only those nations have a good chance of avoiding Communist or other dictatorships, and the West therefore ought to offer them all the help necessary to put them solidly out of danger.

Elsewhere, some hard-boiled choices have to be made. In making them it would be well to remember that free men are engaged in two struggles, parallel but not identical: one is against the Sino-Soviet bid for world empire; the other is against the cultural regression represented by totalitarian systems. The first struggle is immediate and urgent and is waged by military-economic-diplomatic means. The second is long-term and must be waged primarily by *educational* means, which are practicable, of course, only in conjunction with economic development. To gain time for education of the masses, the civilized world must win the cold war—which is to say it must frustrate the spread of Soviet and Chinese power. In certain emergent nations this can be done only if we consent to abandon anticommunism as an immediate political goal and concentrate instead on helping to create, defend, and stabilize these viable states. Such states, even when Marxist, can develop outside the Sino-Soviet orbit. And that is the primary goal of the initial struggle.

In the Soviet Union we have noted that the archaic family pattern has been a source and main support of the totalitarian political system. Since the patriarchal family complex exists in other societies that are still in the primitive agricultural stage, typical "Communist" political ideas can develop and flourish independent of the example or influence of the Soviet Union. The closed society of the Soviet type, we have argued, is modeled, both actually and psychologically, after the culturally isolated village in which so many of the leaders of Stalinist times grew up. Evidently, this pattern, too, is home-grown throughout the rural world. From a cultural point of view, therefore, the effort to build external barriers by military pacts against the spread of communism is doomed. Communism in that sense is hardly more an item of export than is democracy. Parenthetically, it may be noted that if the task of Western diplomats is thus complicated, the task of the Kremlin is made no easier. It can count as little on the cooperation of Communist states as we can on the cooperation of democracies.

Successful states have always sought to aggrandize themselves. The political energy necessary to organize a stable, prosperous society seems inevitably to spill over frontiers and, with an arrogance that history has never succeeded in rebuffing, tries to make over the world. The Soviet Union is such a state. In that sense, the observation that communism represents an international aggression directed from Moscow is correct. But, as we have pointed out, this is no fanatic crusade for an idea. Since World War II, the Soviet Union has consistently taken whatever it saw it could get away with at relatively slight risk. Its grabs have, on the whole, been extremely circumspect; the line of retreat has always been left open, however filled with the underbrush of bellicose rhetoric. The dogma that history dooms the capitalist countries, instead of goading the zealous to bolder action, has in fact served to rationalize the typical expediency of the greedy but cautious neighbor. It has also, of course, had a marginal utility as a weapon to panic the enemy or to win over the wavering. The effective response so far has combined a defensive hardness with a willingness to view sympathetically Soviet political and diplomatic problems to which the leader must find solutions for his own security.

Against a shrewd opportunist at the head of a developing nation it is equally dangerous to be weak and to be unreasonable. He cannot stand still. He must move forward. If immovable walls are raised against him he must try to smash them. Nothing in the background of the present Soviet leadership or in its behavior to date suggests that we need fear overt aggression (unless, of course, we should be so foolish as to make it virtually free of risk). The direct approach, the big gambler's all-or-nothing plunge, is not the method congenial to the temperament, position, or philosophy of ex-peasant leaders. In both Communist and peasant eyes, war must appear as an unnecessary risk and, therefore, as a foolish policy. On the other hand, no national leader can let himself be forced into corners where he must surrender not only substantial advantage but national dignity in order to preserve the peace.

The cultural view of communism as a socio-economic anachronism suggests finally, and perhaps most importantly of all, a general warning to those who would fight effectively against it. The essential evil which free men contend against is not of Russian, Chinese, Cuban or, for that matter, rural patent. Historically, the anachronism was produced in the Soviet Union by the Bolshevik revolution. Sociologically, rural culture is everywhere more immature on the time scale of the growth of civilization than the culture of cities. Politically, at this moment in world history the principal threat of Communist revolution is in the technologically undeveloped agricultural nations. Nevertheless, the source of the Communist perversion of humane ideals is the primitive personality of the mass man which is to be found in the lower cultural levels of all civilizations.

Nationalistic interpretations, however subtle, distort the problem. "Socialism," wrote the Russian philosopher Nikolai Berdiaev, "is deeply rooted in the Russian character." Another Russian writer, Mikhail Koriakov, proclaimed just as confidently, "The idea of socialism has been entirely alien to the Russian people." Granting, perhaps too generously, that each said something, what was the good of either?

It needed a wholly different perspective to produce the vision and true appreciation of the reality to come. Frederic Le Play in 1879 wrote this: "The revolution of 1848 . . . spread the spirit of discord to the lower subdivisions of society . . . Now the West is the principal center of contagion, but unexpected changes are before us. The evil is now being propagated from the west to the east. In the east it becomes aggravated because the naive faith of the populations which it overtakes has not given them the strength or experience necessary to resist the corruption.

"For sixteen years of labor on the eastern frontiers of Europe I studied the conditions of stability and peace of those simple populations. I now learn that forms of discord, unknown to our western populations, are developing rapidly among them. *Would it not seem that a counter-current of evil is going to be produced in eastern Europe? In the future might we not have a movement of 'enlightenment' from the Ural regions to the Atlantic?* The disorganization will come back from the east to the west."[3]

Gustave Le Bon, a few years later, from a similar view of the structure of society rather than the spirit of nations, wrote with

[3] Le Play (159); italics supplied.

still more precise prescience: "Though the barbarians may seem to be very distant, they are in reality very close, far closer than at the time of the Roman emperors. The fact is that they exist in the very bosom of civilized nations. . . . It is not necessary to go to the pure savages, *since the lowest strata of European societies are homologous with primitive man.* . . . It is doubtless Russia that will one day furnish the irresistible flood of barbarians destined to destroy the old civilizations of the West."[4]

Le Bon chose Russia as the probable wellhead of the flood not because of the peculiar characteristics of that enigmatic "Russian soul" but because, for historical reasons, Russia contained the largest number of the domestic "barbarians" that he foresaw must some day be set on the march. "Each people," he noted, "contains an immense number of inferior elements incapable of adapting themselves to a civilization that is too superior for them. There results an enormous waste population, and the peoples who come to be invaded by it will have reason to dread the experience."[5]

Modern communism is only one species of an older, more durable, and far more pervasive challenge to civilization by the great mass of the culturally depressed. In that mass, which does not constitute a social or economic class, are discontented peasants and restless city poor, white collar workers and millionaires, and a notable sprinkling of frustrated intellectuals.[6] What they have in common, as Le Bon put it, is the inability to share in the ruling civilization within which they are cast. For the most part, the bulk is passive except when released by some such cataclysms as the Bolshevik, Nazi, or Fascist revolutions or when momentarily stirred by some such hysteria as McCarthyism. At these moments, the latent hostility against the superior culture which they do not share is set loose, and they become the destroyers.

If the problem of civilization is to resist the destroyers—and surely that must be what matters in our war against communism—then it also matters supremely how civilization responds to the challenge, what allies it calls up, and what battle flags it raises. On the European continent, where the stratification of society has been defended by ancient, though not necessarily legal, barriers to

[4] Le Bon (158); italics supplied.
[5] *Ibid.* Cf. also *supra,* p. 113, footnote.
[6] Cf. Almond (4) and Hoover (105); see Bibliographical Notes.

social and cultural mobility, the societies have been almost chronically threatened by invasion from below and have experimented with various countermeasures. In Mussolini's Italy and Hitler's Germany, the old society, hoping to save something of its values (not to mention its properties) negotiated surrender to the Fascist cultural underworld. There seemed to both sides to be certain advantages in the bargain in preference to violent revolution—advantages which, despite the lesson of history, continue to persuade many that dictatorships of the right are acceptable defenses against dictatorships of the left. The Fascist-Nazi invader gained legal title to rule and a working state machine manned by trained administrators. The old cultured classes, by terms of the surrender, were available to help curb the masses and thus save themselves along with their new masters from the excess fury of those who bitterly remain the have-nots through all political change. The nation, so organized, could not be immediately challenged by its neighbors, who were bound to recognize the new government as legitimate. Making it easier for the conquerors seemed also to help the old culture survive. There was no sharp break with the past. Many of the old leaders continued in positions of power. Their works were not immediately destroyed nor their example immediately decried.

Yet civilization has no reason to be grateful for the Fascist or Nazi experiments. The terms of surrender actually were seen to be intolerable by the truly civilized, who either fled the country or ceased contributing to it. In fact, the restraints on barbarian fury were more plausible than real. Surrender did not help the German Jews, characteristically persecuted not only as an alien race or as economic competitors but as outstanding bearers of urban culture. Neither the arts nor the institutions of civilization were saved under the dictatorships, despite the preservation of models from the past. Primitive tastes and primitive drives for power everywhere foisted on the old order the same paraphernalia of reactionary borrowings from precivilized culture.

In fact it has mattered little under what forms civilization has from time to time been defeated. The delusion that it does matter —that political *creeds* are reliable guides to the quality of political movements—is perhaps the most dangerous of civilized notions. Democracy, believing that the central issues of the cold war are

160

ideological, is constantly tempted to throw in its lot with the uncultured right against the uncultured left.

If McCarthyism had been seen culturally in its true colors, instead of in the assumed garb of anti-Communist ideology, it would never have climbed out of the gutter. The decent people who in honest confusion assented to chaos, saying "I don't like his methods, but—," would instead have seen at once that methods were of the cultural essence. Culturally, what the senator represented was not opposition to communism at all but another path into the same ethical jungle.

There may, indeed, be reasons of expediency for certain dubious alliances, but the clear lesson of history is that they lead into the wrong kinds of battle for the wrong causes. Faulty Western strategy was not to blame for the fact that victory in the war against Hitler resulted only in aggrandizement of the empire of Stalin. The truth is simply that war by its nature cannot give victory to the civilized. Barbarians fight on both sides, fattening on the conditions of strife. Whatever their professions of faith, they fight for the spoils of the world that each forever dreams of conquering. After each war they make their grab in the name of whatever rationalization is currently popular, while those who fought only to put down evil enjoy for a little while the illusion that they have done so.

We began by observing that we were to describe the peasant basis of Soviet society at the moment when peasant features had begun to merge, blur, and tangle with contradictions in the minds of increasingly sophisticated Soviet citizens. To a society no longer peasant[7] the peasant remnants have clung in ways baffling to the outsider and to the Soviet citizen himself. A British observer recently noted that in the Soviet Union today "one may hear townspeople speak of what is 'peasant' as *ipso facto* dirty and to be swept away in due course." At the same time, "industrial Russia is sufficiently established already to feel the need of a green echo"— a touch of back-to-nature. "To have peasant roots may recall the

[7] One is reminded, however, that the peasantry on land still make up 52 per cent of the whole population of the Soviet Union (as of January 15, 1959); cf. *Ezhegodnik* (71) for 1960, p. 6.

bad old days of bugs and illiteracy, of uncertain feeding and cramped living, of the unlighted life in the 'bears' corner,' but they can also be the good old days; they are the link with the father-figure who sings old folk-songs and raises honey . . ."[8] The very young are absorbed in escaping their present; the very old, in recalling their past. In between lie all the uncomfortable kinds of ambivalent desire that go along with growth. We may conclude by reviewing the mixture of old and new, with emphasis on the alteration of the basic material as it affects particularly relations with the outside world.

Stalin was a true primitive. The society he presided over like a tyrannical father was closed to outsiders and as rigidly organized to obey as the rural totalitarian household. Preoccupied with internal development and the consolidation of power, which was not after all completed until 1938—hardly more than a year before the war—he could not be more than a desultory imperialist. Success in the war, however, proved Soviet might and its responsiveness to command and so liberated the leader's megalomania. For a few convulsive years, the barbarian threatened to spring at the throat of weakened Western Europe. These years of open aggression and signs of internal madness burst on the democracies like a climax to the apocalyptic course of the Bolshevik revolution. Socialism bloodily triumphant in one country seemed ready at last openly to take on the world. The West, with the United States for the first time in the lead, girded for defense. Success between 1947 and 1954 in frustrating the Stalinist bid for empire contributed to the sense of having at last come to grips with an elusive problem which like a desperate itch just out of reach had been inflaming democratic nerves for years.

Yet, in fact, the apotheosis of Stalinism was anticlimax, even, in a sense, the convulsive shuddering of a system already dead. American reaction had hardly taken shape in the Truman Doctrine, the Marshall Plan, the North Atlantic Treaty Organization (NATO), before it was out of date. The mobilization of European resources and the initiation of European union under the spur of Soviet aggressiveness were wise and successful as policy of the day and had also long consequences for Europe's development. But so far as relations with the Soviet Union were concerned they closed an era.

[8] Wright W. Miller, *Russians as People* (New York, 1961), p. 62.

Stalin's death brought to an end the period when the cultural gulf between East and West was for all practical purposes absolute. In dying, he uncovered—and liberated—the cultural development of the transplanted traditionalist world of the village toward the diversity and individualism (however timidly expressed) characteristic of urban industrial society. That development, though still spotty, goes forward.

As the cultural gap between maturing Soviet society and the West is narrowed and bridged, the democracies face a more hopeful but at the same time more difficult relationship. In form, the opening of the Soviet Union to increasing cultural exchange has been a political decision suggesting a new leniency on Khrushchev's part or a new sense of security, or both. In substance, however, it looks rather like an unavoidable consequence of maturity. At least for the West, that is its significant aspect. The opportunities offered by freer access to the Soviet people would be muffed if they were thought of as primarily political chances to propagandize for democracy.

No honest observer, not even the most bitterly anti-Communist, has discovered in the Soviet Union today material for political counterrevolution. Few have seen any convincing signs pointing even to evolution toward democratic institutions. The young ex-Soviet school teacher, quoted before, in extreme revulsion against the vulgarity she found in Soviet life, writes of her recollection of a group of Soviet young people critically discussing "the new class." An embittered girl said that she would give her life to see the Soviet government swept away by a new revolution. "One of the boys asked, 'Whom would you strike first?'—and we all laughed." It is misleading to talk about an opposition to the regime, the schoolteacher comments. Not only can an opposition not be identified, but even the distinction between a "we" and a "they" can hardly be sustained in fact: "In the Soviet Union, everybody is discontented with something or other, but not necessarily with the same thing or with the same people."[9]

Thus the hated *they* are almost as indefinable as in the customary usage of disgruntled citizens of a democracy, who wonder why "they" don't fix the hole in the street. The opposing *we* is hardly more comprehensive than in similar complaints by editors. Intel-

[9] A. P. K.; see Bibliographical Notes.

lectuals (old style—chiefly scientists, writers, and artists) of course want more cultural freedom and continually push for it. But there is no indication that they would choose a democratic system on the Western model if they could get it, or that they could agree on any other. The new style intelligentsia, who are technicians, must be too conscious both of how far they have risen and of how great are their opportunities under the present regime to be considered promising recruits for revolutionary leadership.

As for the peasant mass still working the land in virtual serfdom, its political temper is difficult to judge. Unquestionably, the rural world has moved out of the physical and cultural isolation of the old days. The towns which have drawn off so many from the land remain as a magnet for the rest. More peasants can read. Movies, radio, and television, though hardly scattered about the country with an American or British prodigality, nevertheless do reach some.

How have the men and women themselves reacted to their new situation? By all accounts, the older generation who were moved to collective farms universally detest them.[10] Those too young to have known anything else seem less hostile. Less hostile but not, one gathers, more content. Complaints are frequent in the Soviet press against the slowness of peasants in following Party direction and against their tendency to relapse into the old ways, to observe church holidays, fasts, celebrations, local customs. Despite the clear gain of rather better education (though not so much better as generally believed in the West), relief from surplus labor (absorbed now by industry) and from the loan sharks (whose scissorhold on the peasant's personal economy, however, has been taken over by the Party), the multitude remain as before the great mass of the repressed. They appear now, as in the past, to seek refuge from oppression in recreating their isolation (aided more generally than before by alcohol) and transferring to new masters the old distrustful, uncooperative attitudes which they had always displayed to policemen, landlords, and kulaks. With customary peasant resourcefulness they have worked out their own mixture of old and new—a fascinating matter, incidentally, for detailed study

[10] This is the unanimous testimony of Soviet defectors; cf. Bauer (15), Inkeles (116), and Fainsod (72). For peasants in Belorussia and Ukraine during the war, see Dallin (55) and Vakar (295).

if one could be free to investigate it. In considering the Soviet peasantry as stuff for revolution, however, all the traditional reservations on the score of political passivity, disunity, and limited vision apply along with a new one: Soviet industrialization has reduced the peasantry from 85 per cent to 52 per cent of the whole population.[11]

For those who yearn for revolution, whether conceived of as righting wrong or as turning the rascals out, the dispersion of social protest and its almost total lack of political focus are discouraging. Yet considering the development of Russia and the peace of the world they ought not to be. Nonpolitical protest is the least likely to incur reaction and the most likely to promote just that sort of nonconformity which everywhere has been the support of freedom. It has, therefore, the best chance of destroying communism by making it culturally obsolete. So far as outsiders in their multiplying contacts with the Soviet Union can contribute to the process at all, it ought to be in nonpolitical ways, similarly designed to stimulate and satisfy the cultural curiosity of individuals whose own maturity is making the maturity of their society.

Peaceful co-existence, Khrushchev has announced, is just what communism needs to fulfill its manifest destiny of taking over the world. The Chinese Communists do not agree and so oppose the notion of co-existence. A good many Americans, curiously, do seem to agree; and so they also oppose co-existence, seeking either to redefine it in such a way as to eliminate the Marxist stigma or even questioning whether peace itself can be safely recommended. Such is the confusion wrought by the myth of a demonic Communist ideology.

Both Khrushchev and the professional anti-Communist who agree that one idea, one way of life, must fight all others to the death have misread history. History demonstrates the opposite. Ideological

[11] Note that the thesis that Stalinism was culturally a peasant revolution is not contradicted by the fact that the peasant as economic class suffered much and gained little. The truth is that the peasant was both the maker and the victim of the revolution exactly as he was maker and victim of his own village world. The kulaks prospered; the batraks suffered. So it was in the past, and so it came to be again when the kulaks turned into commissars and the batraks into kolkhozniki.

crusades not only fail universally but ordinarily within a few generations become irrelevant. It is difficult now even to imagine what once seemed so obviously irreconcilable in the irreconcilable conflict between, for instance, Christian and Moslem, or Catholic and Protestant. Nothing dates like fanaticism. Universal schemes for ordering the world are not defeated by rival schemes: all founder on the shoals of diversity, where the universality of human error is marked by a thousand monuments to a thousand different truths.

For purposes of this argument the point is that the truth or falsity of doctrine has had little to do with problems of co-existence. The most disparate faiths can—and do—co-exist with only so much uneasiness as testifies to their own vitality. America's dealings with dictatorships past and present may be endlessly argued on moral and practical grounds, but two things cannot be sensibly argued: First, a readiness to live peacefully together cannot be considered tantamount to moral surrender because, to be virtuous, we should then all be committed to endless violence over the most trivial differences; and second, as a practical matter, opposing ideologies need not interfere with peaceful relations between nations—in fact, they are more often than not irrelevant.

Ideological conflict is the least of the practical problems of co-existence. Much more difficult is the psychological gulf between men of different cultural experience and outlook. Across that gulf, communication has never been easy and is sometimes impossible. Increasing contacts with the Soviet Union, both diplomatic and cultural, have not meant an automatic narrowing of the gulf, but only a multiplication of the opportunities to confront it.

Correspondingly, the opportunities for exasperating failure have also multiplied. During the era of John Foster Dulles, failures were more notable than successes. The reasons were many, but a fundamental one was the Dulles diplomatic style, which mistook its adversary. The highly civilized American Secretary of State attempted to deal with shrewd, practical, blunt ex-peasant Russian leaders as though they were relapsed Presbyterian elders or shyster lawyers. Dulles legalisms could be brilliant; Dulles morality could be stern and true (if somewhat inclined to ice over with righteousness); but it tragically missed the mark and, in the end, achieved only explosive frustrations on both sides and deeper mutual distrust.

There is reason to believe, on the other hand, that Khrushchev's personal contact with President Eisenhower did open communication of a sort that might have been useful had the usefulness been better understood. Summit diplomacy has been defended on grounds that one might as well deal directly with the one man on the Soviet side who can commit his side to agreement. It has been attacked on grounds that reaching any sort of agreement in the exposed and rarefied atmosphere of summits is difficult and hazardous. Both arguments lie entirely within the traditional Western view of diplomacy. There is another consideration outside that view: that leaders of Khrushchev's background and experience neither respond to nor trust procedures in which the bases of accommodation are worked out by technicians, submitted for editing and approval to higher functionaries, and at last, in nearly final form, reach the chiefs of state for decision. The trouble with this process from Khrushchev's standpoint may be less the slight risk he takes in relying on the skill and honesty of his subordinates than his own inability to get the feel of what the other side is up to. Because his sense of reality is activated by what he can see with his own eyes and touch with his hands, he is impatient to confront his adversaries, particularly their leaders, to see where and how far he may put his trust. Psychologically, for him it is not the signature on a document that seals the bargain but the handshake of those who have personally undertaken it. In Eisenhower, it appeared as though Khrushchev had met a man whose handshake he might value even though it was by no means clear what bargain he had in mind, if any. He said he thought he could trust the President, and he seemed to believe so. Histrionic and politically motivated as the final blowup over the U-2 incident clearly was, it could have been wrapped around a kernel of genuine personal disappointment. At least, Khrushchev speaking to his world himself pretended that a sufficient explanation of the diplomatic break was that President Eisenhower personally had let him down.

One should not, of course, push too far speculations as to the constructive possibilities of personal contacts between Communist and Western leaders. Nothing in our analysis of Soviet communism or its leadership suggests that the warm glow of harmonious personalities is likely to melt the cold war. We argue rather the reverse: that the legalistic approach, the effort with words and diplomatic instruments to find compromises between opposing interests, fits neither the temper of Soviet leaders nor the nature of our quarrel with them. The notion of agreements binding on the sovereign power is, as we have seen, dependent on the concept of the rule of law, which is not recognized either in the Kremlin or in the village. The preconditions of adjusting disagreements by diplomacy, moreover, are either a basic community of interest or a readiness to accept certain rules of the game. Neither condition is to be found in conflicts of interest between ourselves and the Soviets, which dispute directly or indirectly each other's right to survive. The sole reason for not coming to blows is the desire on both sides to avoid the costly, if not disastrous, consequences of nuclear war. The sole reason for expecting progress toward a more stable relationship in the future is that the prospering and cultural maturing of the Soviet Union ought normally to make war still less desirable and the impulse to aggression less potent.

In these circumstances, "negotiation" with the U.S.S.R. cannot resemble the maneuvers of attorneys desiring to settle out of court. It must be more like a poker game or a bargaining session between kulaks in the village, where personal confrontation, with its mutual weighing of personalities, and strength of wit and will are of the very substance of the play. What is sought in this is not agreement but the pot. Assuming a fair balance of power and luck, however, the game need not end, and its practical consequence could be prolonged mutual forbearance. This is the essential exercise to buy time—time for further growth toward maturity—on both sides, for that matter. At the rate the processes of maturity now move we may need relatively little time. In any event the rewards of patience have never been so rich nor the costs of hot-headedness so catastrophic.

BIBLIOGRAPHICAL NOTES

TO TRY TO SET DOWN IN SCHOLARLY FORM THE SOURCES FROM WHICH
a point of view has been developed over a period of many years
would be difficult for the author and unrewarding for the reader.
It has seemed more sensible to me to supplement the particular
footnote references with some chapter-by-chapter discussion of
reading along the way, in order to help the reader pursue whatever special points may interest him and to indicate the areas
in which scholarly investigation has been well and richly done
and the areas in which it is scanty or altogether missing.

Russian sources, wherever possible, are referred to in existing
English translation, even though in some cases (e.g. Kliuchevsky,
Pushkin) I have preferred to use my own translation in the text.
Needless to say, the great bulk of the sources has never been published in English. More Americans are studying Russian nowadays
and, for their own attention, some of the more important native
studies also are mentioned here. The parenthetical numbers refer to
the entries in the appended Bibliography.

Chapter I—In order not to clog the argument unduly it has been
necessary to assume some knowledge of the course of Russian and
Soviet history. The standard texts are readily available in English—from *A Short History of Russia* by Richard Charques (New
York, 1958) to the more comprehensive histories by Bernard Pares
(New York, 1953), George V. Vernadsky (New Haven, 1954), or
Michael T. Florinsky (New York, 1953); for the Soviet period,
Georg von Rauch, *A History of Soviet Russia* (New York, 1960), or
Donald W. Treadgold (284) and Merle Fainsod (72) among many
others.

The story of the Bolshevik revolution is told in utmost detail by
E. H. Carr in his *History of Soviet Russia* (New York, 1950-59),

169

the first six volumes of which bring us to 1926. Events, of course, are seen in a different light by Soviet official historians or by Leon Trotsky (285) or Paul N. Miliukov (189) or N. N. Sukhanov (270). The fateful day of November 7 (October 25, Old Style) is best described by Sergei P. Melgunov in "Osada Zimnego dvortsa [Storming the Winter Palace]," *Novy Zhurnal*, XVII (New York, 1947); see also his carefully documented summary, *Kak bolsheviki zakhvatili vlast* [How the Bolsheviks Seized Power] (Paris, 1953); and, for the reaction of the leftist groups and organized labor, R. Abramovich's personal reminiscences in *Socialisticheski Vestnik* [The Socialist Courier] (New York, 1960).

The transformation of the Communist Party under Stalin has been observed by all students of Soviet history, albeit from different vantage points; cf. E. H. Carr (39), Trotsky (285), Brzezinski (36), Fainsod (72, 73), Avtorkhanov (10), Reshetar (235), Schapiro (242). The official portrait of Stalin has been retouched by Trotsky (286), Souvarine (261), Serge (245), Basseches (14), Ludwig (171), Lyons (174), Deutscher (59), and others.

For the civil war, early Soviet fiction has inestimable documentary value. Narratives and commentaries are in Struve (268) and Zavalishin (318); consult also *The American Bibliography of Slavic and East European Studies* (Indiana University, annual) for new translations and studies. The ordeal of the middle-class intelligentsia is best described by Ossorgin (210), and some readers may find it a better novel than Pasternak (215). For the White side see Denikin (58) and the relevant chapters in Miliukov (189); for the "Greens," the accounts gathered from scattered sources by Footman (84). No comprehensive history of the anti-Communist movements in Russia has yet been attempted.

For characterizations of the new Soviet élite, see notes to Chapters 6-10.

Chapter 2—Until the mid-nineteenth century Russian literature virtually ignored the peasant. Then three books—*Derevnia* [The Village] and *Anton Goremyka* by Dmitri Grigorovich and *Zapiski okhotnika* [Sketches of a Sportsman] by Ivan Turgenev, published in 1846, 1847, and 1852, respectively—seem to have touched off a romantic interest akin to the Western European excitement over the "noble savage." The image of the Russian peasant as the humble *syn zemli* (son of the soil) and *bogonosets* (vessel of God's grace), embodying the lost virtues of natural and Christian innocence, was quickly and firmly planted in literature where, even to this day, it has proved resistant to the harsher realities. These realities, though ably and early described by writers who observed the village more closely, like Gleb Uspensky (1843-1902) and P. Melnikov-Pechersky (1819-1891), never shook the general admiration for the child of nature or faith in his natural goodness. *The Cossacks* by Leo Tolstoy and the figure of Platon Karatayev in *War and Peace* (Part XII, Chapter 8) consecrated his image. Data about the real rural world piled up, however, during the last half of the century, to make an impressive mass of documentation; but it impressed the liberal intelligentsia so little that when Ivan Bunin published *Derevnia* [The Village] in 1910, and *Sukhodol,* in 1911, he was universally held to be slandering the unfortunate peasant. No one wished to believe that the primitive was himself largely responsible for the evils that plagued his life. It was as though the intelligentsia felt they had to hold to the myth of peasant nobility or lose faith in the future of Russia.

As for the Muscovite state, no comprehensive study comparable to our surveys of medieval Europe exists in English or other western languages. *Le moyen âge russe* (Paris, 1933) by Alexander Eck, however valuable as a pioneering effort, does not fill the gap. Of the three-volume history of the Muscovite period, undertaken by Professor George V. Vernadsky of Yale, only the first volume has so far appeared, *Russia at the Dawn of the Modern Age* (New Haven, 1959). Native sources both primary and secondary are abundant, but attempts at an integrated picture are rare. Illuminating are the historical novels, plays, epics, and poems (classic works by Alexander Pushkin, Mikhail Lermontov, Alexei K. Tolstoy, Mikhail Zagoskin; and more recent works by S. Borodin, A. Chapygin, V. Kostylev, G. Storm, Alexei N. Tolstoy, V. Yazvitsky)— some are available in English translations. Reports by foreign residents in, or visitors to, the city of Moscow in the sixteenth and seventeenth centuries are especially valuable. These are generally accessible in the original Latin, English, German, or French, and in translations. A broad picture can be found in Kliuchevsky (133), and a condensed one, in relevant chapters of the standard histories by Pares (214), Platonov (221), and others.

Works in English about the Dissent are few. Two with bibliographies are A. F. Heard, *The Russian Church and Russian Dissent* (New York, 1887), and F. C. Conybeare, *Russian Dissenters* (Cambridge, Mass., 1921). A succinct narrative of the movement by Sir Donald Mackenzie Wallace in *Russia* (revised and enlarged edition, London, 1912) stresses its significance and importance in the life of peasantry; some new light is thrown on it by studies of Zenkovsky (319, 320). *The Life of Archpriest Avvakum by Himself*, translated by Helen A. Isvolsky, is included in Fedotov (75). A dramatic description of *krasnaia smert* (usually translated "red," but in ancient parlance "excellent" or "handsome" death) can be found in Chapter Two of *Peter and Alexis,* a historical novel by Dimitri Merezhkovsky (New York, 1931); it is presented still more dramatically in *Khovanshchina,* the opera by Mussorgsky. For a Russian bibliography of the movement, see B. Anderson, *Staroobriadchestvo i sektantstvo* [The Old Believers and other Sectarians] St. Petersburg, 1915). Post-revolutionary Russian literature has made no significant contribution to the subject.

As general works about Russian culture and civilization before the revolution, one may suggest Masaryk (178), Miliukov (190), and Weidle (303); see also Kornilov (139), and the brief summary by Karpovich (124) for 1801-1917.

Chapters 3-4—Civilized societies seem to show little general concern about their peasantry. Agriculture is treated as an economic matter, and the farmer is taken for granted. Despite the recent expansion of anthropological studies and attempts to treat rural sociology and culture as separate disciplines, such works as W. I. Thomas and F. Znaniecki, *The Polish Peasant in Europe and America,* 4 vols. (Boston, 1918-20; reprint in two volumes, New York, 1959), are rare. One reason may be that, for the anthropologist, the study of the peasantry raises problems of definition and methodology; cf. Redfield (232).

Outstanding in the meager literature in English, Stepniak (265) remains as illuminating as sixty-five years ago, when it was written in protest against the degradation of peasants under Tsarist policy. Although the author shares the typical nineteenth-century admiration for the simple countryman, he portrays all the more vigorously the brutal reality which he saw, in shocking contrast to the ideal, which he believed to have been the reality of earlier and happier days. Sir Donald M. Wallace made some keen observations in his *Russia*. The English reader may find interesting information in such less well-known writings as B. L. Tollemache, *Russian Sketches, Chiefly from Peasant Life* (London, 1913), Kennard (127), or E. Poole, *The Village: Russian Impressions* (New York, 1919), as well as in translations of Russian fiction before and after the Revolution. A comprehensive study by Y. M. Sokolov, *Russian Folklore* (New York, 1950), and several collections of proverbs, such as Guershoon (97), are available in English, as well as in French and German. Stern (267) contains a unique and fascinating collection of profanities. Among the works by historians, the best known are Robinson (237) and Maynard (181, 182).

Russian special studies before and after the Revolution require careful critical evaluation. It took a German traveler (101) to discover for the Russians their peasant commune, known as *mir* or *obshchina*, which has since been regarded as a specifically and uniquely Russian phenomenon. That view has persisted in spite of the discoveries that a similar order once existed in Western Europe and still exists in China, India and Africa. Large peasant households considered typically Slavic, have been observed as far from the Slavic world as Madagascar; cf. Mosely (196), Linton (166), and Bossard (30). It would seem that peasant experience is much the same in all agricultural communities at a given level of development. The level in Russia was not generally higher than elsewhere. In fact, at the time of the Revolution, there were tribes in Siberia which still lived in a precivilized state. For characteristics common to primitive agricultural societies, see Redfield (233) and Kroeber (146). Russian anthropologists and ethnographers, so far as I know, have attempted no comparative studies on the scale found in western literature.

There exists no complete history of the Russian peasantry. B. Grekov's work, *Krestiane na Rusi* [Peasants in Russia], ends at the seventeenth century (Moscow, 1947; reprinted, 1954). For modern times, useful information can be found in such studies as A. Efimenko, *Issledovania narodnoy zhizni* [Inquiries into the Life of the People] (1884); A. Dzhivilegov *et al.*, *Velikaia reforma* [The

173

Great Reform], 4 vols. (1911); A. Kornilov *et al., Krestiansky stroy* [The Structure of Peasant Communities] (1905); V. Semevsky, *Krestiane v tsarstvovanie Ekateriny II* [Peasants under Catherine II], 2 vols. (1901-03); R. Kocharovsky, *Krestianskaia obshchina* [The Peasant Commune] (1908); A. Leontiev, *Krestianskoe pravo* [Peasant Law] (1909); E. Pakhman, *Obychnoe pravo* [Customary Law] (1913); A. Meiendorf, *Krestiansky dvor* [The Peasant Household] (1909); M. Kovalevsky, *Zakon i obychay na Kavkaze* [Law and Custom in the Caucasus], 2 vols. (1890); A. Khriashcheva, *Gruppy i klassy v krestianstve* [Social Stratification of the Peasantry], 2nd ed., (Moscow, 1926). In addition, a wealth of information is to be found in Russian newspapers, professional periodicals, and fiction from the 1840's to the present.

As one would expect, the Revolution seems to have changed the individual man little, if at all. In the Soviet novel, familiar peasant faces crowd up wherever the propagandist screen of "socialist realism" slips even slightly. The closed society has notably tried to hide its villages (except those organized for show) from outside view. Direct evidence is therefore patchy. An American anthropologist, allowed to live for a year among the Yugoslavian peasants (1953-54), found no evidence that communism, by changing institutions, had altered local habits or customs or had significantly affected the people's world outlook; cf. Joel M. Halpern, *A Serbian Village* (New York, 1958). Compare the Russian village thirty years after the Revolution, described by Konovalov (135), and forty years after, by Alexandr Andreyev ("Grachi prileteli [The Rooks Arrived]," *Oktiabr,* Moscow, 1960). A recent Soviet ex-citizen testifies that "rereading *Muzhiki* [The Peasants] by Anton Chekhov (42) would give you the most complete idea of what life in the remote Soviet villages is today"; cf. *Novoe Russkoe Slovo* (New York), 5 March 1961. In fact, looking at the photographs of Soviet common men and women in *Harper's Magazine* (May 1961, pp. 106, 115) one would not know, but for the captions, whether the pictures had been taken in 1960 or in 1910. In the Soviet press, the backwardness of "individual kolkhozes" is exposed more frequently than before, and it can even be detected in propaganda literature; cf. Valentin Ovechkin, *Collective Farm Sidelights* (Moscow, 1958).

The best descriptions of the homes into which most Soviet leaders were born can be found in such autobiographical works as Gladkov

(89) or Novikova-Vashentsova (204). The English reader will find illuminating Soviet novels such as L. Leonov, *The Badgers* (London, 1946) and *Sot,* published as *Soviet River* (New York, 1931); F. Panferov (213); B. Pilniak (217, 219); M. Sholokhov (253); he also may wish to reread Maxim Gorky's *Childhood* and Maurice Hindus (103).

Chapter 5—Although the Russian peasant communities had their own peculiarities, the parallels of peasant experience elsewhere are striking and illuminating. See, for instance, Kung-chuan Hsiao, *Rural China* (Seattle, 1960), and, for the Middle East, the brilliant summary account by F. Esfandiary in *The New York Times Magazine,* 24 March 1957.

Broad perspectives on peasant culture, stimulating if not wholly acceptable, may be found in René Porak, *Un village de France: Psycho-physiologie du paysan* (Paris, 1943). Kroeber (146), and Redfield (232). Barrington Moore (194) finds that "the entire framework of totalitarian controls existed before industrialism," but fails to identify the origins of totalitarianism in the traditional agricultural household.

Chapter 6—Among the many works describing the origins of Soviet communism, stimulating and provocative are Berdiaev (18), Weidle (303). Soviet historiography is largely an exercise in the invention of myths. For histories available in English, see the selective bibliography in Treadgold (284), pp. 421-434. Formal accounts are illuminated by reports of native and foreign observers and by the Soviet press and literature of the 1920's.

For Stalin's "land consciousness," see quotations in Ushakov (292), III, 1089, as well as his biographies. Svanidze (272) is significant, whether a fabrication or not. For the Party's sense of "ownership," as evidenced in their linguistic usage, see Vakar (298).

Among the Soviet historical fiction referred to in the text are the following: thirteenth century—Aleksandr Yugov, *Ratobortsy* [The Champions] (1949); V. Yan, *Alexander Nevsky* (Part III of the trilogy *Chengiz-Khan*); and the film *Alexander Nevsky* by Sergei Eisenstein; fourteenth century—*Dimitry Donskoy* by Sergei Borodin (awarded the Stalin Prize of literature); fifteenth century—*Ivan III* by V. Yazvitsky, 2 vols.; sixteenth century—Alexei N. Tolstoy, *Ivan Grozny* [Ivan the Terrible], a play, Part I, *Oriol i orlitsa* [The Eagle and His Mate] (1942); Part 2, *Trudnye gody* [The Hard Years] (1943); *Veliky Gosudar* [The Great Sovereign], a play by Vladimir Soloviev; and *Ivan Grozny*, a novel by Valentin Kostylev, 3 vols. (1941-45). (For a contrasting characterization of Ivan the Terrible, cf. *Smert Ioanna Groznogo* [The Death of Ivan the Terrible] by Alexei K. Tolstoy, 1866.) The most famous is *Piotr Pervy* [Peter the First], the monumental novel by Alexei N. Tolstoy: Book I, 1929; Book II, 1933; Book III, 1944; and six additional chapters, 1945 posthumous; an English version, *Peter the First* (New York, 1959). For comments see Karpovich (125), Twarog (290, 291), and Backer (12).

The by-laws of the Communist Party of the Soviet Union (English text) can be found in Meisner (186); see also Avtorkhanov (10), Reshetar (235), and Schapiro (242). What makes a Communist is discussed by Monnerot (193), Almond (4), Gates (87), Hoffer (104), and Hoover (105), among others. A companion to *Darkness at Noon* by Arthur Koestler is Victor Serge (246).

The text, generally accepted as authentic, of Khrushchev's address to the Twentieth Party Congress has been widely published abroad, but not in the Soviet Union. His other public statements have already been translated into 198 languages—according to the UNESCO survey of literature in translations for 1959, Lenin runs second with 174 languages, then the Bible—171, Leo Tolstoy—130, Jules Verne—124, Dostoevsky—114, Agatha Christie—104, etc. An attempt at a political biography, George Paloczi-Horvath, *Khrushchev: The Road to Power* (London, 1960), is rather abstract and unsatisfactory.

Chapter 7—Hardly a day passes without new reports from the Soviet scene, their worth depending on the observer's sensibility and perspective. Unusual in this regard are the impressions of Zinaida Schakhovskoy (241) who, after some forty years, revisited the country she had left at the age of sixteen. Among other works bringing out the contrast between the pre- and postrevolutionary cultures are Simmons (256) and Weidle (303). For a comparative perspective in evaluating Soviet reality, see Masaryk (178), Miliukov (190), Karpovich (124), and Kornilov (139).

The old Russian intelligentsia, a phenomenon in many regards unique in the history of Western civilization, has been subject of the most diverse definitions and interpretations. A collection of the views of American scholars has been published in *Daedalus,* Journal of the American Academy of Arts and Sciences (Summer 1960), and reprinted as *The Russian Intelligentsia,* ed. Richard Pipes (New York, 1961). The Russians' own critical and highly contradictory views are sampled in the collection of articles *Vekhi* [Signposts] (Moscow, 1909); the discussion was continued in *émigré* literature by Ilya Bunakov, Nikolai Berdiaev, George Fedotov, Mark Vishniak, Nikolai Ulianov, and others; and the views are as sharply opposed today as ever before. The portrait of the intellectual in the Russian novel has common features but many different shadings. The reader may find illuminating such studies as Hare (100), Carr (40), Bowman (31), Billington (28). The plight of the old intelligentsia under the Soviets has been described in many works; among them, worthy of fresh attention, are Aldanov (1) and Ossorgin (210).

The new Soviet intelligentsia is of a different breed. Among the numerous attempts at describing it, the most penetrating are Isaiah Berlin (27) and L. (152); for Soviet scientists, see Turkevich (288, 289); many keen observations have been made by Bryner (35), Feuer (79), Haimson (98), Inkeles (115), Labedz (153), Seton-Watson (247, 248), and Shils (251). For the Russian educational system before and after the Revolution, see Kaidanova (122) and Johnson (121); for subsequent changes, Counts (47, 48, 49), Kline (132), Shore (254), Alt (5), Bereday (25), and others.

Useful guides to what "proletarian culture" meant in the twenties and the thirties are Struve (268) and Zavalishin (318), as well as the monograph by Edward J. Brown, *The Proletarian Episode in Russian Literature, 1928-1932* (New York, 1953); see also Gorchakov (90) and Kurt London (168). Insights into the contemporary cultural scene are to be found in Berlin (27), Jelagin (119), Laqueur (155), and Struve (268). Soviet policy toward books and writers has been authoritatively expounded by Alexei Zhdanov, Maxim Gorky *et al.* in *Problems of Soviet Literature: Reports and Speeches at the First Soviet Writers' Congress* (Moscow, 1935); by Alexei Zhdanov, *Essays on Literature, Philosophy and Music* (1948); and by Nikita S. Khrushchev in his address to the Third Congress of Soviet Writers (1959). Soviet achievements in forty

177

years are summed up by Kim (130); statistical data are collected in *Kulturnoe stroitelstvo* (149). For an evaluation by outsiders, see "Soviet Literature Yesterday and Today," a collection of articles in *Soviet Survey*, No. 36 (April-June 1961).

Soviet linguistic usage has not been systematically examined since Selishchev (244). Valuable observations are scattered among various Soviet publications. An attempt to organize the data has been made by Fesenko (78); see also Hunt (111) and Vakar (296, 297, 298). The field of comprehensive linguistic analysis has been hardly touched.

The campaign against "bad taste" is especially vigorous in the pages of *Komsomolskaia Pravda* (Moscow). A leading article, "Aesthetic Training in Shaping the New Man," was published by *Kommunist* in May, 1959. It has been presently followed by a detailed manual on good manners, *O tom, chto prilichno i neprilichno* [About What Is Seemly and Unseemly] (Moscow, 1960). In the press, as well as in specialized periodicals, discussions of the western tastes in fine arts, music, architecture, furniture, etc., are more frequent than before.

Chapter 8—The contrasts between Marxist theory and Communist practice provide an inexhaustible theme in western literature. For discussion from a philosophical point of view, see Wetter (307) and Marcuse (177); books written from political, economic, sociological, or psychological points of views are too many to be listed here; but see Hunt (109, 110) and Monnerot (193). Soviet Communist theory today is discussed by Lichtheim (165) and Wolfe (312). The currently accepted tenets of Party orthodoxy are set forth in *Fundamentals of Marxism-Leninism,* edited by O. Kuusinen, (Moscow, 1961); it is noteworthy that the only authorities now recognized are Marx, Engels, and Lenin.

On the similarities between communism and Christianity, see Hordern (106). For the impact of Marxism-Leninism on the Christian mind, see Cuninggim (52), West (306), and René Rémond, *Les Catholiques, le Communisme, et les Crises, 1929-1939* (Paris, 1960). The Communists, of course, reject those views; cf. Timasheff (274, 275). As to the Communist Russian mind, Berdiaev's works (18 to 24) are full of stimulating insights.

The mind of the Russian peasant, his customs and practices, and

especially his attitude toward religion and the clergy are documented by studies in ethnography, church history and folklore and,
more widely and dramatically, in the Russian novel. The English
reader can find some information summed up in Stepniak (265)
and in S. Bolshakov, *Russian Nonconformity* (Philadelphia, 1950).
Especially interesting are descriptions (by P. Melnikov-Pechersky
and G. Grebenshchikov, for instance) of life in the communities
of Old Believers; see Shiriaev (252). The peasants' simple religiousness, admired by many Russian writers before the Revolution, impressed some foreign travelers as well; cf. Stephen Graham,
The Way of Martha and the Way of Mary (London, 1915). For
similar views of the contemporary scene, see C. Krypton, "Secret
Religious Organizations in the U.S.S.R.," *The Russian Review*, 14
(April 1955), pp. 121-127. Anticlerical folklore has been collected
by Vishnevskaia (300); see also (224) and (267). The source for
religious data from the 1937 Soviet general census is Emelian Yaroslavsky, President of the Union of the Godless, as quoted in Timasheff (274); see also Curtiss (53). *Religion in the U.S.S.R.* (Munich,
1960) is an attempt to appraise the present state of religion under
the Soviets.

Chapter 9—Information on the origins and structure of the
Soviet Communist elite can be found in Fainsod (72, 73), Bauer
(15), Brzezinski (36), Avtorkhanov (10), Armstrong (7), Meisner
(186), Reshetar (235), and Schapiro (242); see also Kitaeff (131).
The emergence of new social classes or castes in Soviet society has
been discussed by Dallin (56, 57), Feldmesser (76), Inkeles (114,
115), Kulski (148), Pool (223), Sandomirsky (240), and Seton-
Watson (247); pertinent are Djilas (63) and Dudintsev (66).
Recent studies are Ernst Halperin, "The Metamorphosis of the
New Class," *Problems of Communism*, VIII, 4 (July-August 1959),
pp. 17-22; Arcadius Kahan, "The Peasant, the Party and the
System," *Problems of Communism*, IX, 4 (July-August 1960), pp.
27-36; Paul Barton, "The Current Status of the Soviet Worker,"
ibid, pp. 18-36; for reader discussions, see *Problems of Communism*,
IX, 6 (November-December 1960), pp. 38-47.

However clouded by the dictates of "socialist realism," the
Soviet press and Soviet literature often give illuminating pictures
of the ruling class, particularly of the middle-aged group. (The

seniors who remain are too high up to be mirrored even obliquely, and the juniors have only begun to enter the scene.) Pertinent data have been extracted by Simmons (255), Cook (46), Matthewson (180), Haimson (98), and others already cited.

The story of the waifs of the twenties and thirties is the part of Soviet history the least investigated in western literature. For the twenties, the only noteworthy study is Zenzinov (321)—all the more impressive as it was based exclusively on Soviet official sources; see also Makarenko (175), an account by a Soviet educator of that time. For the thirties, when the situation was worse, sources are scattered and scant. In English literature, the autobiographical story by Voinov (301) stands out as a document unique of its kind. Fisher (83) is a study of the Komsomol and affiliated youth organizations, from 1918 to 1954, based on official sources. The institute for the Study of the USSR has published a collection of articles by six ex-Komsomol members, *Komsomol* (Munich, 1960); and, in English, *Soviet Youth. Twelve Komsomol Histories* (Munich, 1959). Feuer (79) also has used personal stories to describe the younger generation, and Vera Alexandrova has gleaned facts from Soviet printed sources in "Soviet Youth in Life and Literature," *Problems of Communism*, VIII, 4 (July-August 1959), pp. 30-35. Articles on juvenile delinquency, parasitism, and snobbery are frequent in the Soviet press; for sociological discussion, see Field (80).

Foreign visitors have generally been favorably impressed with Soviet youth and are often enthusiastic. Wright W. Miller, *Russians as People* (New York, 1961), is a penetrating and sympathetic report. Tim Callaghan gives a soberer picture, at least of the Soviet students with whom he spent the academic year 1958-59 at Moscow University, in "Studying the Students," *Soviet Survey*, 33 (July-September 1960), pp. 12-19. Recent Soviet defectors in that age group tend to be either cautiously critical (e.g. David Burg, "Observations on Soviet University Students," *Daedalus* (Summer 1960), pp. 520-540, and "The Voice of a Dissenter: An Interview with a Graduate of Moscow University," *Harper's Magazine* (May 1961), pp. 122-131, or bitterly adverse, e.g. A. P. K. in a series of articles in *Novoe Russkoe Slovo* (March-April 1961). The latter author, a young ex-schoolteacher in Moscow, depicts the privileged Soviet youth in devastating terms. Her articles aroused impassioned discussion in the Russian *émigré* press, and the facts she has related are minimized or downright denied. But the Soviet press confirms that "in Moscow province alone there are 15,000 young men and women," who graduated from the best Soviet schools, but who "do not work and live off their parents"; cf. *Kommunist,* No. 9 (1960), p. 55.

Chapter 10—There have been many inquiries into the "Russian character" or the "Russian mind" or the "Russian soul" both by foreigners and by Russians themselves. Among the more recent are Berdiaev (21), Gorer (91), Arseniev (9), Lossky (169), and Miller, *op. cit.* The most pessimistic view has been expressed by a Pole—Duchinski (65)—the most optimistic by a German: Schubart (243). Russian seekers have oscillated between bright visions and despair, never lingering in a middle ground where consensus might be possible.

The search for national essences, in whatever form, has so far contributed little to an understanding of the Russian scene. Far more light is thrown by broader sociological perspectives, as in Le Play (159), Le Bon (157, 158), Ortega y Gasset (207, 208), and the works of Wilfredo Pareto, Gaetano Mosca, and Nikolai Berdiaev, even though these tend to be dismissed nowadays as hopelessly outdated and, in any case, irrelevant to the state of Soviet affairs. In fact, their surprising relevance today reinforces the view that in Soviet communism one is dealing in substance with universal cultural phenomena. So there has developed a quite unexpected affinity among Russian, Chinese, Congolese, and Cuban souls.

The story related on page 163 is published in *Novy Zhurnal,* 63 (New York, 1961), pp. 7-59. For general information, books on communism published in English since 1945 are listed in Hunt (112).

These books and articles have been referred to in text; others are given in footnotes.

1. ALDANOV, MARK. *The Fifth Seal,* a novel (New York, 1943).
2. ———. *Samoubistvo* [Suicide], a novel (New York, 1959).
3. ALEKSANDROV, G.; GALIANOV, V.; and RUBINSTEIN, N. (eds.). *Politicheski slovar* [Political Dictionary] (Moscow, 1940).
4. ALMOND, GABRIEL, *et al. The Appeals of Communism* (Princeton, N.J., 1954).
5. ALT, HERSCHEL and EDITH. *Russia's Children* (New York, 1959).
6. ANDERSON, M. S. *Britain's Discovery of Russia, 1553-1815* (New York, 1958).
7. ARMSTRONG, JOHN A. *The Soviet Bureaucratic Elite* (New York, 1959).
8. ARON, RAYMOND. *The Opium of the Intellectuals* (New York, 1958).
9. ARSENIEV, N. S. "Russkie prostory i narodnaia dusha [Russia's Vastness and the National Soul]." *Grani,* 17 (West Germany, 1953), 118-132.
10. AVTORKHANOV, ABDURAKHMAN. *Tekhnologia vlasti. Protsess obrazovania KPSS;* published in English as *Stalin and the Soviet Communist Party: A Study in the Technology of Power* (New York, 1959).
11. AVVAKUM, ARCHPRIEST. *The Life of Archpriest Avvakum by Himself,* in FEDOTOV (75), 134-181.
12. BACKER, G. *The Deadly Parallel: Stalin and Ivan the Terrible* (New York, 1950).
13. BAHDER, EGON VON. *Osteuropa,* 3 (West Germany, 1952).
14. BASSECHES, NIKOLAUS. *Stalin.* Translated from the German by E. W. DICKES (London-New York 1952).
15. BAUER, RAYMOND A.; INKELES, ALEX; and KLUCKHOHN, CLYDE. *How the Soviet System Works* (Cambridge, Mass., 1956).
16. BELINSKY, VISSARION. "Letter to Gogol," in *Treasury of Russian Literature,* ed. BERNARD G. GUERNEY (New York, 1953); see also BOWMAN (31).
17. BENEDICT, RUTH. "Marital Property Rights in Bilateral Society," *American Anthropologist,* 38 (1936), 369-372; also in STERN (266), 13-16.

18. BERDIAEV, NIKOLAI A. *The Origin of Russian Communism* (London, 1937; reprints, 1948, 1955).
19. ———. *The General Line of Soviet Philosophy* (London, 1933).
20. ———. *The Realm of Spirit and the Realm of Caesar* (New York, 1952).
21. ———. *The Russian Idea* (New York, 1948).
22. ———. *Russkaia religioznaia psikhologia i kommunisticheski ateizm* [Russian Philosophy of Religion and the Communist Atheism] (Paris, 1931).
23. ———. *Marksizm i religia* [Marxism and Religion] (Paris, 1928).
24. ———. "Gogol v russkoi revolutsii [The Gogolian Element in the Russian Revolution]," in the collection of articles *Iz glubiny* [De Profundis] (published privately, Moscow, 1921); reprinted, *Vestnik Russkogo Studencheskogo Christianskogo Dvizhenia,* Vol. II, No. 53 (Paris, 1959).
25. BEREDAY, GEORGE Z. F. and PENNAR, JAAN (eds.). *The Politics of Soviet Education* (New York, 1960).
26. BERMAN, HAROLD J., review of CARSON (41) in *Annals of the American Academy of Political and Social Science* (May 1956).
27. BERLIN, ISAIAH. "The Silence in Russian Culture," *Foreign Affairs,* 36 (October 1957).
28. BILINGTON, JAMES H. *Mikhailovsky and Russian Populism* (New York, 1958); for more extensive treatment of the period, see VENTURI (299).
29. BORODIN, SERGEI. *Dmitry Donskoy,* a historical novel (Moscow, 1949).
30. BOSSARD, JAMES H. S. and BELL, ELEANOR S. *The Large Family System* (Philadelphia, 1956).
31. BOWMAN, HERBERT S. *Vissarion Belinsky, 1811-1848: A Study in the Origins of Social Criticism in Russia* (Cambridge, Mass., 1955).
32. BOYKOV, MIKHAIL. *Uzniki sovetskikh tiurem* [The Inmates of Soviet Prisons] (Buenos Aires, 1957).
33. BRESHKO-BRESHKOVSKY, CATHERINE. "Vospominania [Memoirs]," *Novy Zhurnal,* 38 (New York, 1954).
34. BRINTON, CRANE. *The Anatomy of Revolution,* (New York, rev. ed., 1957).
35. BRYNER, C. "Lenin and the Search for an Elite," *Canadian Slavonic Papers,* II (Toronto, 1958).
36. BRZEZINSKI, Z. K. *The Permanent Purge: The Purge as a Technique of Soviet Totalitarian Politics from the Rise of Stalin to the Fall of Malenkov* (Cambridge, Mass., 1956).
37. BUNIN, IVAN A. *The Village.* Translated by ISABEL F. HAPGOOD from the Russian *Derevnia,* published in 1911 (New York, 1933).
38. CALHUN, ARTHUR W. "The Early American Family," *The Annals of the American Academy of Political and Social Science,* 160 (March 1932): also in STERN (266).

39. CARR, EDWARD HALLETT. *A History of Soviet Russia*—monumental work, of which six volumes have so far appeared; Vol. VI, *Socialism in One Country*, covers 1924-1926 (New York, 1958).

40. ———. *Romantic Exiles* (New York, paperback reprint, 1952).

41. CARSON, GEORGE B., JR. *Electoral Practices in the USSR* (New York, 1955); see also BERMAN (26).

42. CHEKHOV, ANTON. "Peasants," *Portable Chekhov*, ed. AVRAHM YARMOLINSKY (New York, 1947).

43. ———. *Ward No. 6*, in GUERNEY (96), 244-322.

44. CHETVERIKOV, DMITRY. *Liuban*, a novel (Moscow, 1928).

45. COMMAGER, HENRY STEELE. *The American Mind: An Interpretation of American Thought and Character since the 1880s* (New Haven, 1950).

46. COOK, PHILIP BRUCE. "The Party Secretary in the Post-War Soviet Novel," *Soviet Survey*, 23 (January-March 1958), 42-46.

47. COUNTS, GEORGE S. *The Challenge of Soviet Education* (New York, 1957).

48. COUNTS, GEORGE S. and LODGE, NUCIA P. *The Country of the Blind: The Soviet System of Mind Control* (Boston, 1949).

49. ———. *"I Want To Be Like Stalin."* Translated from the Russian (New York, 1947).

50. CPSU History. *History of the Communist Party of the Soviet Union;* an English translation of the standard Soviet textbook (Moscow, 1938; revised, 1960).

51. *Criminal Code of the R.S.F.S.R.*, revised as of March 1, 1957; references appended (Moscow, 1957).

52. CUNNINGGIM, MERRIMON (ed.). *Christianity and Communism: An Inquiry into Relationships* (Dallas, Texas, 1958).

53. CURTISS, JOHN S. *The Russian Church and the Soviet State, 1917-1950* (Boston, 1953).

54. DAHL, VLADIMIR. *Tolkovy slovar zhivogo velikorusskogo yazyka* [Explanatory Dictionary of the Spoken Russian Language] (Moscow, 1955, reprint).

55. DALLIN, ALEXANDER. *German Rule in Russia, 1941-1945: A Study of Occupation Policies* (New York, 1957).

56. DALLIN, DAVID J. *The Real Soviet Russia* (New Haven, 1944).

57. ———. "Classes among the Soviets," *Catholic World*, 160 (1945), 363-364.

58. DENIKIN, ANTON I. *Ocherki russkoi smuty* [Story of the Russian Civil War] published in English as *The White Army* (London, 1930).

59. DEUTSCHER, ISAAC. *Stalin: A Political Biography* (New York, 1949).

60. ———. *The Prophet Armed* (New York, 1954).

61. DICKS, HENRY V. "Observations on Contemporary Russian Behavior," *Human Relations*, 5 (1952), 111-175.

62. DINERSTEIN, HERBERT S. *Communism and the Russian Peasant* (Glencoe, Ill., 1955).

63. DJILAS, MILOVAN. *The New Class: An Analysis of the Communist System* (New York, 1957).

64. DOSTOEVSKY, FEDOR. *The Idiot,* a novel (New York, 1916).

65. DUCHINSKI, FR. *Peuples âryas et tourans. Nécessité des reformes dans l'exposition de l'histoire des peuples âryas-européens et tourans, particulièrement des Slaves et des Moscovites* (Paris, 1864).

66. DUDINTSEV, VLADIMIR. *Not by Bread Alone,* a novel (London-New York, 1957).

67. EARLE, ALICE M. *Child Life in Colonial Days* (New York, 1909).

68. ECKARDT, HANS V. *Ivan the Terrible* (New York, 1949).

69. ELISSÉEFF, SERGE. "The Orthodox Church and the Russian Merchant Class," *Harvard Theological Review,* XLIX, 4 (October 1956).

70. EHRENBURG, ILYA. *Out of Chaos,* a novel (Moscow, 1930).

71. *Ezhegodnik* [Year Book] of the Great Soviet Encyclopedia, 1958, 1959, 1960.

72. FAINSOD, MERLE. *How Russia Is Ruled* (Cambridge, Mass., 1953).

73. ———. *Smolensk under Soviet Rule* (Cambridge, Mass., 1958).

74. FAIRCHILD, MILDRED. "The Russian Family Life Today," *Journal of the American Association of University Women,* XXX, 3 (April 1937), 142-148; also in STERN (266), 400-411.

75. FEDOTOV, GEORGE P. (ed.). *A Treasury of Russian Spirituality* (New York, 1948).

76. FELDMESSER, ROBERT A. "The Persistence of Status Advantages in Soviet Russia," *The American Journal of Sociology,* 59 (July 1953), 19-27.

77. FENNELL, J. L. I. (ed.). *The Correspondence between Prince A. M. Kurbsky and Tsar Ivan IV of Russia, 1564-1579* (Cambridge, Engl., 1956).

78. FESENKO, ANDREI and TATIANA. *Russki yazyk pri Sovetakh* [Russian Language under the Soviets]; a useful bibliography (New York, 1955).

79. FEUER, KATHRYN. "Russia's Young Intellectuals," *Encounter,* 8 (February 1957), 10-25.

80. FIELD, MARK G. "Alcoholism, Crime and Delinquency in Soviet Society," *Social Problems,* 3 (October 1955), 100-108.

81. FIRTH, RAYMOND. *Human Types* (New York, paperback, 1960).

82. FISHER, GEORGE. *Soviet Opposition to Stalin* (Cambridge, Mass., 1952).

83. FISHER, RALPH T., JR. *Pattern for Soviet Youth* (New York, 1959).

84. FOOTMAN, DAVID (ed.). *Soviet Affairs,* No. 2 (St. Anthony's Papers, No. 6, London 1959).

85. FRIEDRICH, CARL J. (ed.). *Totalitarianism* (Cambridge, Mass., 1954).

86. FRIEDRICH, CARL J., and BRZEZINSKI, Z. K. *Totalitarian Dictatorship and Autocracy* (Cambridge, Mass., 1956).

87. GATES, JOHN. *The Story of an American Communist* (London, 1959).

88. GLADKOV, FEDOR. *Cement,* a novel (Moscow, 1925).

89. ———. *Povest o detstve* [The Story of a Childhood] (Moscow, 1953).

90. GORCHAKOV, NIKOLAI. *Istoria sovetskogo teatra* (New York, 1956); an English translation, *The Theatre in Soviet Russia* (New York, 1957).

91. GORER, GEOFFREY. *The People of Great Russia: A Psychological Study* (New York, 1949).

92. GORKY, MAXIM. *O literature* [About Literature]; a collection of articles and speeches, 1926-1936; 3rd. ed. (Moscow, 1937).

93. *Gorki i voprosy sovetskoi literatury* [Gorky and the Problems of Soviet Literature]; a collection of articles (Leningrad, 1956).

94. GREBENSHCHIKOV, GEORGE D. *Churaevy* [The Churaevs], a family chronicle in several volumes. One volume translated into English as *The Turbulent Giant: An Epic Novel on Russian Peasantry* (Churaevka, Conn., 1940).

95. GSOVSKY, VLADIMIR. "The Soviet Union's Revised Criminal Code," *New Leader,* 27 April 1959.

96. GUERNEY, BERNARD G. *The Portable Russian Reader* (New York, 1947).

97. GUERSHOON, ANDREW. *Russian Proverbs* (London, 1941).

98. HAIMSON, LEOPOLD H. "Three Generations of the Soviet Intelligentsia," *Foreign Affairs* (January 1959), 235-246.

99. HANDLIN, OSCAR. *The Uprooted* (Boston, 1951).

100. HARE, RICHARD. *Pioneers of Russian Social Thought* (London, 1951).

101. HAXTHAUSEN, AUGUST V. *Studien ueber die innern Zustaende, das Volksleben und insbesondere die laendliche Einrichtung Russlands,* 3 vols. (Hannover, Germany, 1847).

102. HERBERSTEIN, BARON SIGISMUND. *Rerum moscovitarum commentarii* (Basel, 1551); quoted by WOLFF (313).

103. HINDUS, MAURICE. *Broken Earth* (New York, 1926); further pictures of peasant life can be found in his *Humanity Uprooted* (1929), *Red Bread* (1931), and *Mother Russia* (1942).

104. HOFFER, ERIC. *The True Believer* (New York, 1951).

105. HOOVER, EDGAR J. *Masters of Deceit: The Story of Communism in America and How to Fight It* (New York, 1958).

106. HORDERN, WILLIAM. *Christianity, Communism and History.* (London, 1957).

107. HORKHEIMER, MAX. "The Problem and Its Setting," *Studien*

ueber Autoritaet und Familie, Schriften des Instituts fuer Sozial-
forschung, XV Band (Paris 1936), 905-907; also in STERN (266).
108. HUIZINGA, JOHAN. *Homo Ludens. Versuch einer Bestimmung
des Spielelementes der Kultur* (1939); appeared in English as
Homo Ludens: A Study of the Play-Element in Culture (New
York, 1949); see also ORTEGA Y GASSET (207, 208).
109. HUNT, R. N. CAREW. *The Theory and Practice of Communism*
(New York, 1950).
110. ———. *Marxism: Past and Present.* New York, 1955.
111. ———. *A Guide to Communist Jargon* (New York, 1957).
112. ———. *Books on Communism* (London, 1959).
113. ILF, I., and PETROV, E. *Zolotoy telets* (Moscow, 1927); published
in English as *The Little Golden Calf: A Satiric Novel* (London-
New York, 1932); excerpts in KUNITZ (151).
114. INKELES, ALEX. "Social Stratification and Mobility in the Soviet
Union, 1940-1950," *The American Sociological Review,* 15
(August 1950), 465-479.
115. ———. "Images of Class Relations among Former Soviet Citizens," *Social Problems,* 3 (January 1956), 181-196.
116. INKELES, ALEX, and BAUER, RAYMOND A. *The Soviet Citizen:
Daily Life in a Totalitarian Society* (Cambridge, Mass., 1959).
117. IVANOVICH, STEPAN O. *Rossiskaia Kommunisticheskaia partia* [The
Russian Communist Party] (Berlin, 1924).
118. IZUTZU, TOSHIHIKO. *Language and Magic: Studies in the Magical Function of Speech* (Tokyo, 1956).
119. JELAGIN, YURI. *Taming of the Arts* (New York, 1951).
120. JENKINS, M. "Pisemsky's 'Bitter Fate': The First Outstanding
Drama of Russian Peasant Life," *Canadian Slavonic Papers,* III
(Toronto 1959).
121. JOHNSON, WILLIAM H. E. *Russia's Educational Heritage* (New
Brunswick, N. J., 1950).
122. KAIDANOVA-BERVY, OLGA. *History of Public Education in Russia:
I. Imperial Regime; II . Under Soviet Government* (New York,
1948).
123. KALB, MARVIN L. *Eastern Exposure* (New York, 1958); his diary
quoted, *The New York Times Magazine,* 28 July 1957.
124. KARPOVICH, MICHAEL M. *Imperial Russia, 1801-1917* (New York,
1932).
125. ———. "Soviet Historical Novel," *The Russian Review,* Vol. 5,
No. 2 (Spring 1946).
126. KASENKINA, OKSANA. *Leap to Freedom* (Philadelphia, 1949).
127. KENNARD, HOWARD P. *The Russian Peasant* (Philadelphia, 1908).
128. KHLEBNIKOV, N. *Obshchestvo i gosudarstvo v do-mongolski period
russkoi istorii* [Society and Government in the Pre-Mongolian
Period of Russian History] (St. Petersburg, 1872).
129. *Khoziaistvo Sovetskogo Soiuza v 1958 godu* [Soviet Economy in
1958]; official statistics (Moscow, 1959).

130. KIM, M. P. *40 let sovetskoi kultury* [Forty Years of Soviet Culture] (Moscow, 1957).

131. KITAEFF, MIKHAIL. *Communist Party Officials: A Group of Portraits* (New York, 1954).

132. KLINE, GEORGE L. (ed.). *Soviet Education* (New York, 1957).

133. KLIUCHEVSKY, V. O. *Kurs russkoi istorii* [Lectures on Russian History] 2nd ed. (Moscow, 1937); American reprint, 5 vols. (1944-49). An English translation, *The History of Russia*, 5 vols. (London, 1910-11; new edition, 1960).

134. *Komsomol* [The Communist Youth League]; a collection of articles by ex-Komsomol members (Munich, 1960); an English version, *Soviet Youth. Twelve Komsomol Histories* (Munich, 1959).

135. KONOVALOV, GRIGORI. *Stepnoy mayak* [A Lighthouse in the Steppe], a novel (Moscow, 1949).

136. KLUCKHOHN, CLYDE; BAUER, RAYMOND A.; and INKELES, ALEX. *The Soviet System: Cultural, Psychological and Social Themes* (Cambridge, Mass., 1956).

137. KOPTIAEVA, ANTONINA. *Ivan Ivanovich*, a novel, winning Stalin Prize for Literature (Moscow, 1949).

138. KORIAKOV, MIKHAIL. *I'll Never Go Back*. Translated from the Russian by NICHOLAS WREDEN (New York, 1948).

139. KORNILOV, A. A. *Modern Russian History*, 2 vols, (New York, 1917).

140. KOSTYLEV, VALENTIN. *Ivan Grozny* [Ivan the Terrible], a historical novel; 3 vols. (Moscow, 1941-45).

141. KRASNOV, N. N., JR. *Nezabyvaemoe* [Unforgettable]; ten years in the Soviet slave labor camps, 1946-1956 (Buenos Aires 1957).

142. KRAVCHENKO, VICTOR. *I Chose Freedom: The Personal and Political Life of a Soviet Official* (New York, 1946).

143. *Kravchenko versus Moscow*, ed. TRAVERS HUMPHREYS (New York, 1950); report of the Paris libel case.

144. KRAVCHINSKY, S. (STEPNIAK). *The Russian Peasantry: The Agrarian Conditions, Social Life and Religion*, 2 vols. (London, 1888); see STEPNIAK (265).

145. KRIZHAN, *O tom, chto prilichno i neprilichno* [About What Is Seemly and Unseemly]; a book of good manners (Moscow, 1960).

146. KROEBER, ALFRED L. *Anthropology: Race, Language, Culture, Psychology, Pre-history* (New York, 1948).

147. KROEBER, ALFRED L., and KLUCKHOHN, CLYDE. *Culture: A critical Review of Concepts and Definitions of Culture*. Papers of the Peabody Museum of Anthropology and Ethnology, XLVII, 1. (Cambridge, Mass., 1952).

148. KULSKI, W. W. "Class Stratification in the Soviet Union," *Foreign Affairs*, 32 (October 1953), 145-153.

149. *Kulturnoe stroitelstvo SSSR* [Building Culture in the USSR]; official statistics (Moscow, 1956).

150. KUNG-CHUAN HSIAO, *Rural China* (Seattle, 1960).

151. KUNITZ, JOSHUA (ed.). *Russian Literature since the Revolution* (New York, 1948).

152. L. "The Soviet Intelligentsia," *Foreign Affairs* (October 1957), 122-130.

153. LABEDZ, L. "The New Soviet Intelligentsia," *Soviet Survey*, 29 (July-September 1959), 103-111.

154. LAMB, HAROLD. *The March of Muscovy* (New York, 1948).

155. LAQUEUR, WALTER Z., and LICHTHEIM, GEORGE. *The Soviet Cultural Scene, 1956-1957* (New York, 1959).

156. LAVROV, P. *Istoricheskie pisma* [Historical Letters]; published under the pseudonym MIRTOV (Moscow, 1870).

157. LE BON, GUSTAVE. *The Crowd: A Study of the Popular Mind.* Translated from the French (London, 1896; 17th ed., 1930).

158. ———. *The Psychology of Peoples.* Translated from the French (New York, 1898), especially pp. 29, 160, and 228.

159. LE PLAY, FRÉDÉRIC. *Les ouvriers européens;* English translation in ZIMMERMAN (332), Part IV.

160. LEITES, NATHAN. *The Operational Code of the Politbureau* (New York, 1951).

161. LEITES, NATHAN, and BERNAUT, ELSA. *Ritual of Liquidation* (Glencoe, Ill., 1954).

162. LEKHIN, I. V., and PETROV, F. N. (eds.). *Slovar inostrannykh slov* [Foreign Words Dictionary], 4th ed. (Moscow, 1954).

163. LEONOV, LEON. *Skutarevsky,* a novel (Moscow, 1932).

164. LESKOV, NIKOLAI S. *The Steel Flea,* a short story; adapted from the Russian by BABETTE DEUTCH and AVRAHM YARMOLINSKY (New York, 1943).

165. LICHTHEIM, GEORGE. "Marxist Doctrine in Perspective," *Problems of Communism*, 6 (November-December 1958), 32-38, and "Soviet Marxism: From Theory to Ideology," *Soviet Survey*, 27 (January-March 1959), 69-74.

166. LINTON, RALPH. *The Tanala, a Hill Tribe of Madagascar* (Chicago, 1933); excerpts in STERN (266).

167. *Literaturnaia Moskva* [Literary Moscow], Nos. 1-2; collections of poetry and short stories (Moscow, 1956-57).

168. LONDON, KURT. *The Seven Soviet Arts* (New Haven, 1937).

169. LOSSKY, NIKOLAI O. *Kharakter russkogo naroda* [The Character of Russian People] (West Germany, 1957).

170. LOWREY, LAWSON G. "The Family as a Builder of Personality," *The American Journal of Orthopsychiatry*, VI, 1 (January 1936), 118-124; excerpts in STERN (266), 412-413.

171. LUDWIG, EMIL. *Stalin* (New York, 1942).

172. LUKE, LOUISE E. *Marxian Woman: Soviet Variants;* in SIMMONS (255).

173. LUMPKIN, KATHERINE D. *The Family: A Study of Member Roles* (Chapel Hill, N. C., 1933); excerpts in STERN (266).

174. LYONS, EUGENE. *Stalin, Czar of All the Russians* (Philadelphia, 1940).

175. MAKARENKO, ANTON. *Road to Life*. Parts 1-3 (Moscow, 1954).

176. MAKLAKOV, VASSILY A. *Vtoraia gosudarstvennaia duma* [The Second State Duma] (Paris, 1946).

177. MARCUSE, HERBERT. *Soviet Marxism: A Critical Analysis* (New York, 1957).

178. MASARYK, THOMAS G. *The Spirit of Russia: Studies in History, Literature and Philosophy*, 2 vols. (New York, 1955).

179. MASSING, HEDE. *This Deception: The Story of a Woman Agent* (New York, 1950).

180. MATHEWSON, RUFUS W., JR. "The Soviet Hero and the Literary Heritage," *American Slavic and East European Review*, 12 (December 1953), 506-523.

181. MAYNARD, Sir JOHN. *Russia in Flux* (New York, 1948).

182. ———. *The Russian Peasant, and Other Stories* (New York, 1942).

183. MEAD, MARGARET. "Contrasts and Comparisons from Primitive Society," *The Annals of the American Academy of Political and Social Science*, 160 (March 1932), 1-6; also in STERN (266).

184. ———. *Soviet Attitudes Toward Authority* (New York, 1951).

185. MEHNERT, KLAUS. *Soviet Man and His World* (New York, 1959).

186. MEISNER, BORIS. *The Communist Party of the U.S.S.R.* Translated from the German by FRED HOLLING; ed. JOHN S. RESHETAR, JR. (New York, 1955).

187. MEYER, ALFRED G. *The Use of the Term Culture in the Soviet Union;* in KROEBER. (147).

188. MILIUKOV, PAVEL N. *Glavnye techenia russkoi istoricheskoi mysli* [The Main Trends in Russian Historiography], 2nd ed. (Moscow, 1898).

189. ———. *Istoria vtoroi russkoi revolutsii* [A History of the Second Russian Revolution], 3 vols. (Sofia, 1921-24).

190. ———. *Outlines of Russian Culture*. Translated from the Russian *Ocherki po istorii russkoi kultury* (1930-37), abridged and edited by M. M. KARPOVICH, 3 vols. (Philadelphia, 1941); in one volume (New York, 1948).

191. MITIAEV, S. (ed.). *Khoziaistvo i byt russkikh krestian* [Economy and the Manner of Life of the Russian Peasantry]; a collection of articles and documents (Moscow, 1959).

192. MITRANY, DAVID. *Marx Against the Peasant* (Chapel Hill, N. C., 1951).

193. MONNEROT, JULES. *Sociology and Psychology of Communism*. Translated from the French by JANE DEGRAS and RICHARD REES (Boston, 1953).

194. MOORE, BARRINGTON, JR. *Political Power and Social Theory* (Cambridge, Mass., 1958); especially, Chapter Two: "Totalitarian Elements in Pre-Industrial Societies," pp. 30-88.

191

195. MORGAN, E. *The Puritan Family* (Boston, 1944).
196. MOSELY, PHILIP E. "Adaptation for Survival: The Varzic Zadruga," *The Slavonic and East European Review*, XXI, 56 (March 1943); American Series, II, 147-173.
197. Munich Institute. *Forty Years of the Soviet Regime;* a symposium of the Institute for the Study of the USSR (Munich, 1957).
198. ———. *Soviet Society Today;* a symposium (Munich, 1959).
199. *Narodnoe khoziaistvo SSSR* [National Economy of the USSR]; a statistical survey (Moscow, 1956); see also *Khoziaistvo* (129).
200. NECHKINA, M. (ed.). *Istoria SSSR. Epokha sotsializma, 1917-1957* [History of the USSR: The Epoch of Socialism] (Moscow, 1957).
201. NIEMEYER, GERHART, and RESHETAR, JOHN S., JR. *An Inquiry into Soviet Rationality* (New York, 1955).
202. NOBLE, JOHN, and EVERETT, GLENN D. *I Found God in Soviet Russia* (New York, 1959).
203. NOSS, JOHN B. *Man's Religions* (New York, 1956); especially chapter on religion in prehistoric and primitive cultures, pp. 5 ff.
204. NOVIKOVA-VASHENTSOVA, E. *Marinkina Zhizn* [Marinka's Life]; an autobiographical novel (Moscow, 1939).
205. *Novoe Russkoe Slovo* (New York), a Russian-American daily.
206. O'BRIEN, C. BICKFORD. *Russia under Two Tsars, 1682-1689* (Los Angeles, 1952).
207. ORTEGA Y GASSET, JOSÉ. *The Revolt of the Masses* (London, 1932).
208. ———. *Toward a Philosophy of History* (New York, 1941).
209. ORWELL, GEORGE, *Nineteen Eighty-Four* (New York, 1949).
210. OSSORGIN, MIKHAIL (ILYIN). *The Quiet Street*. Translated from the Russian *Sivtsev Vrazhek*, a novel (New York, 1930).
211. PALEOLOGUE, MAURICE. *Ambassador's Memoirs*. Translated from the French (New York, 1925).
212. PALOCZI-HORVATH, GEORGE. *Khrushchev: The Road to Power* (London, 1960).
213. PANFEROV, FEDOR. *Bruski*, a novel in two parts; published in English as *Bruski: A Tale of Soviet Village Life* (New York, 1930).
214. PARES, Sir BERNARD. *A History of Russia*, 5th ed. (New York, 1947).
215. PASTERNAK, BORIS. *Dr. Zhivago*, a novel (New York, 1958).
216. PETROV, VLADIMIR and EVDOKIA. *Empire of Fear*. (London, 1956).
217. PILNIAK, BORIS. *Goly god* [The Bare Year], a novel (Moscow, 1922).
218. ———. *Tretia stolitsa* [The Third Capital], a novel (Moscow, 1922).
219. ———. *Krasnoe derevo* [Redwood], a novel (Moscow, 1929).
220. PLANT, JAMES S. *Personality and the Cultural Pattern* (New York, 1937).

221. PLATONOV, SERGEI F. *History of Russia.* Translated from the Russian by E. ARONSBERG; ed. F. A. GOLDER (New York, 1925).
222. PONOMAREV, B. N. (ed.). *Politicheski slovar* [Political Dictionary], 2nd ed. (Moscow, 1958).
223. POOL, ITHIEL DE SOLA. *Satellite Generals: A Study of Military Elites in the Soviet Sphere* (Stanford, Calif., 1955).
224. *Pop i Muzhik* [The Priest and the Peasant]; a collection of anti-clerical folklore (Moscow, 1931).
225. POGODIN, NIKOLAI. *The Chimes of the Kremlin,* a play (Moscow, 1941), in Russian.
226. PUSHKIN, ALEXANDER S. "The Captain's Daughter," in *Poems, Prose and Plays of Alexander Pushkin,* ed. AVRAHM YARMOLINSKY (New York, 1936), 599-727.
227. ———. "Dubrovsky," *ibid.,* pp. 787-875.
228. QUEEN, STUART A., and ADAMS, JOHN B. *The Family in Various Cultures* (Philadelphia, 1952).
229. RADIN, PAUL. *Primitive Man as Philosopher* (New York, 1927).
230. RADKEY, OLIVER H. *The Elections to the Russian Constituent Assembly* (Cambridge, Mass., 1950).
231. REDDING, DAVID. "Comparison of Volume and Distribution of Non-Agricultural Employment in the USSR, 1928-1955, with the USA, 1870-1952," *Review of Economics and Statistics* (November 1954).
232. REDFIELD, ROBERT, *Peasant Society and Culture,* 2nd ed. (Chicago, 1958).
233. ———. *The Primitive World and Its Transformation* (Ithaca, N.Y., 1953; paperback, 1959).
234. REMMERS, H. H., and RADLER, D. H. *The American Teenager* (New York, 1958).
235. RESHETAR, JOHN S., JR. *A Concise History of the Communist Party of the Soviet Union* (New York, 1960).
236. REYNOLDS, QUENTIN J. *Only the Stars Are Neutral* (New York, 1947).
237. ROBINSON, GEROID T. *Rural Russia under the Old Regime* (New York, 1932; 2nd ed., 1949).
238. ROZENTAL, M. *et al. Kratki filosofski slovar* [A Brief Philosophical Dictionary], 4th ed. (Moscow, 1954).
239. *Russkaia Pravda,* Troitsky Copy I; especially, Arts. 91 to 95, and 99 to 106. There are several editions, with comments by different scholars; under the Soviets, by B. D. GREKOV (Moscow-Leningrad, 1940) and by A. LIKHACHEV (Moscow-Leningrad, 1955). For an English translation, see GEORGE V. VERNADSKY, *The Russian Medieval Law* (New Haven, 1946).
240. SANDOMIRSKY, VERA. "The Spirit of the New Soviet Middle Class," *The Russian Review,* 13 (Spring 1954), 193-202.
241. SCHAKHOVSKOY, ZINAIDA. *Ma Russie habillée en URSS* (Paris,

1958); published in English as *The Privilege Was Mine* (London, 1959).

242. SCHAPIRO, LEONARD. *The Communist Party of the Soviet Union* (New York, 1960).

243. SCHUBART, WALTER. *Russia and Western Man*. Translated from the German (New York, 1950).

244. SELISHCHEV, A. M. *Yazyk revolutsionnoi epokhi* [The Language of the Revolution]; observations on Russian usage in the years 1917 to 1926 (Moscow, 1928).

245. SERGE, VICTOR. *Staline;* a biography (Paris, 1940).

246. ———. *The Case of Comrade Tulaev.* Translated from the French by WILLARD R. TRASK (New York, 1950).

247. SETON-WATSON, HUGH. "The Soviet Ruling Class," *Problems of Communism*, 3 (May-June 1956).

248. ———. "Intelligentsia and Revolution," *Soviet Survey*, 29 (July-September 1959), 90-96.

249. SHCHERBAKOV, A. V. (ed.). *Istoria SSSR* [History of the USSR], a textbook (Moscow, 1945).

250. SHCHIPACHEV, STEPAN. *Pavlik Morozov,* a poem (Moscow, 1950), in Russian.

251. SHILS, EDWARD. "The Prospects for Intellectuals," *Soviet Survey*, 29 (July-September 1959), 81-89.

252. SHIRIAEV, BORIS. "Urenski tsar," *Vozrozhdenie* (Paris), XI, XII, XIII (1950-51); the story of Old Believers' revolt against the Soviets in Vologda Province.

253. SHOLOKHOV, MIKHAIL. *Podniataia tselina*, Part I (Moscow, 1931); published in English as *Seeds of Tomorrow: Virgin Soil Upturned* (New York, 1934). See also his *And Quiet Flows the Don* and *The Don Flows Home to the Sea* (paperback, 1960); and *Harvest on the Don* (New York, 1961).

254. SHORE, MAURICE J. *Soviet Education, Its Psychology and Philosophy* (New York, 1947).

255. SIMMONS, ERNEST J. (ed.). *Through the Glass of Soviet Literature: Views of Russian Society* (New York, 1953).

256. ———. *Continuity and Change in Russian and Soviet Thought* (New York, 1955).

257. SIMONOV, KONSTANTIN. *Chuzhaia ten* [Someone's Shadow], a play (Moscow, 1949).

258. *Slovar sovremennogo russkogo literaturnogo yazyka* [Dictionary of the Modern Russian Literary Standard] (Moscow-Leingrad, 1956-   ); first ten volumes appeared by 1961.

259. *Slovar russkogo yazyka* [A Dictionary of the Russian Language], 4 vols.; edited by the USSR Academy of Science, Russian Language Institute (Moscow, 1958-61).

260. SMITH, LACEY B. "English Treason Trials and Confessions in the 16th Century," *Journal of the History of Ideas*, 15 (October 1954), 471-498.

261. SOUVARINE, BORIS. *Stalin: A Critical Study of Bolshevism.* Translated from the French (New York, 1939).

262. SPROTT, W. J. H. *Human Groups* (Baltimore, 1958).

263. SREZNEVSKY, I. I. *Materialy dlia slovaria drevnerusskogo yazyka* [Materials for a Dictionary of Old Russian], Vol. I; reprint (Moscow, 1958).

264. STALIN, JOSEPH. *Voprosy leninizma* [Problems of Leninism], 11th ed. (Moscow, 1947); available in English and in most other languages.

265. STEPNIAK—see KRAVCHINSKY (144); quoted from one-volume edition (London, 1905).

266. STERN, BERNHARDT J. (ed.). *The Family, Past and Present* (New York, 1938).

267. ————. *Geschichte der oeffentlichen Sittlichkeit in Russland,* 2 vols. (Berlin, 1907-08).

268. STRUVE, GLEB. *Soviet Russian Literature, 1917-1950* (Norman, Oklahoma, 1951).

269. SU, SING GING. *The Chinese Family System* (New York, 1922); excerpts in STERN (266).

270. SUKHANOV, N. N. *The Russian Revolution 1917: A Personal Record;* edited, abridged, and translated by JOEL CARMICHAEL from *Zapiski o revolutsii* (New York, 1955).

271. SUMNER, B. N. *A Short History of Russia* (New York, 1942).

272. SVANIDZE, BUDU. *Stalin v nochnykh tufliakh* [Stalin in Slippers]; an account of doubtful veracity, by a pretended relative (Paris, 1953).

273. TAO-TAI HSIA, "Justice and the Law," *New Leader,* 22 June 1959.

274. TIMASHEFF, NIKOLAI S. *Religion in Soviet Russia, 1917-1942* (New York, 1942).

275. ————. "Religion in Russia Today," *Thought,* XXXII, 126 (Autumn 1957).

276. TOCQUEVILLE, ALEXIS DE. *Democracy in America* (New York, 1954), reprint; especially, I, 273-275.

277. TOLSTOY, ALEXEI N. *Ivan Grozny* [Ivan the Terrible], a play (Moscow, 1942-43).

278. ————. *Peter the First,* a historical novel (New York, 1959).

279. TOLSTOY, LEO N. *War and Peace,* 2 vols. (Baltimore, 1957).

280. ————. *The Cossacks* (Baltimore, paperback, 1960).

281. ————. *Utro pomeshchika* [A Landlord's Morning] Complete Works, II, 76 ff. (Moscow, 1948).

282. TOMKINS, STUART R. *The Russian Intelligentsia: Makers of the Revolutionary State* (Norman, Oklahoma, 1957). See also the collection of articles in *Daedalus* (Summer 1960), especially, "The Structure of the Soviet Intelligentsia," by LEOPOLD LABEDZ; "Observations on Soviet University Students," by DAVID BURG; and "The Solitary Hero and the Philistines," by LEOPOLD H.

HAIMSON. Reissued as *The Russian Intelligentsia,* ed. RICHARD PIPES (New York, 1961).

283. TOUMANOFF, C. "Moscow and the Third Rome: Genesis and Significance of a Politico-Religious Idea," *Catholic Historical Review,* 40 (January 1955), 411-447; see also WOLFF (313).

284. TREADGOLD, DONALD W. *Twentieth Century Russia* (Chicago, 1959).

285. TROTSKY, LEON. *The History of the Russian Revolution.* Translated from the Russian by MAX EASTMAN (New York, 1932); one-volume edition quoted here (Philadelphia, 1958).

286. ———. *Stalin* (New York, 1946).

287. TURGENEV, IVAN S. *Zapiski okhotnika* [Sketches of a Sportsman]. (New York, paperback, 1961).

288. TURKEVICH, JOHN. "Soviet Science in the Post-Stalin Era," *The Annals of the American Academy of Political and Social Science* (January 1956).

289. ———. "Soviet Science: Achievements and Problems," *Soviet Survey,* 29 (July-September 1959), 38-43; see also articles by DAVID JORAVSKY and GUSTAV WETTER in *Daedalus* (Summer 1960), 562-603.

290. TWAROG, LEON. *Studies in the Soviet Historical Novel;* unpublished Ph.D. dissertation (Harvard University, 1952).

291. ———. "A Novel in Flux: V. Kostylev's 'Ivan Grozny,'" *The American Slavic and East European Review* (October 1955).

292. USHAKOV, D. N. (ed.). *Tolkovy slovar russkogo yazyka* [A Comprehensive Dictionary of Russian Usage], 4 vols. (Moscow, 1935-1940).

293. USPENSKY, GLEB. *Vlast zemli* [Power of the Soil], a novel (1882); section "Ivan Petrov" translated by LEO WIENER, *Anthology of Russian Literature,* Part 2 (1903), pp. 407-417.

294. U. S. S. R. *Polozhenie selskogo khoziaistva i krestianstva v koloniakh i drugikh slaborazvitykh stranakh* [Agriculture and the Peasantry in Colonial and Other Underdeveloped Countries] (Moscow, 1958).

295. VAKAR, NICHOLAS. *Belorussia: The Making of a Nation* (Cambridge, Mass., 1956).

296. ———. "Words and Meanings," *The AATSEEL Journal,* XII, 3 (October 1954), 44-51 (The quarterly of the American Association of Teachers of Slavic and East European Languages.)

297. ———. "Communism and Language: Soviet Psycholinguistics," *ibid.,* XIV, 1 (March 1956), 13-19.

298. ———. "The Mass Communication Index: Some Observations on Communist Russian Discourse," *Symposium,* X (Spring 1956), 42-59.

299. VENTURI, FRANCO. *Roots of Revolution: A History of the Russian Populist and Socialist Movements in the 19th Century.* Translated from the Italian (New York, 1959).

300. VISHNEVSKAIA, E. *Antireligioznye skazki narodov SSSR* [Anti-religious Folklore of the Peoples of the USSR] (Moscow, 1939).
301. VOINOV, NICHOLAS. *The Waif* (New York, 1955).
302. VOINOVA, A. I. *Samotsvety* [Precious Stones], a novel (Moscow, 1930).
303. WEIDLE, WLADIMIR. *Russia: Absent and Present* (New York, 1952).
304. WEISSBERG-CYBULSKI, ALEXANDER. *Russland im Schmelztiegel der Saeuberungen* (Frankfurt, 1951); published in Great Britain as *Conspiracy of Silence* (London, 1951), and in the United States, as *The Accused* (New York, 1951).
305. WERTENBAKER, THOMAS J. *The Puritan Oligarchy: The Foundation of American Civilization* (New York, 1938).
306. WEST, CHARLES C. *Communism and the Theologians* (London, 1958).
307. WETTER, GUSTAVUS. *Il Materialismo Dialectico Sovietico* (Turin, 1950); published in English as *The Dialectical Materialism of the Soviet Union* (New York, 1956).
308. WILLAN, T. S. *The Muscovy Merchants of 1555* (Manchester, Engl., 1953).
309. ———. *The Early History of the Russian Company, 1553-1603* (Manchester, Engl., 1956).
310. WIPPER, R. *Ivan Grozny,* translated from the Russian (Moscow, 1947).
311. WOLFE, BERTRAM D. *Three Who Made a Revolution* (New York, 1948).
312. WOLFE, BERTRAM D., and LICHTHEIM, GEORGE. "Marxism-Leninism: Marxism—Yesterday and Today," *Problems of Communism,* 6 (November-December 1958), 24-37.
313. WOLFF, ROBERT LEE. "The Three Romes: The Migration of an Ideology and the Making of an Autocrat," *Daedalus* (Spring 1959); see also TOUMANOFF (283).
314. WU, CHING CHAO. "The Chinese Family: Organization, Names, and Kinship Terms," *American Anthropologist,* 29 (1927), 316-318.
315. YARMOLINSKY, AVRAHM. *Road to Revolution: A Century of Russian Radicalism* (New York, 1959); see also VENTURI (299).
316. YASHIN, A. "Rychagi [The Levers]," a short story, in *Literaturnaia Moskva* (167); an English translation in E. STILLMAN (ed.), *Bitter Harvest,* collection of writings from behind the Iron Curtain (New York, 1959).
317. YUGOV, ALEXANDER. *Ratobortsy* [The Champions], a historical novel (Moscow, 1949).
318. ZAVALISHIN, VYACHESLAV. *Early Soviet Writers* (New York, 1958).
319. ZENKOVSKY, SERGE. "The Old Believer Avvakum: His Writings," *Indiana Slavic Studies,* I (1956), 1-52.

320. ———. "The Ideological World of the Denisov Brothers," *Harvard Slavic Studies*, III (1957), 49-66.
321. ZENZINOV, VLADIMIR M. *Besprizornye* [The Waifs]; with a list of Soviet primary sources (Paris, 1929).
322. ZIMMERMAN, CARLE C. *Family and Society: A Study of the Sociology of Reconstruction* (New York, 1935).

INDEX

199

Class war, 4
Classless society, 79
Cold war, 156-157, 163-168
"Collective leadership," 26
Collectivization, collective farms, 12, 15, 47, 49, 54-58, 79, 137; *See also* Kolkhoz
Comintern, 15, 21 *n*
Committees of the Poor, 55
Comte, Auguste, 109
Communist Manifesto, The, 3, 154 *n*
Communist Youth League, *see* Komsomol
Connecticut "blue laws," 39
Constantinople, fall of, 20, 23
Constituent Assembly, 6, 10
Constitution of the U.S.S.R., 38
Cossaks, the, 24, 41
Courts of Justice, 75-76; *See also* Law, concept of
Crankshaw, Edward, 101, 115-116
Czechs, the, 94, 111

Danilevsky, N. J., 29
Democratic African Union, 48
Democracy, concept of, 26, 42, 45, 47-50, 57-58, 155, 160-161, 163-164
Denisov, Brothers, 25-27
Deutscher, I., 6 *n*
Dissent, the, *see* Old Believers, Raskol
Don (region), 55
Dostoevsky, Fedor, 11, 70, 176
Dudintsev, Vladimir, 80, 106, 142-143
Dulles, John Foster, vii, 166
Durnovo, P., 56 *n*

East Germans, 111
Education, 18, 19, 27-28, 35, 40, 63, 139, 146-152, 156, 164, 177, 180-181
Eisenhower, Dwight D., 70, 167
Elders, the, 26, 35, 45, 51-52, 92-93, 140, 143
Elisséeff, Serge, 121-122
Emancipation Act, 30, 46
Embassies, Soviet, 81-82

Engels, Friedrich, ix, x, 86-87, 126
England, 4, 64, 66 *n*, 77, 99-100
Essenin, Sergei, 33 *n*, 69, 95

Family, patterns of, 31-44, 62-63, 67 72, 79, 82-93, 108, 118, 137, 152, 156, 172-175
Fascism, 111, 159, 160
Fedor, Tsar, 22
Fedoseyev, A., 128
Fedotov, G., 177
First Secretary, 92, 93, 117
Five-Year-Plan, 25, 55
Folklore, 32, 61-62, 73, 87-88, 173
Foreigners, ix, 2, 19, 24, 60, 66, 74-75, 109, 151
France, 117 *n*
French Guinea, 48
French Revolution, 117

Gaulle, Charles de, 85
German invasion, 43, 51 *n*, 55, 69
Germans, the, 87, 88, 99, 160
Gladkov, Fedor, 37, 42
Gogol, Nikolai, 120
Gorchakov, Nikolai, 103
Gorky, Maxim, 84, 97 *n*, 131
Gosudar, title of, 21
Greeks, the, 18, 23, 119-120

Hinduism, 116
Hitler, Adolf, viii, 160, 161
Holy Russia, 18, 19, 87
Huizinga, Johan, 104, 127
Human rights, concept of, 32-49, 52-57, 61-66, 72, 75-78, 81-84
Humanism, 71
Humphrey, Hubert H., 108 *n*, 115
Hungary, and the Hungarians, 73, 119, 129, 130
Hutchinson, Paul, 117

Ilf and Petrov, 102
Illiteracy, 11, 28
India, 128
Industrialization, 94, 155, 165
Intelligentsia, the old, 14-16, 28-30,

200

201

203